MW01052436

Java™ Student Solutions Manual

to Accompany

Java How To Program, Fifth Edition

Deitel® Books, Cyber Classrooms, Complete Tra
published by

How To Program Series

Advanced Java™ 2 Platform How to Program

C How to Program, 3/E

C++ How to Program, 4/E

C# How to Program

e-Business and e-Commerce How to Program

Internet and World Wide Web How to Program, 2/E

Java™ How to Program, 5/E

Perl How to Program

Python How to Program

Visual Basic® 6 How to Program

Visual Basic® .NET How to Program, 2/E

Wireless Internet & Mobile Business How to Program

XML How to Program

Deitel® Developer Series

C# A Programmer's Introduction
C# for Experienced Programmers
Java™ Web Services for Experienced Programmers
Web Services A Technical Introduction
Visual C++ .NET for Experienced Programmers

.NET How to Program Series

C# How to Program
Visual Basic® .NET How to Program, 2/E

For Managers Series

e-Business and e-Commerce for Managers

Visual Studio® Series

C# How to Program
Visual Basic® .NET How to Program, 2/E
Getting Started with Microsoft® Visual C++® 6 with an Introduction to MFC
Visual Basic® 6 How to Program

Coming Soon

e-books and e-whitepapers
Premium CourseCompass, WebCT and Blackboard Multimedia Cyber Classroom versions

ining Courses and Web-Based Training Courses Prentice Hall

Multimedia Cyber Classroom and *Web-Based Training* Series

C++ Multimedia Cyber Classroom, 4/E
C# Multimedia Cyber Classroom
e-Business and e-Commerce Multimedia Cyber Classroom
Internet and World Wide Web Multimedia Cyber Classroom, 2/E
Java™ 2 Multimedia Cyber Classroom, 5/E
Perl Multimedia Cyber Classroom
Python Multimedia Cyber Classroom
Visual Basic® 6 Multimedia Cyber Classroom
Visual Basic® .NET Multimedia Cyber Classroom, 2/E
Wireless Internet & Mobile Business Programming Multimedia Cyber Classroom
XML Multimedia Cyber Classroom

The Complete Training Course Series

The Complete C++ Training Course, 4/E
The Complete C# Training Course
The Complete e-Business and e-Commerce Programming Training Course
The Complete Internet and World Wide Web Programming Training Course, 2/E
The Complete Java™ 2 Training Course, 5/E
The Complete Perl Training Course
The Complete Python Training Course
The Complete Visual Basic® 6 Training Course
The Complete Visual Basic® .NET Training Course, 2/E
The Complete Wireless Internet & Mobile Business Programming Training Course
The Complete XML Programming Training Course

To follow the Deitel publishing program, please register at:

`www.deitel.com/newsletter/subscribe.html`

for the *DEITEL® BUZZ ONLINE* e-mail newsletter.

To communicate with the authors, send e-mail to:

`deitel@deitel.com`

For information on corporate on-site seminars offered by Deitel & Associates, Inc. worldwide, visit:

`www.deitel.com`

For continuing updates on Prentice Hall and Deitel publications visit:

`www.deitel.com`,
`www.prenhall.com/deitel` or
`www.InformIT.com/deitel`

Java™ Student Solutions Manual

to Accompany

Java How To Program, Fifth Edition

H. M. Deitel
Deitel & Associates, Inc.

P. J. Deitel
Deitel & Associates, Inc.

PEARSON
Prentice Hall

PRENTICE HALL, Upper Saddle River, New Jersey 07458

Library of Congress Cataloging-in-Publication Data

On file

Vice President and Editorial Director, ECS: ***Marcia J. Horton***
Acquisitions Editor: ***Petra J. Recter***
Assistant Editor: ***Sarah Parker***
Editorial Assistant: ***Michael Giacobbe***
Associate Editor: ***Jennifer Cappello***
Vice President and Director of Production and Manufacturing, ESM: ***David W. Riccardi***
Executive Managing Editor: ***Vince O'Brien***
Managing Editor: ***Tom Manshreck***
Production Editor: ***John F. Lovell***
Production Editor, Media: ***Bob Engelhardt***
Director of Creative Services: ***Paul Belfanti***
Creative Director: ***Carole Anson***
Cover Designer: ***Geoffrey Cassar***
Manufacturing Manager: ***Trudy Pisciotti***
Manufacturing Buyer: ***Ilene Kahn***
Marketing Manager: ***Pamela Shaffer***
Marketing Assistant: ***Barrie Reinhold***

Printed in the United States of America

10 9 8 7 6 5 4 3 2 1

ISBN 0-13-142579-X

Pearson Education Ltd., *London*
Pearson Education Australia Pty. Ltd., *Sydney*
Pearson Education Singapore, Pte. Ltd.
Pearson Education North Asia Ltd., *Hong Kong*
Pearson Education Canada, Inc., *Toronto*
Pearson Educacion de Mexico, S.A. de C.V.
Pearson Education–Japan, *Tokyo*
Pearson Education Malaysia, Pte. Ltd.
Pearson Education, Inc., *Upper Saddle River, New Jersey*

Trademarks

Contents

1

Introduction to Computers, the Internet and the Web

Solutions to Selected Exercises

1.4 Categorize each of the following items as either hardware or software:

a) CPU

ANS: *hardware*

b) Java compiler

ANS: *software*

c) Java interpreter

ANS: *software*

d) input unit

ANS: *hardware*

e) editor

ANS: *software*

1.8 Fill in the blanks in each of the following statements (based on Sections 1.15 and 1.16):

a) ________ design patterns describe techniques to instantiate objects (or groups of objects).

ANS: *Creational*

b) The ________ is now the most widely used graphical representation scheme for modeling object-oriented systems.

ANS: *Unified Modeling Language*

c) Java classes contain ________ (which implement class behaviors) and ________ (which implement class data).

ANS: *methods, fields*

d) ________ design patterns allow designers to organize classes and objects into larger structures.

ANS: *Structural*

e) ________ design patterns assign responsibilities to objects.

ANS: *Behavioral*

f) In Java, the unit of programming is the ________, from which ________ are eventually instantiated.

ANS: *class, objects*

1.9 Why is it valuable to study design patterns?

ANS: *Using design patterns can substantially reduce the complexity of the design process. Design patterns benefit system developers by: helping to construct reliable software using proven architectures and accumulated industry expertise; promoting design reuse in future systems; helping to identify common mistakes and pitfalls that occur when building systems; helping to design systems independently of the language in which they will ultimately be implemented; establishing a common design vocabulary among developers, and shortening the design phase in a software-development process.*

2

Introduction to Java Applications

Solutions to Selected Exercises

2.7 Fill in the blanks in each of the following statements:

a) __________ are used to document a program and improve its readability.

ANS: *Comments*

b) An input dialog capable of receiving input from the user is displayed with method of class __________.

ANS: `showInputDialog`, `JOptionPane`.

c) A decision can be made in a Java program with a/an __________.

ANS: **`if statement`**

d) Calculations are normally performed by __________ statements.

ANS: *assignment*

e) A dialog capable of displaying a message to the user is displayed with method __________ of class __________.

ANS: `showMessageDialog`, `JOptionPane`

2.9 State whether each of the following is *true* or *false*. If *false*, explain why.

a) Java operators are evaluated from left to right.

ANS: *False. Some operators (e.g., assignment, =) evaluate from right to left.*

b) The following are all valid variable names: `_under_bar_`, `m928134`, `t5`, `j7`, `her_sales$`, `his_$account_total`, `a`, `b$`, `c`, `z`, `z2`.

ANS: *True.*

c) A valid Java arithmetic expression with no parentheses is evaluated from left to right.

ANS: *False. The expression is evaluated according to operator precedence.*

d) The following are all invalid variable names: `3g`, `87`, `67h2`, `h22` and `2h`.

ANS: *False. Identifier* `h22` *is a valid variable name.*

2.11 What displays in the message dialog when each of the given Java statements is performed? Assume that `x = 2` and `y = 3`.

a) `JOptionPane.showMessageDialog( null, "x = " + x );`

ANS: *x* = 2

b)
```
JOptionPane.showMessageDialog( null,
    "The value of x + x is " + ( x + x ) );
```

ANS: *The value of x + x is 4*

c) `JOptionPane.showMessageDialog( null, "x =" );`

ANS: *x* =

d)
```
JOptionPane.showMessageDialog( null,
    ( x + y ) + " = " + ( y + x ) );
```

ANS: 5 = 5

2.12 Which of the following Java statements contain variables whose values are changed or replaced?

a) `p = i + j + k + 7;`

b)
```
JOptionPane.showMessageDialog( null,
    "variables whose values are destroyed" );
```

c) `JOptionPane.showMessageDialog( null, "a = 5" );`

d) `stringVal = JOptionPane.showInputDialog( "Enter string:" );`

ANS: *(a) and (d).*

2.13 Given that $y = ax^3 + 7$, which of the following are correct Java statements for this equation?

a) `y = a * x * x * x + 7;`

b) `y = a * x * x * ( x + 7 );`

c) `y = ( a * x ) * x * ( x + 7 );`

d) `y = ( a * x ) * x * x + 7;`

e) `y = a * ( x * x * x ) + 7;`

f) `y = a * x * ( x * x + 7 );`

ANS: *(a), (d) and (e).*

2.17 Write an application that asks the user to enter two integers, obtains the numbers from the user and displays the larger number followed by the words "`is larger`" in an information message dialog. If the numbers are equal, print the message "`These numbers are equal.`" Use the techniques shown in Fig. 2.20.

ANS:

```
// Exercise 2.17 Solution: Larger.java
// Program that determines the larger of two numbers.

```

Fig. S2.1 Solution to Exercise 2.17. (Part 1 of 3.)

```java
import javax.swing.JOptionPane;

public class Larger {

   // main method begins execution of Java application
   public static void main( String args[] )
   {
      String firstNumber;
      String secondNumber;   // second string entered by user
      String result;
      int number1;
      int number2;

      // read first number from user as a string
      firstNumber = JOptionPane.showInputDialog( "Enter first integer:" );

      // read second number from user as a string
      secondNumber =
         JOptionPane.showInputDialog( "Enter second integer:" );

      // convert numbers from type String to type int
      number1 = Integer.parseInt( firstNumber );
      number2 = Integer.parseInt( secondNumber );

      // initialize result to empty String
      result = "";

      if ( number1 > number2 )
         result = number1 + " is larger.";

      if ( number1 < number2 )
         result = number2 + " is larger.";

      if ( number1 == number2 )
         result = "These numbers are equal.";

      // Display results
      JOptionPane.showMessageDialog( null, result, "Comparison Results",
         JOptionPane.INFORMATION_MESSAGE );

      System.exit( 0 ); // terminate application

   } // end method main

} // end class Larger
```

Fig. S2.1 Solution to Exercise 2.17. (Part 2 of 3.)

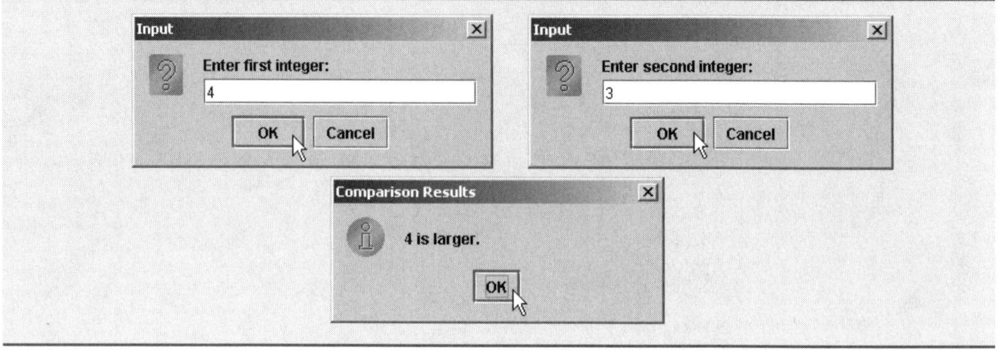

Fig. S2.1 Solution to Exercise 2.17. (Part 3 of 3.)

2.19 Write an application that inputs from the user the radius of a circle as an integer and prints the circle's diameter, circumference and area. Use the value 3.14159 for π. Use the GUI techniques shown in Fig. 2.9. [*Note*: You may also use the predefined constant `Math.PI` for the value of π. This constant is more precise than the value 3.14159. Class `Math` is defined in the `java.lang` package, so you do not need to `import` it.] Use the following formulas (r is the radius):

$$diameter = 2r$$
$$circumference = 2\pi r$$
$$area = \pi r^2$$

Do not store the results of each calculation in a variable. Rather, add the result of each directly to a string that will be used to display the results.

ANS:

```java
// Exercise 2.19 Solution: Circle.java
// Program that calculates area, circumference
// and diameter for a circle.

import javax.swing.JOptionPane;

public class Circle {

   // main method begins execution of Java application
   public static void main( String args[] )
   {
      String input;     // string entered by user
      String result;    // output display string
      int radius;       // radius of circle

      // read from user as a string
      input = JOptionPane.showInputDialog( "Enter radius:" );

      // convert number from type String to type int
      radius = Integer.parseInt( input );

```

Fig. S2.2 Solution to Exercise 2.19. (Part 1 of 2.)

```java
      result = "Diameter is " + ( 2 * radius ) +
         "\nArea is " + ( Math.PI * radius * radius ) +
         "\nCircumference is " + ( 2 * Math.PI * radius );

      // Display results
      JOptionPane.showMessageDialog( null, result, "Calculation Results",
         JOptionPane.INFORMATION_MESSAGE );

      System.exit( 0 );  // terminate application

   } // end method main

} // end class Circle
```

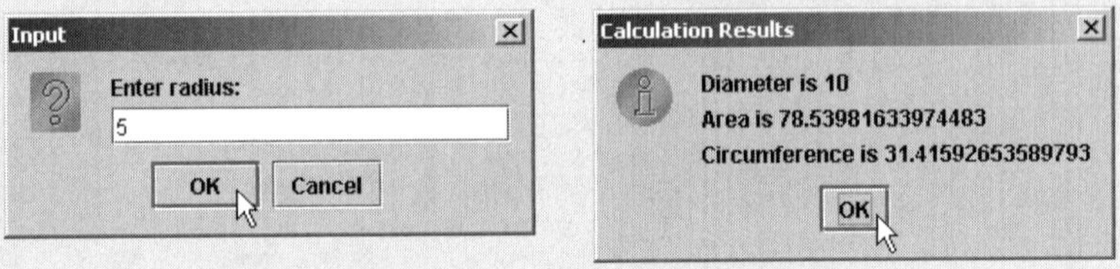

Fig. S2.2 Solution to Exercise 2.19. (Part 2 of 2.)

2.24 What does the following code print?

```java
System.out.print( "*" );
System.out.print( "***" );
System.out.print( "*****" );
System.out.print( "****" );
System.out.println( "**" );
```

ANS:

```
***************
```

Fig. S2.3 Solution to Exercise 2.24.

2.27 Write an application that reads an integer and determines and prints whether it is odd or even. [*Hint*: Use the remainder operator. An even number is a multiple of 2. Any multiple of 2 leaves a remainder of 0 when divided by 2.]

ANS:

```java
// Exercise 2.27 Solution: OddEven.java
// Program that determines if a number is odd or even.

import javax.swing.JOptionPane;

public class OddEven {
```

Fig. S2.4 Solution to Exercise 2.27. (Part 1 of 2.)

```java

   // main method begins execution of Java application
   public static void main( String args[] )
   {
      String input;     // string entered by user
      String result;    // output display string
      int number;       // number

      // read from user as a string
      input = JOptionPane.showInputDialog( "Enter integer:" );

      // convert number from type String to type int
      number = Integer.parseInt( input );

      // initialize result to empty String
      result = "";

      if ( number % 2 == 0 )
         result = "Number is even.";

      if ( number % 2 != 0 )
         result = "Number is odd.";

      // Display results
      JOptionPane.showMessageDialog( null, result, "Calculation Results",
         JOptionPane.INFORMATION_MESSAGE );

      System.exit( 0 );  // terminate application

   } // end method main

} // end class OddEven
```

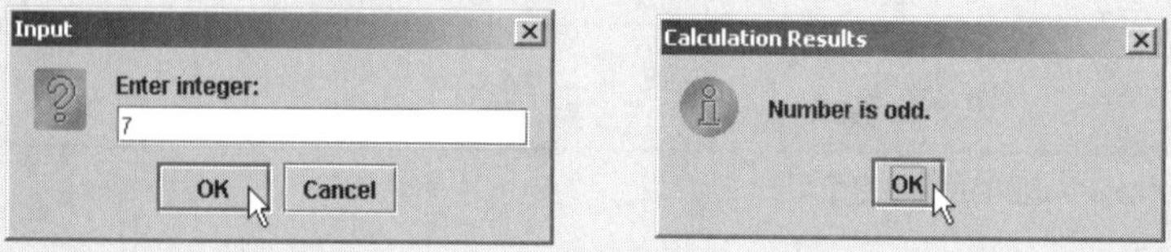

Fig. S2.4 Solution to Exercise 2.27. (Part 2 of 2.)

2.29 Write an application that displays in the command window a checkerboard pattern as follows:

```
* * * * * * * *
 * * * * * * * *
* * * * * * * *
 * * * * * * * *
* * * * * * * *
 * * * * * * * *
* * * * * * * *
 * * * * * * * *
```

ANS:

```
// Exercise 2.29 Solution: Checker.java
// Program that draws a checkerboard.

public class Checker {

   // main method begins execution of Java application
   public static void main( String args[] )
   {
      System.out.println( "* * * * * * * *" );
      System.out.println( " * * * * * * * *" );
      System.out.println( "* * * * * * * *" );
      System.out.println( " * * * * * * * *" );
      System.out.println( "* * * * * * * *" );
      System.out.println( " * * * * * * * *" );
      System.out.println( "* * * * * * * *" );
      System.out.println( " * * * * * * * *" );
   }
}
```

```
* * * * * * * *
 * * * * * * * *
* * * * * * * *
 * * * * * * * *
* * * * * * * *
 * * * * * * * *
* * * * * * * *
 * * * * * * * *
```

Fig. S2.5 Solution to Exercise 2.29.

2.31 Here's a peek ahead. In this chapter, you have learned about integers and the type `int`. Java can also represent uppercase letters, lowercase letters and a considerable variety of special symbols. Every character has a corresponding integer representation. The set of characters a computer uses and the corresponding integer representations for those characters is called that computer's *character set*. You can indicate a character value in a program simply by enclosing that character in single quotes, as in `'A'`.

You can determine the integer equivalent of a character by preceding that character with `(int)`, as in

```
(int) 'A'
```

This form is called a *cast operator.* (We will say more about these in Chapter 4.) The following statement outputs a character and its integer equivalent:

```
System.out.println( "The character " + 'A' +
   " has the value " + ( int ) 'A' );
```

When the preceding statement executes, it displays the character `A` and the value `65` (from the so-called Unicode character set) as part of the string.

Using statements similar to the one shown eariler in this exercise, write an application that displays the integer equivalents of some uppercase letters, lowercase letters, digits and special symbols. Display the integer equivalents of the following: `A B C a b c 0 1 2 $ * + /` and the blank character.

ANS:

```java
// Exercise 2.31 Solution: Display.java
// Program that prints a unicode character
// and its integer equivalent.

public class Display {

   // main method begins execution of Java application
   public static void main( String args[] )
   {
      System.out.println( "The character " + 'A' +
         " has the value " + ( int ) 'A' );
      System.out.println( "The character " + 'B' +
         " has the value " + ( int ) 'B' );
      System.out.println( "The character " + 'C' +
         " has the value " + ( int ) 'C' );
      System.out.println( "The character " + 'a' +
         " has the value " + ( int ) 'a' );
      System.out.println( "The character " + 'b' +
         " has the value " + ( int ) 'b' );
      System.out.println( "The character " + 'c' +
         " has the value " + ( int ) 'c' );
      System.out.println( "The character " + '0' +
         " has the value " + ( int ) '0' );
      System.out.println( "The character " + '1' +
         " has the value " + ( int ) '1' );
      System.out.println( "The character " + '2' +
         " has the value " + ( int ) '2' );
      System.out.println( "The character " + '$' +
         " has the value " + ( int ) '$' );
      System.out.println( "The character " + '*' +
         " has the value " + ( int ) '*' );
      System.out.println( "The character " + '+' +
         " has the value " + ( int ) '+' );
      System.out.println( "The character " + '/' +
         " has the value " + ( int ) '/' );
      System.out.println( "The character " + ' ' +
         " has the value " + ( int ) ' ' );

   } // end method main

} // end class Display
```

Fig. S2.6 Solution to Exercise 2.31. (Part 1 of 2.)

```
The character A has the value 65
The character B has the value 66
The character C has the value 67
The character a has the value 97
The character b has the value 98
The character c has the value 99
The character 0 has the value 48
The character 1 has the value 49
The character 2 has the value 50
The character $ has the value 36
The character * has the value 42
The character + has the value 43
The character / has the value 47
The character   has the value 32
```

Fig. S2.6 Solution to Exercise 2.31. (Part 2 of 2.)

3

Introduction to Java Applets

Solutions to Selected Exercises

3.5 Fill in the blanks in each of the following:

a) Type ________ declares a single-precision floating-point variable.

ANS: `float`

b) If class `Double` provides method `parseDouble` to convert a string to a `double` and class `Integer` provides method `parseInt` to convert a string to an `int`, then class `Float` probably provides method ________ to convert a string to a `float`.

ANS: `parseFloat`

c) Type ________ is used to declare double-precision, floating-point variables.

ANS: `double`

d) The ________ or a browser can be used to execute a Java applet.

ANS: *appletviewer*

e) To load an applet into a browser, you must first define a(n) ________ file.

ANS: *HTML*

f) The ________ and ________ HTML tags specify that an applet should be loaded into an applet container and executed.

ANS: **`<applet>, </applet>`**.

3.8 Write an applet that asks the user to enter two floating-point numbers, obtains the numbers from the user and displays the larger number followed by the words "`is larger`" as a string on the applet. If the numbers are equal, print the message "`These numbers are equal`." Use the techniques shown in Fig. 3.13.

ANS:

```
<html>
<applet code = "Larger.class" width = "300" height = "100" >
</applet>
</html>
```

```
// Exercise 3.8 Solution: Larger.java
// Program accepts two floating point numbers as input
// and determines which number is larger.

import java.awt.Graphics;    // import class Graphics
import javax.swing.*;        // import package javax.swing

public class Larger extends JApplet {
   String result;   // String containing the output

   // initialize applet by obtaining values from user
   public void init()
   {
      String firstNumber;     // first String entered by user
      String secondNumber;    // second String entered by user
      double number1;         // first number to compare
      double number2;         // second number to compare

      // read first number from user as a String
      firstNumber = JOptionPane.showInputDialog(
         "Enter first floating-point number:" );

      // read second number from user as a String
      secondNumber = JOptionPane.showInputDialog(
         "Enter second floating-point number:" );

      // convert numbers from type String to type double
      number1 = Double.parseDouble( firstNumber );
      number2 = Double.parseDouble( secondNumber );

      if ( number1 > number2 )
         result = number1 + " is larger.";

      if ( number1 < number2 )
         result = number2 + " is larger.";

      if ( number1 == number2 )
         result = "These numbers are equal.";
```

Fig. S3.1 Solution to Exercise 3.8. (Part 1 of 2.)

```java

    } // end method init

    // draw results in a rectangle on applet's background
    public void paint( Graphics g )
    {
       // draw rectangle starting from (15, 10) that is 270
       // pixels wide and 20 pixels tall
       g.drawRect( 15, 10, 270, 20 );

       //draw result as a String at (25, 25)
       g.drawString( result, 25, 25 );

    } // end method paint

 } // end class Larger
```

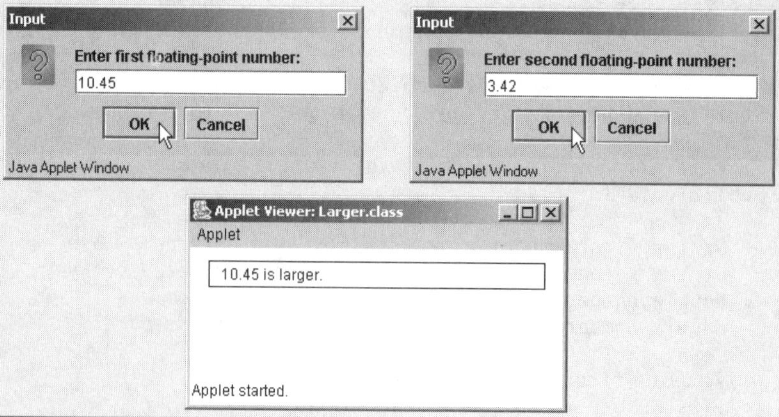

Fig. S3.1 Solution to Exercise 3.8. (Part 2 of 2.)

3.10 Write an applet that asks the user to input the radius of a circle as a floating-point number and draws the circle's diameter, circumference and area. Use the value 3.14159 for π. Use the techniques shown in Fig. 3.13. [*Note*: You may also use the predefined constant `Math.PI` for the value of π. This constant is more precise than the value 3.14159. Class `Math` is defined in the `java.lang` package, so you do not need to `import` it.] Use the following formulas (r is the radius):

$diameter = 2r$

$circumference = 2\pi r$

$area = \pi r^2$

ANS:

```html
<html>
<applet code = "Circle.class" width = "300" height = "100" >
</applet>
</html>
```

```java
// Exercise 3.10 Solution: Circle.java
// Program calculates the area, circumference
// and diameter for a circle

import java.awt.Graphics;   // import class Graphics
import javax.swing.*;       // import package javax.swing

public class Circle extends JApplet {

   // Strings for output
   String line1;
   String line2;
   String line3;

   // initialize applet by obtaining values from user
   public void init()
   {
      String input;   // String entered by user
      double radius;     // radius of circle

      // read from user as String
      input = JOptionPane.showInputDialog( "Enter radius:" );

      // convert number from type String to type int
      radius = Double.parseDouble( input );

      line1 = "Diameter is " + ( 2 * radius );
      line2 = "Area is " + ( Math.PI * radius * radius );
      line3 = "Circumference is " + ( 2 * Math.PI * radius );

   } // end method init

   // draw results on applet's background
   public void paint( Graphics g )
   {
      //draw line1 as a String at (25, 30)
      g.drawString( line1, 25, 30 );

      //draw line2 as a String at (25, 45)
      g.drawString( line2, 25, 45 );

      //draw line3 as a String at (25, 60)
      g.drawString( line3, 25, 60 );

   } // end method paint

} // end class Circle
```

Fig. S3.2 Solution to Exercise 3.10. (Part 1 of 2.)

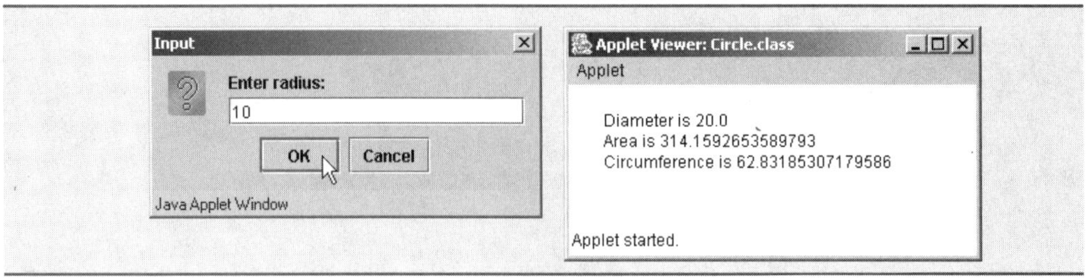

Fig. S3.2 Solution to Exercise 3.10. (Part 2 of 2.)

3.12 What does the following code print?

```
g.drawString( "*", 25, 25 );
g.drawString( "***", 25, 55 );
g.drawString( "*****", 25, 85 );
g.drawString( "****", 25, 70 );
g.drawString( "**", 25, 40 );
```

ANS:

```
*
**
***
****
*****
```

Fig. S3.3 Solution to Exercise 3.12.

3.13 Write an applet that draws a checkerboard pattern as follows:

```
* * * * * * * *
 * * * * * * * *
* * * * * * * *
 * * * * * * * *
* * * * * * * *
 * * * * * * * *
* * * * * * * *
 * * * * * * * *
```

ANS:

```
<html>
<applet code = "Checker.class" width = "50" height = "50" >
</applet>
</html>
```

```java
// Exercise 3.13 Solution: Checker.java
// Program draws a checkerboard.

import java.awt.Graphics;    // import class Graphics
import javax.swing.*;        // import package javax.swing

public class Checker extends JApplet {

   // draw Strings on applet's background
   public void paint( Graphics g )
   {
      g.drawString( "* * * * * * * *", 25, 20 );
      g.drawString( " * * * * * * * *", 25, 28 );
      g.drawString( "* * * * * * * *", 25, 36 );
      g.drawString( " * * * * * * * *", 25, 44 );
      g.drawString( "* * * * * * * *", 25, 52 );
      g.drawString( " * * * * * * * *", 25, 60 );
      g.drawString( "* * * * * * * *", 25, 68 );
      g.drawString( " * * * * * * * *", 25, 76 );
   }

} // end class Checker
```

Fig. S3.4 Solution to Exercise 3.13.

3.16 Class `Graphics` contains method `drawOval`, which takes as arguments the same four arguments as method `drawRect`. The arguments for method `drawOval` specify the "bounding box" for the oval—the sides of the bounding box are the boundaries of the oval. Write a Java applet that draws an oval and a rectangle with the same four arguments. The oval will touch the rectangle at the center of each side.

ANS:

```html
<html>
<applet code = "Draw3.class" width = "200" height = "100" >
</applet>
</html>
```

```java
// Exercise 3.16 Solution: Draw3.java
// Program draws an oval inside a rectangle on the applet.

import java.awt.Graphics;    // import class Graphics
import javax.swing.*;        // import package javax.swing
```

Fig. S3.5 Solution to Exercise 3.16. (Part 1 of 2.)

```java

public class Draw3 extends JApplet {

   // draw shapes on applet's background
   public void paint( Graphics g )
   {
      // draw rectangle starting at (10, 10) that is 50
      // pixels wide and 50 pixels tall
      g.drawRect( 10, 10, 50, 50 );

      // draw oval starting at (10, 10) that is 50 pixels
      // wide and 50 pixels tall
      g.drawOval( 10, 10, 50, 50 );
   }

} // end class Draw3
```

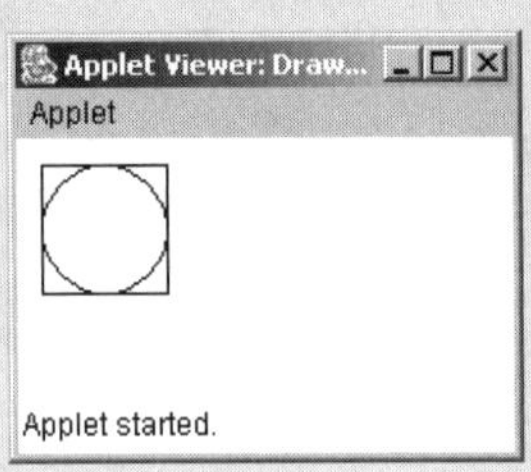

Fig. S3.5 Solution to Exercise 3.16. (Part 2 of 2.)

4

Control Statements: Part 1

Solutions to Selected Exercises

4.10 What does the following program print?

```
public class Mystery {

   public static void main( String args[] )
   {
      int y, x = 1, total = 0;

      while ( x <= 10 ) {
         y = x * x;
         System.out.println( y );
         total += y;
         ++x;
      }

      System.out.println( "Total is " + total );

   } // end main

} // end class Mystery
```

ANS:

```
1
4
9
16
25
36
49
64
81
100
Total is 385
```

Fig. S4.1 Solution to Exercise 4.10.

For Exercise 4.11 and Exercise 4.13, perform each of the following steps:

a) Read the problem statement.
b) Formulate the algorithm using pseudocode and top-down, stepwise refinement.
c) Write a Java program.
d) Test, debug and execute the Java program.
e) Process three complete sets of data.

4.11 Drivers are concerned with the mileage their automobiles get. One driver has kept track of several tankfuls of gasoline by recording miles driven and gallons used for each tankful. Develop a Java application that will input the miles driven and gallons used (both as integers) for each tankful. The program should calculate and display the miles per gallon obtained for each tankful and print the combined miles per gallon obtained for all tankfuls up to this point. All averaging calculations should produce floating-point results. Use input dialogs to obtain the data from the user.

ANS:

```
// Exercise 4.11 Solution: Gas.java
// Program calculates average mpg
import java.text.DecimalFormat;
import javax.swing.JOptionPane;

public class Gas {

   public static void main( String args[] )
   {
      int miles, gallons, totalMiles = 0, totalGallons = 0;
      float milesPerGallon, totalMilesPerGallon;
      String inputMiles, inputGallons, result = "";

      // read first number from user as a string
      inputMiles = JOptionPane.showInputDialog(
         "Enter miles (-1 to quit):" );

      // convert miles from type String to type int
      miles = Integer.parseInt( inputMiles );

      // exit if the input is -1 otherwise, proceed with the program
      while ( miles != -1 ) {
         // read second number from user as String
         inputGallons = JOptionPane.showInputDialog( "Enter gallons:" );

         // convert gallons from type String to type int
         gallons = Integer.parseInt( inputGallons );

         totalMiles += miles;
         totalGallons += gallons;

         DecimalFormat twoDigits = new DecimalFormat( "0.00" );

```

Fig. S4.2 Solution to Exercise 4.11. (Part 1 of 2.)

```
         if ( gallons != 0 ) {
            milesPerGallon = (float) miles / gallons;
            result = "MPG this tankful: " +
               twoDigits.format( milesPerGallon ) + "\n";
         }

         totalMilesPerGallon = (float) totalMiles / totalGallons;
         result += "Total MPG: " +
            twoDigits.format( totalMilesPerGallon ) + "\n";

         JOptionPane.showMessageDialog( null, result, "Milage",
            JOptionPane.INFORMATION_MESSAGE );

         // input new value for miles and convert from String to int
         inputMiles = JOptionPane.showInputDialog(
            "Enter miles (-1 to quit):" );
         miles = Integer.parseInt( inputMiles );

      } // end while loop

      System.exit( 0 );

   } // end method main

} // end class Gas
```

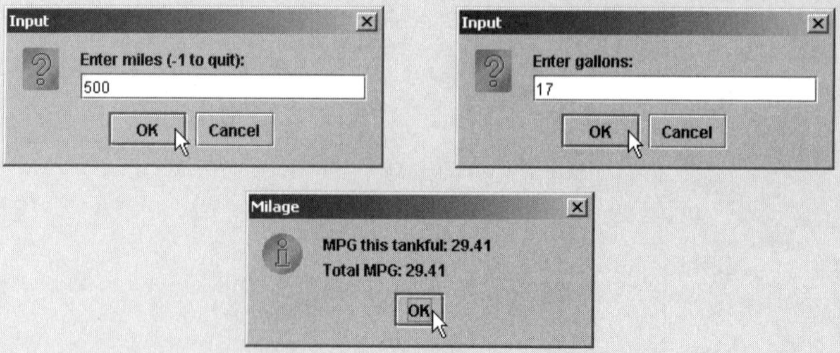

Fig. S4.2 Solution to Exercise 4.11. (Part 2 of 2.)

4.13 A large company pays its salespeople on a commission basis. The salespeople receive $200 per week, plus 9% of their gross sales for that week. For example, a salesperson who sells $5000 worth of merchandise in a week receives $200 plus 9% of $5000, or a total of $650. You have been supplied with a list of items sold by each salesperson. The values of these items are as follows:

```
ItemValue
1   239.99
2   129.75
3    99.95
4   350.89
```

Develop a Java application that inputs one salesperson's items sold for last week and calculates and displays that salesperson's earnings. There is no limit to the number of items that can be sold by a salesperson.

ANS:

```java
// Exercise 4.13 Solution: Sales.java
// Program calculates commissions based on sales.
import java.text.DecimalFormat;
import javax.swing.JOptionPane;

public class Sales {

   public static void main( String args[] )
   {
      double gross = 0.0, earnings;
      int product = 0, numberSold;
      String input;

      while ( product < 4 ) {
         product++;

         // read number from user as String
         input = JOptionPane.showInputDialog(
            "Enter number sold of product #" + product + ":" );

         // convert numbers from type String to type int
         numberSold = Integer.parseInt( input );

         // determine gross of each individual product and add to total
         if ( product == 1 )
            gross += numberSold * 239.99;

         else if ( product == 2 )
            gross += numberSold * 129.75;

         else if ( product == 3 )
            gross += numberSold * 99.95;

         else if ( product == 4 )
            gross += numberSold * 350.89;

      } // end while

      DecimalFormat twoDigits = new DecimalFormat( "0.00" );

      earnings = 0.09 * gross + 200;
      String result = "Earnings this week: " +
         twoDigits.format( earnings );

      JOptionPane.showMessageDialog( null, result, "Sales",
```

Fig. S4.3 Solution to Exercise 4.13. (Part 1 of 2.)

```
            JOptionPane.INFORMATION_MESSAGE );

         System.exit( 0 );

      } // end method main

   } // end class Sales
```

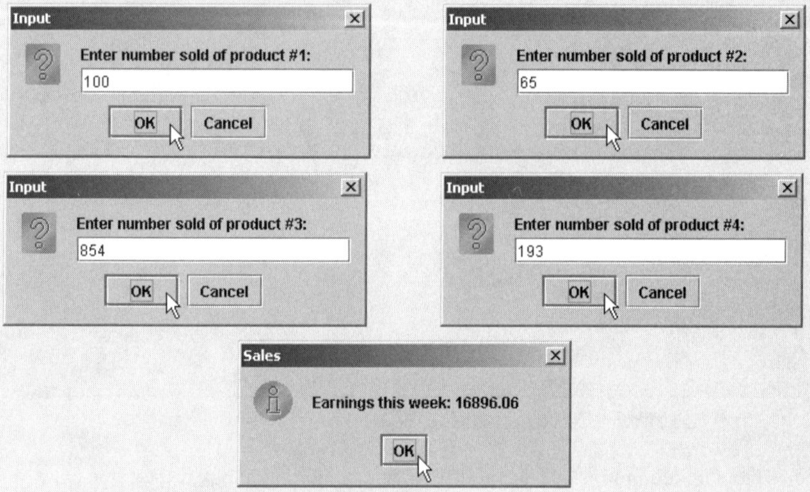

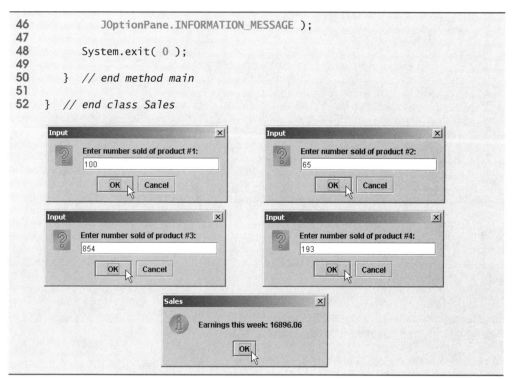

Fig. S4.3 Solution to Exercise 4.13. (Part 2 of 2.)

4.16 Write a Java application that uses looping to print the following table of values:

```
N     10*N   100*N   1000*N

1     10     100     1000
2     20     200     2000
3     30     300     3000
4     40     400     4000
5     50     500     5000
```

ANS:

```
// Exercise 4.16 Solution: Table.java
// Program prints a table of values using a while loop.

public class Table {

   public static void main( String args[] )
```

Fig. S4.4 Solution to Exercise 4.16. (Part 1 of 2.)

```
   {
      int n = 1;

      System.out.println( "N\t10*N\t100*N\t1000*N\n" );

      while ( n <= 5 ) {
         System.out.println( n + "\t" + ( 10 * n ) +
            "\t" + ( 100 * n ) + "\t" + ( 1000 * n ) );
         n++;
      }
   }

} // end class Table
```

```
N       10*N    100*N   1000*N

1       10      100     1000
2       20      200     2000
3       30      300     3000
4       40      400     4000
5       50      500     5000
```

Fig. S4.4 Solution to Exercise 4.16. (Part 2 of 2.)

4.18 Modify the program in Fig. 4.11 to validate its inputs. For any input, if the value entered is other than 1 or 2, keep looping until the user enters a correct value.

ANS:

```
// Exercise 4.18 Solution: Analysis.java
// Program performs analysis of examination results.
import javax.swing.JOptionPane;

public class Analysis {

   public static void main( String args[] )
   {
      // initializing variables in declarations
      int passes = 0, failures = 0, student = 1, result;
      String input, output;

      // process 10 students; counter-controlled loop
      while ( student <= 10 ) {
         input = JOptionPane.showInputDialog(
            "Enter result (1=pass,2=fail): " );

         result = Integer.parseInt( input );

         if ( result == 1 ) {       // if...else nested in while
```

Fig. S4.5 Solution to Exercise 4.18. (Part 1 of 2.)

```
            passes++;
            student++;
         }

         else if ( result == 2 ) {
            failures++;
            student++;
         }

         else
            JOptionPane.showMessageDialog( null, "Invalid Input",
               "Error", JOptionPane.ERROR_MESSAGE );
      }

      output = "Passed: " + passes + "\nFailed: " + failures;

      if ( passes > 8 )
         output += "\nRaise tuition ";

      JOptionPane.showMessageDialog( null, output,
         "Results", JOptionPane.INFORMATION_MESSAGE );

      System.exit( 0 );

   } // end method main

} // end class Analysis
```

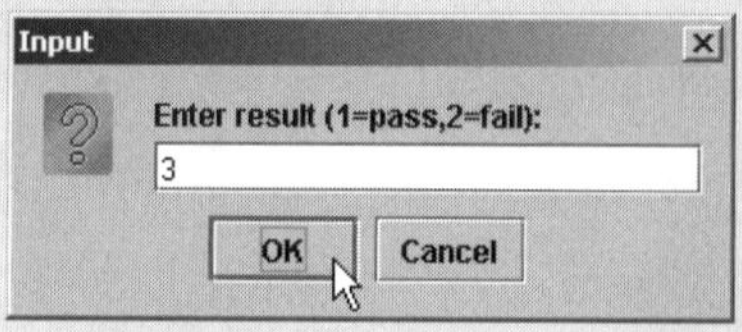

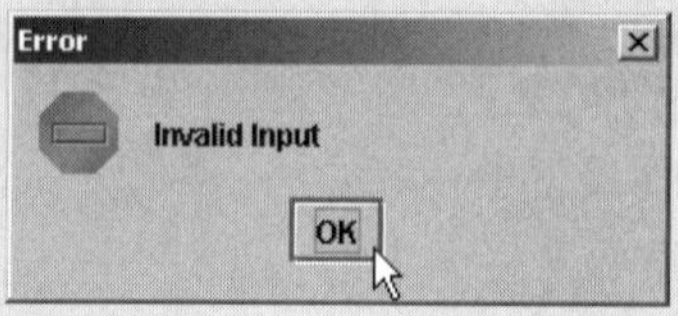

Fig. S4.5 Solution to Exercise 4.18. (Part 2 of 2.)

4.23 Write an applet that reads in the size of the side of a square and displays a hollow square of that size out of asterisks, by using the `drawString` method inside your applet's `paint` method. Use an input dialog to read the size from the user. Your program should work for squares of all side lengths between 1 and 20.

ANS:

```
// Exercise 4.23 Solution: Hollow.java
// Program prints a hollow square.
import java.awt.Graphics;
import javax.swing.*;

public class Hollow extends JApplet {
```

Fig. S4.6 Solution to 4.23. (Part 1 of 3.)

```
   int stars;

   // initializes applet by obtaining value from user
   public void init()
   {
      String input;   // String entered by user

      // read number from user as String
      input = JOptionPane.showInputDialog( "Enter length of side:" );

      // convert numbers from type String to type int
      stars = Integer.parseInt( input );

      if ( stars < 1 ) {
         stars = 1;
         JOptionPane.showMessageDialog( null,
            "Invalid Input\nUsing default value 1",
            "Error", JOptionPane.ERROR_MESSAGE );
      }
      if ( stars > 20 ) {
         stars = 20;
         JOptionPane.showMessageDialog( null,
            "Invalid Input\nUsing default value 20",
            "Error", JOptionPane.ERROR_MESSAGE );
      }

   } // end method init

   // draw Strings on applet's background
   public void paint( Graphics g )
   {
      super.paint( g ); // call inherited version of method paint

      int xCoordinate = 5, yCoordinate = 70, row = 1, column = 1;

      // repeat for as many rows as the user entered
      while ( row <= stars ) {

         // and for as many columns as rows
         while ( column <= stars ) {
            if ( row == 1 )
               g.drawString( "*", xCoordinate, yCoordinate );

            else if ( row == stars )
               g.drawString( "*", xCoordinate, yCoordinate );

            else if ( column == 1 )
               g.drawString( "*", xCoordinate, yCoordinate );

            else if ( column == stars )

               g.drawString( "*", xCoordinate, yCoordinate );
```

Fig. S4.6 Solution to 4.23. (Part 2 of 3.)

```java

            else
               g.drawString( " ", xCoordinate, yCoordinate );

            xCoordinate += 5;
            column++;
         }

         column = 1;
         row++;
         yCoordinate += 5;
         xCoordinate = 5;

      } // end while

   } // end method paint

} // end class Hollow
```

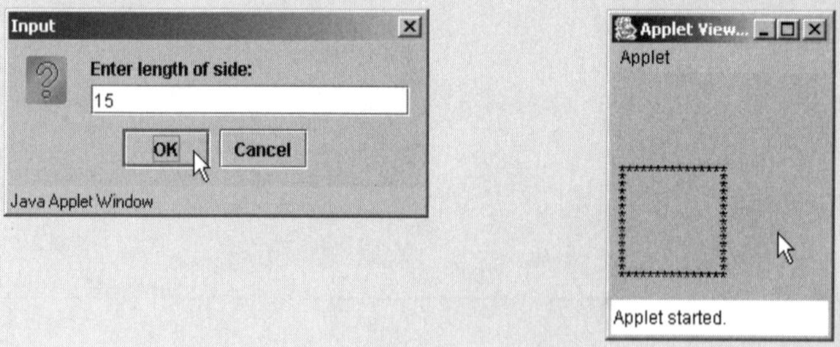

Fig. S4.6 Solution to 4.23. (Part 3 of 3.)

4.26 Write an application that uses only the output statements

```java
System.out.print( "* " );
System.out.print( " " );
System.out.println();
```

to display the checkerboard pattern that follows. Note that a `System.out.println` method call with no arguments causes the program to output a single newline character. [*Hint*: Repetition structures are required.]

```
* * * * * * * *
 * * * * * * * *
* * * * * * * *
 * * * * * * * *
* * * * * * * *
 * * * * * * * *
* * * * * * * *
 * * * * * * * *
```

ANS:

```java
// Exercise 4.26 Solution: Stars.java
// Program prints a checkerboard pattern.
public class Stars {

   public static void main( String args[] )
   {
      int row = 1;

      while ( row <= 8 ) {
         int column = 1;

         if ( row % 2 == 0 )
            System.out.print( " " );

         while ( column <= 8 ) {
            System.out.print( "* " );
            column++;
         }

         System.out.println();
         row++;
      }

   } // end method main

} // end class Stars
```

```
* * * * * * * *
 * * * * * * * *
* * * * * * * *
 * * * * * * * *
* * * * * * * *
 * * * * * * * *
* * * * * * * *
 * * * * * * * *
```

Fig. S4.7 Solution to Exercise 4.26.

4.27 Write an application that keeps displaying in the command window the multiples of the integer 2—namely, 2, 4, 8, 16, 32, 64, etc. Your loop should not terminate (i.e., create an infinite loop). What happens when you run this program?

ANS:

```java
// Exercise 4.27 Solution: Infinite.java
// Program creates an infinite loop.

public class Infinite {
```

Fig. S4.8 Solution to Exercise 4.27. (Part 1 of 2.)

```

   public static void main( String args[] )
   {
      int x = 1;

      while ( true ) {
         x *= 2;
         System.out.println( x );
      }
   }

} // end class Infinite
```

```
2
4
8
16
32
64
128
256
512
1024
2048
4096
8192
16384
32768
65536
131072
262144
524288
1048576
2097152
4194304
8388608
16777216
33554432
67108864
134217728
268435456
536870912
1073741824
-2147483648
0
0
0
```

Fig. S4.8 Solution to Exercise 4.27. (Part 2 of 2.)

4.30 Write an application that reads three nonzero integers and determines whether and prints if they could represent the sides of a right triangle.

ANS:

```java
// Exercise 4.30 Solution: Triangle2.java
// Program takes three integers and determines if they
// form the sides of a right triangle.
import javax.swing.JOptionPane;

public class Triangle2 {

   public static void main( String args[] )
   {
      int side1,          // length of side 1
          side2,          // length of side 2
          side3;          // length of side 3
      String input,       // user input
             result;      // output String

      // read number from user as String
      input = JOptionPane.showInputDialog( "Enter length of side 1:" );

      side1 = Integer.parseInt( input );

      // read number from user as String
      input = JOptionPane.showInputDialog( "Enter length of side 2:" );

      side2 = Integer.parseInt( input );

      // read number from user as String
      input = JOptionPane.showInputDialog( "Enter length of side 3:" );

      side3 = Integer.parseInt( input );

      int side1Square = side1 * side1;
      int side2Square = side2 * side2;
      int side3Square = side3 * side3;

      result = "These do not form a right triangle.";

      if ( ( side1Square + side2Square ) == side3Square )
         result = "These are the sides of a right triangle.";

      if ( ( side1Square + side3Square ) == side2Square )
         result = "These are the sides of a right triangle.";

      if ( ( side2Square + side3Square ) == side1Square )
         result = "These are the sides of a right triangle.";

      JOptionPane.showMessageDialog( null, result, "Result",
```

Fig. S4.9 Solution to Exercise 4.30. (Part 1 of 2.)

```
                JOptionPane.INFORMATION_MESSAGE );

        System.exit( 0 );

    } // end method main

} // end class Triangle2
```

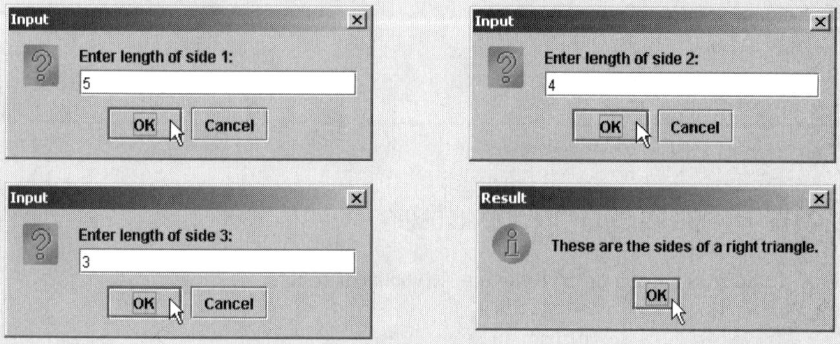

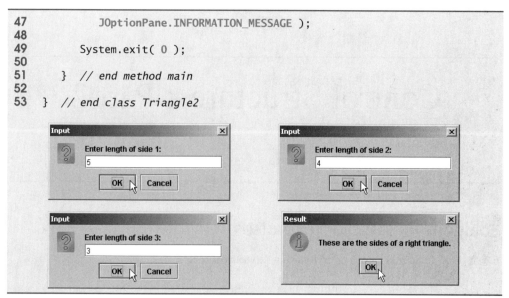

Fig. S4.9 Solution to Exercise 4.30. (Part 2 of 2.)

5

Control Structures: Part 2

Solutions to Selected Exercises

5.4 Find the error(s) in each of the following segments of code:

a)
```
For ( i = 100, i >= 1, i++ )
    System.out.println( i );
```

ANS: *The F in* **For** *should be lowercase. Semicolons should be used in the* **For** *header instead of commas. ++ should be --.*

b) The following code should print whether integer `value` is odd or even:

```
switch ( value % 2 ) {

   case 0:
      System.out.println( "Even integer" );

   case 1:
      System.out.println( "Odd integer" );
}
```

ANS: *A* **break** *statement should be placed in* **case** 0.

c) The following code should output the odd integers from 19 to 1:

```
for ( i = 19; i >= 1; i += 2 )
   System.out.println( i );
```

ANS: += *should be* -=.

d) The following code should output the even integers from 2 to 100:

```
counter = 2;

do {
   System.out.println( counter );
   counter += 2;
} While ( counter < 100 );
```

ANS: *The W in* **`while`** *should be lowercase. < should be <=.*

5.6 Write an application that finds the smallest of several integers. Assume that the first value read specifies the number of values to input from the user.

ANS:

```java
// Exercise 5.6 Solution: Small.java
// Program finds the smallest of several integers.

import javax.swing.JOptionPane;

public class Small {

   // main method begins execution of Java application
   public static void main( String args[] )
   {
      int smallest = 0,    // smallest number
          number = 0,      // number entered by user
          integers;        // number of integers
      String input;        // user input

      input = JOptionPane.showInputDialog( "Enter number of integers:" );
      integers = Integer.parseInt( input );

      for ( int counter = 1; counter <= integers; counter++ ) {
         input = JOptionPane.showInputDialog( "Enter integer:" );
         number = Integer.parseInt( input );

         if ( counter == 1 )
            smallest = number;

         else if ( number < smallest )
            smallest = number;

      } // end for loop

      JOptionPane.showMessageDialog( null, "Smallest Integer is: " +
         smallest, "Result", JOptionPane.INFORMATION_MESSAGE );

      System.exit( 0 );

   }  // end of main method

}  // end of class Small
```

Fig. S5.1 Solution to Exercise 5.6. (Part 1 of 2.)

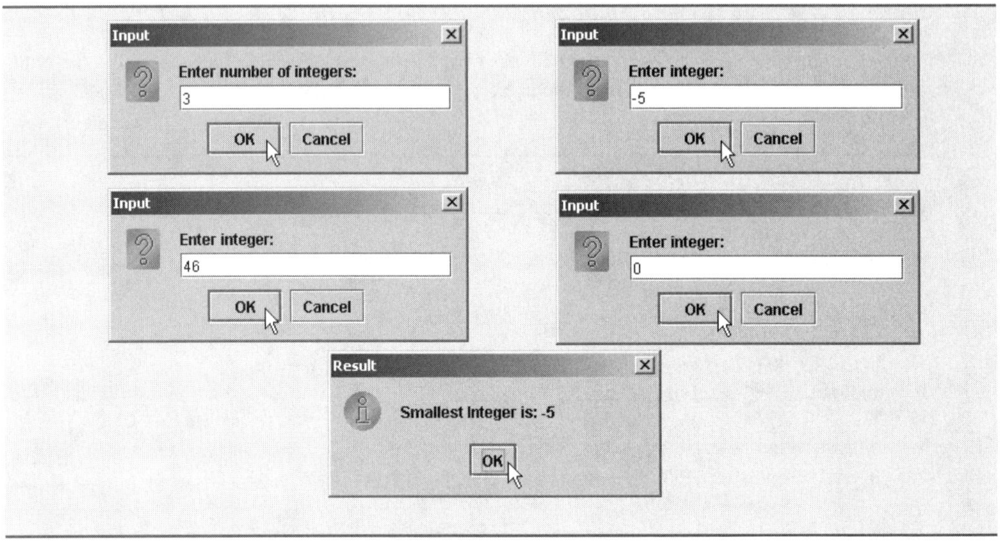

Fig. S5.1 Solution to Exercise 5.6. (Part 2 of 2.)

5.8 *Factorials* are used frequently in probability problems. The factorial of a positive integer *n* (written *n!* and pronounced "*n* factorial") is equal to the product of the positive integers from 1 to *n*. Write an application that evaluates the factorials of the integers from 1 to 5. Display the results in tabular format in a `JTextArea` that is displayed on a message dialog. What difficulty might prevent you from calculating the factorial of 20?

ANS:

```
// Exercise 5.8 Solution: Factorial.java
// Program calculates factorials.

import javax.swing.*;

public class Factorial {

   // main method begins execution of Java program
   public static void main( String args[] )
   {
      JTextArea outputArea = new JTextArea( 5, 10 );
      String outputString = "X\tX!\n";

      for ( int number = 1; number <= 5; number++ ) {
         int factorial = 1;

         for ( int smaller = 1; smaller <= number; smaller++ )
            factorial *= smaller;

         outputString += "\n" + number + "\t" + factorial;
      }
```

Fig. S5.2 Solution to Exercise 5.8. (Part 1 of 2.)

```java

      outputArea.setText( outputString );
      JOptionPane.showMessageDialog( null, outputArea,
         "Factorial", JOptionPane.INFORMATION_MESSAGE );

      System.exit( 0 );
   }

} // end class Factorial
```

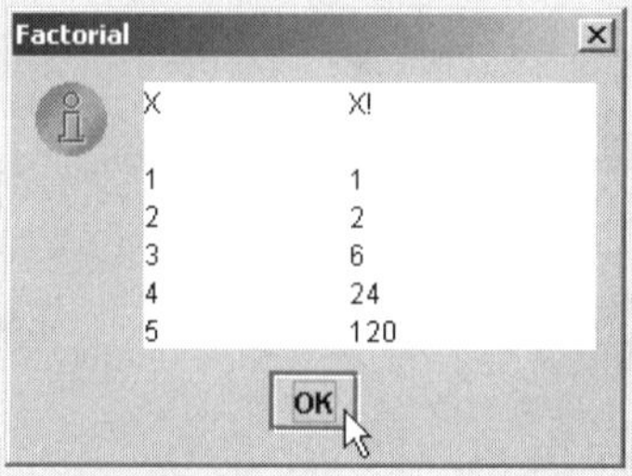

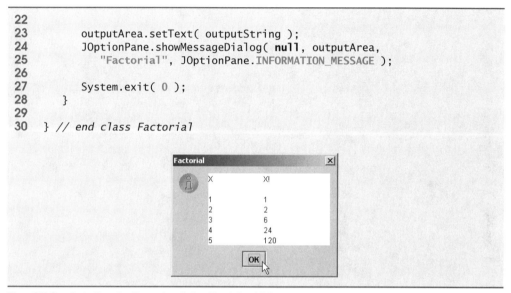

Fig. S5.2 Solution to Exercise 5.8. (Part 2 of 2.)

5.11 One interesting application of computers is drawing graphs and bar charts (sometimes called "histograms"). Write an applet that reads five numbers, each between 1 and 30. For each number read, your program should draw that number of adjacent asterisks. For example, if your program reads the number 7, it should display *******. [*Hint:* All asterisks on one line should be drawn with the same *y*-coordinate.]

ANS:

```java
// Exercise 5.11 Solution: Graphs.java
// Program prints 5 histograms with lengths determined by user.

import java.awt.Graphics;
import javax.swing.*;

public class Graphs extends JApplet {
   int number1, number2, number3, number4, number5;

   // initialize applet by obtaining values from user
   public void init()
   {
      String inputString;
      int inputNumber, counter = 1;

      while ( counter <= 5) {
         inputString = JOptionPane.showInputDialog( "Enter number:" );
         inputNumber = Integer.parseInt( inputString );

         // define appropriate num if input is between 1-30
         if ( inputNumber >= 1 && inputNumber <= 30 ) {
```

Fig. S5.3 Solution to Exercise 5.11. (Part 1 of 4.)

```

            switch ( counter ) {

               case 1:
                  number1 = inputNumber;
                  break;   // done processing case

               case 2:
                  number2 = inputNumber;
                  break;   // done processing case

               case 3:
                  number3 = inputNumber;
                  break;   // done processing case

               case 4:
                  number4 = inputNumber;
                  break;   // done processing case

               case 5:
                  number5 = inputNumber;
                  break;   // done processing case
            }

            counter++;

         } // end if

         else
            JOptionPane.showMessageDialog( null,
               "Invalid Input\nNumber should be between 1 and 30",
               "Error", JOptionPane.ERROR_MESSAGE );

      } // end while

   } // end method init

   // draw histograms on applet's background
   public void paint( Graphics g )
   {
      // call inherited version of method paint
      super.paint( g );

      int xCoordinate, yCoordinate = 0, value = 0;

      // print histograms
      for ( int counter = 1; counter <= 5; counter++ ) {

         switch ( counter ) {

```

Fig. S5.3 Solution to Exercise 5.11. (Part 2 of 4.)

```
            case 1:
               value = number1;
               break;   // done processing case

            case 2:
               value = number2;
               break;   // done processing case

            case 3:
               value = number3;
               break;   // done processing case

            case 4:
               value = number4;
               break;   // done processing case

            case 5:
               value = number5;
               break;   // done processing case
         }

         xCoordinate = 5;
         yCoordinate = counter * 10 + 40;

         for ( int j = 1; j <= value; j++ )
            g.drawString( "*", xCoordinate += 5, yCoordinate );
      }

   } // end method paint

} // end class Graphs
```

Fig. S5.3 Solution to Exercise 5.11. (Part 3 of 4.)

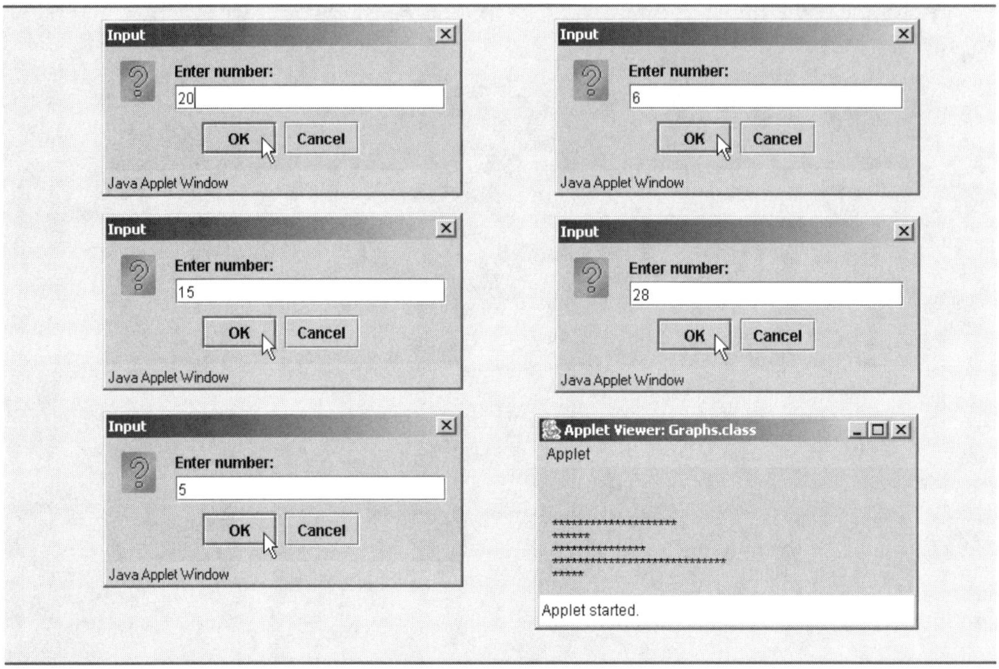

Fig. S5.3 Solution to Exercise 5.11. (Part 4 of 4.)

5.14 Assume that `i = 1`, `j = 2`, `k = 3` and `m = 2`. What does each of the following statements print?

a) `System.out.println( i == 1 );`

ANS: *True.*

b) `System.out.println( j == 3 );`

ANS: *False.*

c) `System.out.println( i >= 1 && j < 4 );`

ANS: *True.*

d) `System.out.println( m <= 99 & k < m );`

ANS: *False.*

e) `System.out.println( j >= i || k == m );`

ANS: *True.*

f) `System.out.println( k + m < j | 3 - j >= k );`

ANS: *False.*

g) `System.out.println( !( k > m ) );`

ANS: *False.*

5.16 Calculate the value of π from the infinite series

$$\pi = 4 - \frac{4}{3} + \frac{4}{5} - \frac{4}{7} + \frac{4}{9} - \frac{4}{11} + \cdots$$

Print a table that shows the value of π approximated by computing one term of this series, by two terms, by three terms, etc. How many terms of this series do you have to use before you first get 3.14? 3.141? 3.1415? 3.14159?

ANS:

```java
// Execise 5.16 Solution: Pi.java
// Program calculates Pi from the infinite series.

import javax.swing.*;

public class Pi {

   //method main begins execution of Java application
   public static void main( String args[] )
   {
      double piValue = 0, number = 4.0, denominator = 1.0;
      int accuracy = 400;

      JTextArea outputArea = new JTextArea( 17, 40 );
      JScrollPane scroller = new JScrollPane( outputArea );

      String output = "Accuracy: \n" + accuracy;
      output += "\nTerm\t\tPi\n";

      for ( int term = 1; term <= accuracy; term++ ) {

         if ( term % 2 != 0 )
            piValue += number / denominator;

         else
            piValue -= number / denominator;

         output += "\n" + term + "\t\t" + piValue;
         denominator += 2.0;
      }

      outputArea.setText( output );

      JOptionPane.showMessageDialog( null, scroller, "PI",
         JOptionPane.INFORMATION_MESSAGE );

      System.exit( 0 );
```

Fig. S5.4 Solution to Exercise 5.16. (Part 1 of 2.)

```

    } // end method main

} // end class Pi
```

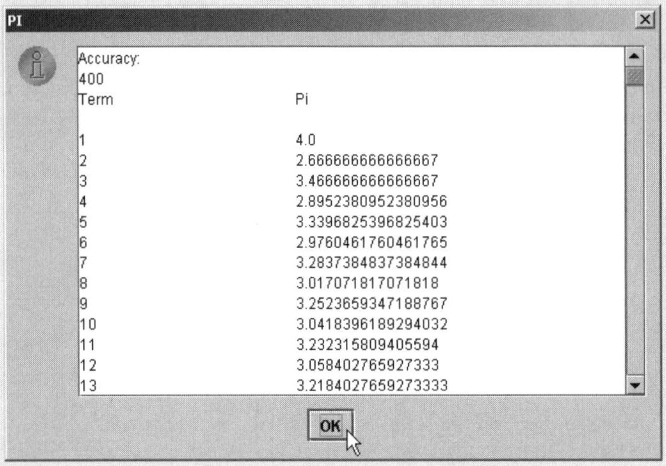

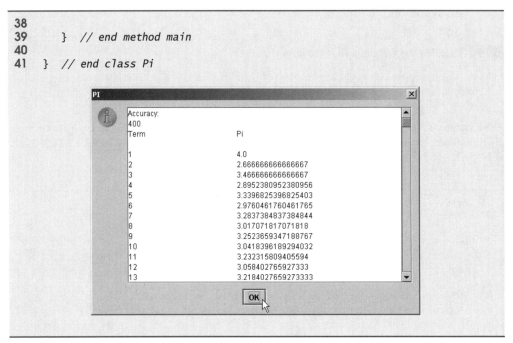

Fig. S5.4 Solution to Exercise 5.16. (Part 2 of 2.)

5.19 (*De Morgan's Laws*) In this chapter, we have discussed the logical operators &&, &, ||, |, ^ and !. De Morgan's Laws can sometimes make it more convenient for us to express a logical expression. These laws state that the expression !(*condition1* && *condition2*) is logically equivalent to the expression (!*condition1* || !*condition2*). Also, the expression !(*condition1* || *condition2*) is logically equivalent to the expression (!*condition1* && !*condition2*). Use De Morgan's Laws to write equivalent expressions for each of the following, then write an application to show that both the original expression and the new expression in each case produce the same value:

a) `!( x < 5 ) && !( y >= 7 )`
b) `!( a == b ) || !( g != 5 )`
c) `!( ( x <= 8 ) && ( y > 4 ) )`
d) `!( ( i > 4 ) || ( j <= 6 ) )`

ANS:

```
// Exercise 5.19 Solution: DeMorgan.java
// Program tests DeMorgan's laws.

import javax.swing.JOptionPane;

public class DeMorgan {

   // method main begins execution of Java application
   public static void main( String args[] )
```

Fig. S5.5 Solution to Exercise 5.19. (Part 1 of 3.)

```
    {
       String result = "";
       int x = 6, y = 0;

       // part a
       if ( !( x < 5 ) && !( y >= 7 ) )
          result += "\n!( x < 5 ) && !( y >= 7 )";

       if ( !( ( x < 5 ) || ( y >= 7 ) ) )
          result += "\n!( ( x < 5 ) || ( y >= 7 )";

       int a = 8, b = 22, g = 88;

       // part b
       if ( !( a == b ) || !( g != 5 ) )
          result += "\n!( a == b ) || !( g != 5 )";

       if ( !( ( a == b ) && ( g != 5 ) ) )
          result += "\n!( ( a == b ) && ( g != 5 ) )";

       x = 8;
       y = 2;

       // part c
       if ( !( ( x <= 8 ) && ( y > 4 ) ) )
          result += "\n!( ( x <= 8 ) && ( y > 4 ) )";

       if ( !( x <= 8 ) || !( y > 4 ) )
          result += "\n!( x <= 8 ) || !( y > 4 )";

       int i = 0, j = 7;

       // part d
       if ( !( ( i > 4 ) || ( j <= 6 ) ) )
          result += "\n!( ( i > 4 ) || ( j <= 6 ) )";

       if ( !( i > 4 ) && !( j <= 6 ) )
          result += "\n!( i > 4 ) && !( j <= 6 )";

       JOptionPane.showMessageDialog( null, result, "DeMorgan's Laws",
          JOptionPane.INFORMATION_MESSAGE );

       System.exit( 0 );

    } // end method main

 } // end class DeMorgan
```

Fig. S5.5 Solution to Exercise 5.19. (Part 2 of 3.)

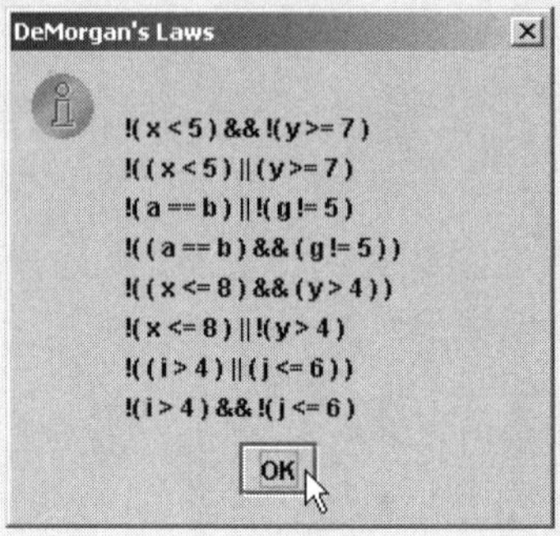

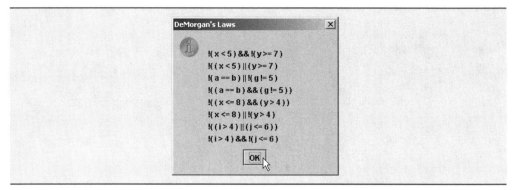

Fig. S5.5 Solution to Exercise 5.19. (Part 3 of 3.)

5.25 (*"The Twelve Days of Christmas" Song*) Write an application that uses repetition and `switch` statements to print the song "The Twelve Days of Christmas." One `switch` statement should be used to print the day (i.e., "First," "Second," etc.). A separate `switch` statement should be used to print the remainder of each verse. Visit the Web site `www.12days.com/library/carols/12daysofxmas.htm` for the complete lyrics to the song.

ANS:

```java
// Exercise 5.25 Solution: Twelve.java
// Program prints the 12 days of Christmas song.

import javax.swing.*;

public class Twelve {

   // method main begins execution of Java application
   public static void main( String args[] )
   {
      JTextArea outputArea = new JTextArea( 17, 40 );
      JScrollPane scroller = new JScrollPane( outputArea );
      String result = "";

      for ( int day = 1; day <= 12; day++ ) {
         result += "\nOn the ";

         // add correct day to String
         switch( day ) {

            case 1:
               result += "first";
               break;

            case 2:
               result += "second";
               break;
```

Fig. S5.6 Solution to Exercise 5.25. (Part 1 of 4.)

```

         case 3:
            result += "third";
            break;

         case 4:
            result += "fourth";
            break;

         case 5:
            result += "fifth";
            break;

         case 6:
            result += "sixth";
            break;

         case 7:
            result += "seventh";
            break;

         case 8:
            result += "eighth";
            break;

         case 9:
            result += "ninth";
            break;

         case 10:
            result += "tenth";
            break;

         case 11:
            result += "eleventh";
            break;

         case 12:
            result += "twelfth";
            break;

      } // end switch

      result += " day of Christmas, my true love gave to me: ";

      // add remainder of verse to String
      switch( day ) {

         case 12:
            result += "  Twelve lords-a-leaping, ";
```

Fig. S5.6 Solution to Exercise 5.25. (Part 2 of 4.)

```java
            case 11:
               result += "  Eleven pipers piping, ";
            case 10:
               result += "  Ten drummers drumming, ";
            case 9:
               result += "  Nine ladies dancing, ";
            case 8:
               result += "  Eight maids-a-milking, ";
            case 7:
               result += "  Seven swans-a-swimming, ";
            case 6:
               result += "  Six geese-a-laying, ";
            case 5:
               result += "  Five golden rings.";
            case 4:
               result += "  Four calling birds, ";
            case 3:
               result += "  Three French hens, ";
            case 2:
               result += "  Two turtle doves, and";
            case 1:
               result += "  a Partridge in pear tree.";
         } // end switch
      } // end for
      outputArea.setText( result );
      JOptionPane.showMessageDialog( null, scroller,
         "Twelve Days of Christmas", JOptionPane.INFORMATION_MESSAGE );
      System.exit( 0 );
   } // end method main
} // end class Twelve
```

Fig. S5.6 Solution to Exercise 5.25. (Part 3 of 4.)

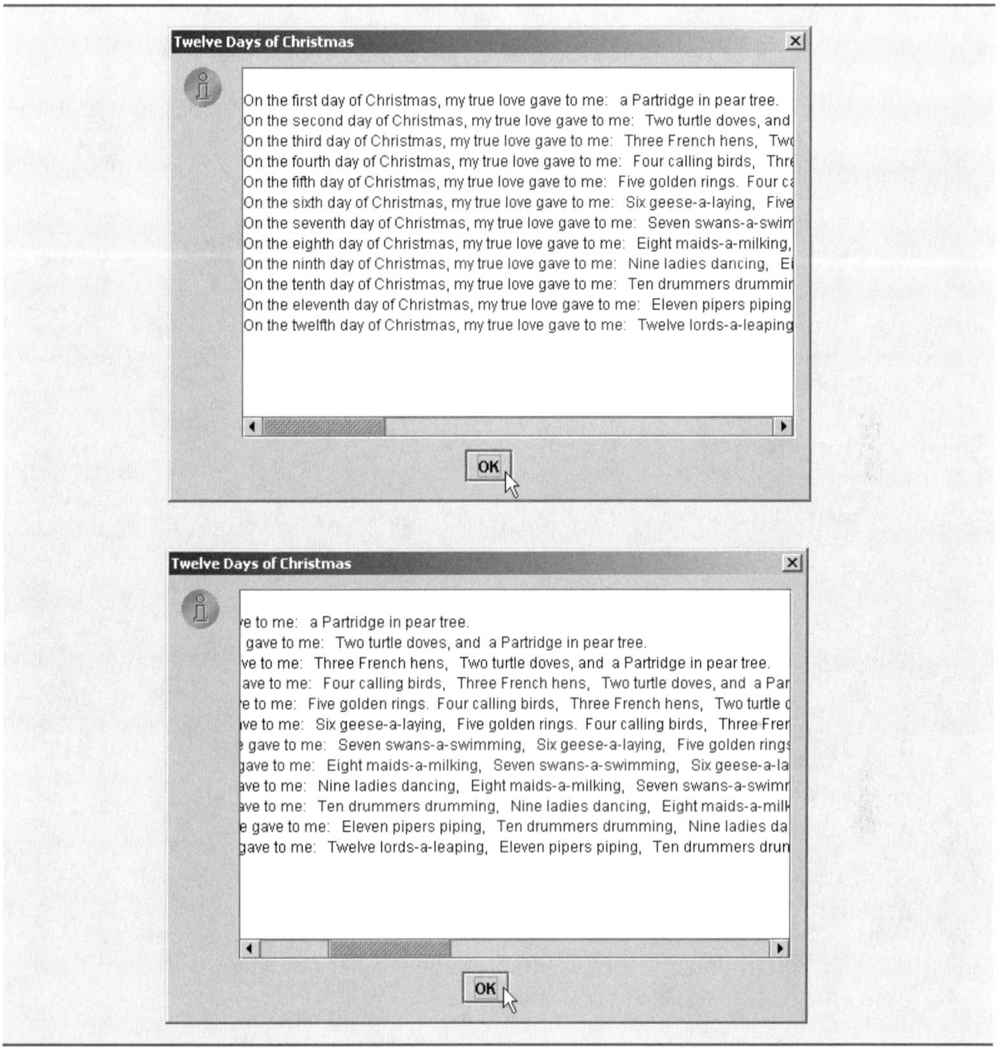
Twelve Days of Christmas
On the first day of Christmas, my true love gave to me: a Partridge in pear tree.
On the second day of Christmas, my true love gave to me: Two turtle doves, and
On the third day of Christmas, my true love gave to me: Three French hens, Two
On the fourth day of Christmas, my true love gave to me: Four calling birds, Thre
On the fifth day of Christmas, my true love gave to me: Five golden rings. Four c
On the sixth day of Christmas, my true love gave to me: Six geese-a-laying, Five
On the seventh day of Christmas, my true love gave to me: Seven swans-a-swim
On the eighth day of Christmas, my true love gave to me: Eight maids-a-milking,
On the ninth day of Christmas, my true love gave to me: Nine ladies dancing, E
On the tenth day of Christmas, my true love gave to me: Ten drummers drummi
On the eleventh day of Christmas, my true love gave to me: Eleven pipers piping
On the twelfth day of Christmas, my true love gave to me: Twelve lords-a-leaping
OK
Twelve Days of Christmas
e to me: a Partridge in pear tree.
gave to me: Two turtle doves, and a Partridge in pear tree.
ve to me: Three French hens, Two turtle doves, and a Partridge in pear tree.
ave to me: Four calling birds, Three French hens, Two turtle doves, and a Par
e to me: Five golden rings. Four calling birds, Three French hens, Two turtle
ve to me: Six geese-a-laying, Five golden rings. Four calling birds, Three Fre
gave to me: Seven swans-a-swimming, Six geese-a-laying, Five golden ring
gave to me: Eight maids-a-milking, Seven swans-a-swimming, Six geese-a-la
ve to me: Nine ladies dancing, Eight maids-a-milking, Seven swans-a-swim
ve to me: Ten drummers drumming, Nine ladies dancing, Eight maids-a-mil
e gave to me: Eleven pipers piping, Ten drummers drumming, Nine ladies da
gave to me: Twelve lords-a-leaping, Eleven pipers piping, Ten drummers dru
OK

Fig. S5.6 Solution to Exercise 5.25. (Part 4 of 4.)

6

Methods

Solutions to Selected Exercises

6.7 What is the value of `x` after each of the following statements is executed?

a) `x = Math.abs( 7.5 );`

ANS: *7.5*

b) `x = Math.floor( 7.5 );`

ANS: *7.0*

c) `x = Math.abs( 0.0 );`

ANS: *0.0*

d) `x = Math.ceil( 0.0 );`

ANS: *0.0*

e) `x = Math.abs( -6.4 );`

ANS: *6.4*

f) `x = Math.ceil( -6.4 );`

ANS: *-6.0*

g) `x = Math.ceil( -Math.abs( -8 + Math.floor( -5.5 ) ) );`

ANS: *-14.0*

6.9 An application of method `Math.floor` is rounding a value to the nearest integer. The statement

```
y = Math.floor( x + 0.5 );
```

will round the number `x` to the nearest integer and assign the result to `y`. Write an applet that reads `double` values and uses the preceding statement to round each of the numbers to the nearest integer. For each number processed, display both the original number and the rounded number.

ANS:

```java
// Exercise 6.9 Solution: Test.java
// Program tests Math.floor.

import java.awt.event.*;
import java.awt.*;
import javax.swing.*;

public class Test extends JApplet implements ActionListener {
   JTextField inputField;
   JLabel inputLabel;

   // set up GUI components
   public void init()
   {
      inputLabel = new JLabel( "Enter a decimal number:" );
      inputField = new JTextField( 4 );
      inputField.addActionListener( this );

      Container container = getContentPane();
      container.setLayout( new FlowLayout() );
      container.add( inputLabel );
      container.add( inputField );
   }

   // execute floor function on input number
   public void actionPerformed( ActionEvent e )
   {
      double x = Double.parseDouble( inputField.getText() );

      showStatus( "Number: " + x + "    Math.floor( x + .5 ): "
         + String.valueOf( Math.floor( x + .5 ) ) );
   }

} // end class Test
```

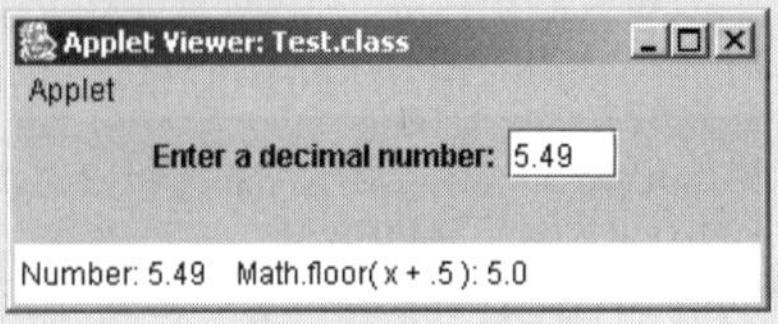

Fig. S6.1 Solution to Exercise 6.9.

6.12 Write statements that assign random integers to the variable *n* in the following ranges:

a) $1 \leq n \leq 2$

ANS: `n = ( int ) ( 1 + Math.random() * 2 );`

b) $1 \leq n \leq 100$

ANS: *n = (int) (1 + Math.random() * 100);*

c) $0 \le n \le 9$

ANS: `n = ( int ) ( Math.random() * 10 );`

d) $1000 \le n \le 1112$

ANS: `n = ( int ) ( 1000 + Math.random() * 113 );`

e) $-1 \le n \le 1$

ANS: `n = ( int ) ( -1 + Math.random() * 3 );`

f) $-3 \le n \le 11$

ANS: `n = ( int ) ( -3 + Math.random() * 15 );`

6.15 Define a method `hypotenuse` that calculates the length of the hypotenuse of a right triangle when the lengths of the other two sides are given. (Use the sample data in Fig. 6.21.) The method should take two arguments of type `double` and return the hypotenuse as a `double`. Incorporate this method into an applet that reads values for `side1` and `side2` from `JTextField` objects and performs the calculation with the `hypotenuse` method. Determine the length of the hypotenuse for each of the triangles in Fig. 6.21. [*Note*: Register for event handling on only the second `JTextField`. The user should interact with the program by typing numbers in both `JTextField`s, but pressing *Enter* only in the second `JTextField`.]

Triangle	Side 1	Side 2
1	3.0	4.0
2	5.0	12.0
3	8.0	15.0

Fig. S6.2 Values for the sides of triangles in Exercise 6.15.

ANS:

```java
// Exercise 6.15 Solution: Triangle.java
// Program calculates the hypotenuse of a right triangle.

import java.awt.event.*;
import java.awt.*;
import javax.swing.*;

public class Triangle extends JApplet implements ActionListener {
   JTextField side1Input, side2Input;
   JLabel side1Prompt, side2Prompt;

   // set up GUI components
   public void init()
   {
      side1Prompt = new JLabel( "Enter side 1: " );
      side2Prompt = new JLabel( "Enter side 2: " );
      side1Input = new JTextField( 4 );
      side2Input = new JTextField( 4 );
```

Fig. S6.3 Solution to Exercise 6.15. (Part 1 of 2.)

```
      side2Input.addActionListener( this );

      Container container = getContentPane();
      container.setLayout( new FlowLayout() );
      container.add( side1Prompt );
      container.add( side1Input );
      container.add( side2Prompt );
      container.add( side2Input );
   }

   // perform calculation of hypotenuse
   public void actionPerformed( ActionEvent actionEvent )
   {
      double side1, side2;

      side1 = Double.parseDouble( side1Input.getText() );
      side2 = Double.parseDouble( side2Input.getText() );

      double result = hypotenuse( side1, side2 );
      showStatus( "Hypotenuse is : " + result );
   }

   // calculate hypotenuse given lengths of two sides
   public double hypotenuse( double side1, double side2 )
   {
      double hypotenuseSquared = Math.pow( side1, 2 ) +
         Math.pow( side2, 2 );

      return Math.sqrt( hypotenuseSquared );
   }

} // end class Triangle
```

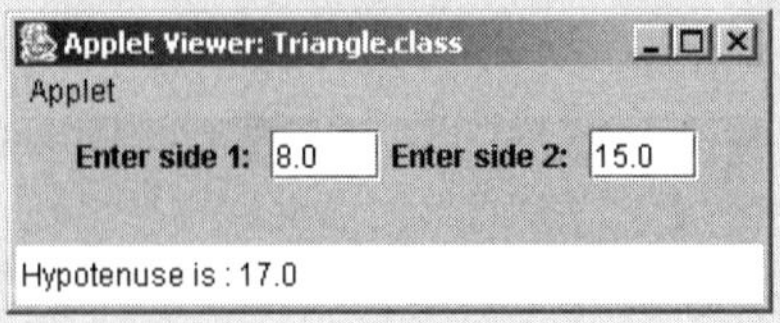

Fig. S6.3 Solution to Exercise 6.15. (Part 2 of 2.)

6.17 Write a method `isEven` that uses the remainder operator (%) to determine whether an integer is even. The method should take an integer argument and return `true` if the integer is even and `false` otherwise. Incorporate this method into an applet that inputs a sequence of integers (one at a time, using a `JTextField`).

ANS:

```
// Exercise 6.17 Solution: EvenOdd.java
// Program determines if a number is odd or even.
```

Fig. S6.4 Solution to Exercise 6.17. (Part 1 of 3.)

```java
import java.awt.event.*;
import java.awt.*;
import javax.swing.*;

public class EvenOdd extends JApplet implements ActionListener {
   JTextField inputField;
   JLabel prompt;

   // set up GUI components
   public void init()
   {
      prompt = new JLabel( "Enter number: " );
      inputField = new JTextField( 4 );
      inputField.addActionListener( this );

      Container container = getContentPane();
      container.setLayout( new FlowLayout() );
      container.add( prompt );
      container.add( inputField );

   } // end method init

   // determine if input is even or odd
   public void actionPerformed( ActionEvent e )
   {
      int number = Integer.parseInt( inputField.getText() );
      String result = "";

      if ( isEven( number ) == true )
         result = number + " is even";

      else
         result = number + " is odd ";

      showStatus( result );

   } // end method actionPerformed

   // return true if number is even
   public boolean isEven( int number )
   {
      if ( number % 2 == 0 )
         return true;

      return false;

   } // end method isEven

} // end class EvenOdd
```

Fig. S6.4 Solution to Exercise 6.17. (Part 2 of 3.)

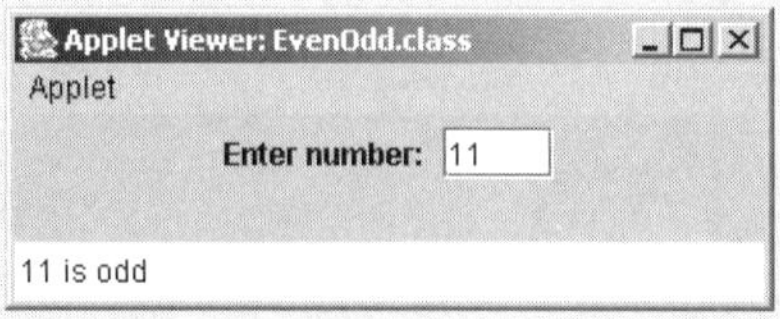

Fig. S6.4 Solution to Exercise 6.17. (Part 3 of 3.)

6.18 Write a method `squareOfAsterisks` that displays a solid square (the same number of rows and columns) of asterisks whose side is specified in integer parameter `side`. For example, if `side` is 4, the method displays the pattern of asterisks at the top of the next page.

```
****
****
****
****
```

Incorporate this method into an applet that reads an integer value for `side` from the user and performs the drawing with the `squareOfAsterisks` method. Note that this method should be called from the applet's `paint` method and should be passed the `Graphics` object from `paint`.

ANS:

```java
// Exercise 6.18 Solution: Square.java
// Program draws a square of asterisks.

import java.awt.*;
import javax.swing.*;

public class Square extends JApplet {
   int inputNumber;

   // obtain value from user
   public void init()
   {
      String inputString = JOptionPane.showInputDialog(
         "Enter square size:" );

      inputNumber = Integer.parseInt( inputString );

   } // end method init

   // draw square of asteriks on applet's background
   public void squareOfAsterisks( Graphics g, int side )
   {
      int y = 50, x = 5;

      for ( int count = 1; count <= side * side; count++ ) {
         g.drawString( "*", x += 5, y );

```

Fig. S6.5 Solution to Exercise 6.18. (Part 1 of 2.)

```
         if ( count % side == 0 ) {
            y += 10;
            x = 5;
         }

      } // end for loop

   } // end method squareOfAsterisks

   // execute method squareOfAsterisks
   public void paint( Graphics g )
   {
      squareOfAsterisks( g, inputNumber );

   } // end method paint

} // end class Square
```

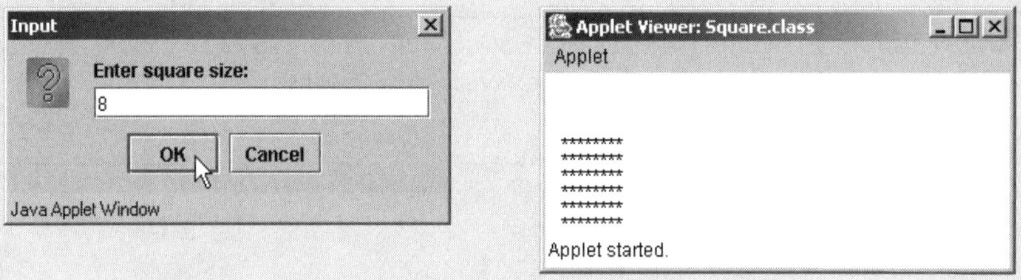

Fig. S6.5 Solution to Exercise 6.18. (Part 2 of 2.)

6.19 Modify the method created in Exercise 6 to form the square out of whatever character is contained in character parameter `fillCharacter`. Thus, if `side` is 5 and `fillCharacter` is "#", the method should print

```
#####
#####
#####
#####
#####
```

ANS:

```
// Exercise 6.19 Solution: Square2.java
// Program draws a square of asterisks

import java.awt.*;
import java.awt.event.*;
import javax.swing.*;

```

Fig. S6.6 Solution to Exercise 6.19. (Part 1 of 3.)

```
public class Square2 extends JApplet {
   int size;
   String fillCharacter;

   public void init()
   {
      // get user-specified square size
      String input = JOptionPane.showInputDialog( "Enter square size:" );
      size = Integer.parseInt( input );

      // choose character to compose the square with
      fillCharacter = JOptionPane.showInputDialog(
         "Enter square character:" );
   }

   // draw a square filled with the specified char
   public void paint( Graphics g )
   {
      fillSquare( g );
   }

   public void fillSquare( Graphics g )
   {
      // set initial position and value of output
      int y = 50, x = 5;

      // draw the square, one value at a time
      for ( int a = 1; a <= size * size; a++ ) {
         g.drawString( fillCharacter, x += 5, y );

         if ( a % size == 0 ) {
            y += 10;
            x = 5;
         }
      }
   }

}  // end class Square2
```

Fig. S6.6 Solution to Exercise 6.19. (Part 2 of 3.)

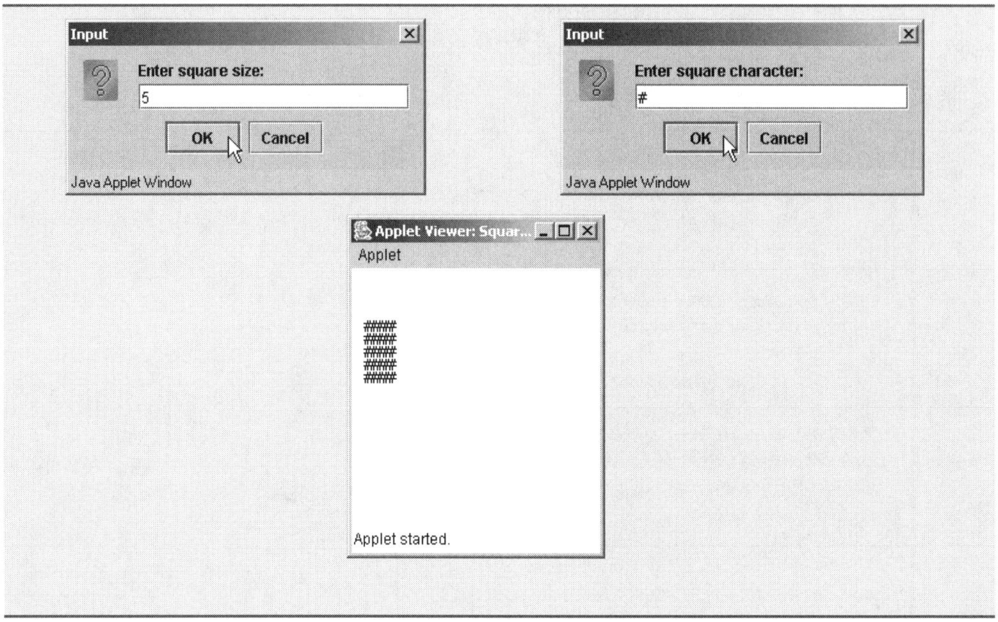

Fig. S6.6 Solution to Exercise 6.19. (Part 3 of 3.)

6.22 Write program segments that accomplish each of the following tasks:

a) Calculate the integer part of the quotient when integer `a` is divided by integer `b`.

b) Calculate the integer remainder when integer `a` is divided by integer `b`.

c) Use the program pieces developed in parts (a) and (b) to write a method `displayDigits` that receives an integer between `1` and `99999` and displays it as a sequence of digits, separating each pair of digits by two spaces. For example, the integer `4562` should appear as

```
4  5  6  2
```

d) Incorporate the method developed in part (c) into an applet that inputs an integer from a textfield and calls `displayDigits` by passing the method the integer entered. Display the results in a second textfield.

ANS:

```java
// Exercise 6.22 Solution: Digits.java
// Program separates a four digit number
// into its individual digits.

import java.awt.*;
import java.awt.event.*;
import javax.swing.*;

public class Digits extends JApplet implements ActionListener {
   JTextField inputField, resultField;
```

Fig. S6.7 Solution to Exercise 6.22. (Part 1 of 3.)

```java
   JLabel inputLabel, resultLabel;

   // set up GUI and obtain value from user
   public void init()
   {
      inputLabel = new JLabel( "Enter the integer (1-99999): " );
      inputField = new JTextField( 5 );
      inputField.addActionListener( this );

      resultLabel = new JLabel( "Result: " );
      resultField = new JTextField( 10 );
      resultField.setEditable( false );

      Container container = getContentPane();
      container.setLayout( new FlowLayout() );
      container.add( inputLabel );
      container.add( inputField );
      container.add( resultLabel );
      container.add( resultField );
   }

   // obtain user input and call method circleArea
   public void actionPerformed( ActionEvent actionEvent )
   {
      int inputNumber =
         Integer.parseInt( inputField.getText() );

      if ( inputNumber <= 99999 && inputNumber >= 1 )
         displayDigits( inputNumber );
      else
         JOptionPane.showMessageDialog( null,
            "Input a number between 1 and 99999",
            "Invalid Number", JOptionPane.ERROR_MESSAGE );
   }

   // part A
   public int quotient( int a, int b )
   {
      return a / b;
   }

   // part B
   public int remainder( int a, int b )
   {
      return a % b;
   }

   // part C
   public void displayDigits( int number )
   {
```

Fig. S6.7 Solution to Exercise 6.22. (Part 2 of 3.)

```java
      int divisor = 1, digit;
      String result = "";

      // Loop for highest divisor
      for( int i = 1; i < number; i *= 10 )
         divisor = i;

      while ( divisor >= 1 ) {
         digit = quotient( number, divisor );

         result += digit + "  ";

         number = remainder( number, divisor );
         divisor = quotient( divisor, 10 );
      }

      resultField.setText( result );
   }

} // end class Digits
```

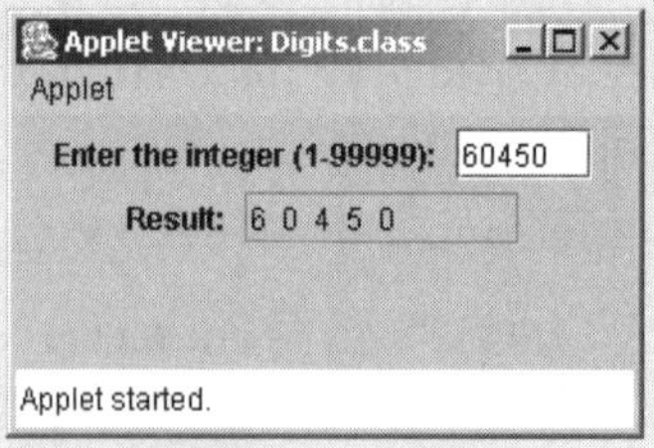

Fig. S6.7 Solution to Exercise 6.22. (Part 3 of 3.)

6.23 Implement the following integer methods:

a) Method `celsius` returns the Celsius equivalent of a Fahrenheit temperature, using the calculation

```
C = 5.0 / 9.0 * ( F - 32 );
```

b) Method `fahrenheit` returns the Fahrenheit equivalent of a Celsius temperature, using the calculation

```
F = 9.0 / 5.0 * C + 32;
```

c) Use the methods from parts (a) and (b) to write an applet that enables the user either to enter a Fahrenheit temperature and display the Celsius equivalent or to enter a Celsius temperature and display the Fahrenheit equivalent.

[*Note*: This applet will require two `JTextField` objects that have registered action events. When `actionPerformed` is called, the `ActionEvent` parameter has method `getSource()` to determine the GUI component with which the user interacted. Your `actionPerformed` method should contain an `if...else` statement of the form

```
if ( actionEvent.getSource() == input1 ) {
   // process input1 interaction here
}
else {  // e.getSource() == input2
   // process input2 interaction here
}
```

where input1 and input2 are JTextField references.]

ANS:

```
// Exercise 6.23 Solution: Convert.java
// Program converts Fahrenheit to Celsius. and vice versa.

import java.awt.event.*;
import java.awt.*;
import javax.swing.*;

public class Convert extends JApplet implements ActionListener {
   JTextField celsiusInput, fahrenheitInput;
   JLabel celsiusLabel, fahrenheitLabel;

   // set up GUI components
   public void init()
   {
      celsiusLabel = new JLabel( "Celcius:" );
      fahrenheitLabel = new JLabel( "Fahrenheit:" );
      celsiusInput = new JTextField( 4 );
      fahrenheitInput = new JTextField( 4 );
      celsiusInput.addActionListener( this );
      fahrenheitInput.addActionListener( this );

      Container container = getContentPane();
      container.setLayout( new FlowLayout() );
      container.add( celsiusLabel );
      container.add( celsiusInput );
      container.add( fahrenheitLabel );
      container.add( fahrenheitInput );

   } // end method init

   // perform conversion
   public void actionPerformed( ActionEvent actionEvent )
   {
      // convert from Celsius to Fahrenheit
      if ( actionEvent.getSource() == celsiusInput ) {
         int celsiusNumber = Integer.parseInt( celsiusInput.getText() );

         fahrenheitInput.setText(
            String.valueOf( fahrenheit( celsiusNumber ) ) );
         showStatus( "Celsius to Fahrenheit" );
      }
```

Fig. S6.8 Solution to Exercise 6.23. (Part 1 of 2.)

```

      // convert from Fahrenheit to Celsius
      else {
         int fahrenheitNumber =
            Integer.parseInt( fahrenheitInput.getText() );

         celsiusInput.setText(
            String.valueOf( celsius( fahrenheitNumber ) ) );
         showStatus( "Fahrenheit to Celsius" );
      }

   } // end method actionPerformed

   // return Celsius equivalent of Fahrenheit temperature
   public int celsius( int fahrenheitTemperature )
   {
      return ( ( int ) ( 5.0 / 9.0 * ( fahrenheitTemperature - 32 ) ) );

   } // end method celcius

   // return Fahrenheit equivalent of Celsius temperature
   public int fahrenheit( int celsiusTemperature )
   {
      return ( ( int ) ( 9.0 / 5.0 * celsiusTemperature + 32 ) );

   } // end method fahrenheit

} // end class Convert
```

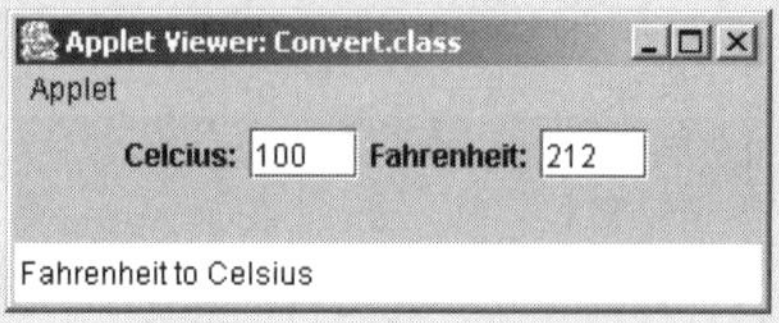

Fig. S6.8 Solution to Exercise 6.23. (Part 2 of 2.)

6.25 An integer number is said to be a *perfect number* if its factors, including 1 (but not the number itself), sum to the number. For example, 6 is a perfect number, because 6 = 1 + 2 + 3. Write a method `perfect` that determines whether parameter `number` is a perfect number. Use this method in an applet that determines and displays all the perfect numbers between 1 and 1000. Print the factors of each perfect number to confirm that the number is indeed perfect. Challenge the computing power of your computer by testing numbers much larger than 1000. Display the results in a `JTextArea` that has scrolling functionality.

ANS:

```
// Exercise 6.25 Solution: PerfectNumber.java
// Program displays all perfect numbers between 1 and 1000.

```

Fig. S6.9 Solution to Exercise 6.25. (Part 1 of 3.)

```
import java.awt.*;
import javax.swing.*;

public class PerfectNumber extends JApplet {
   JTextArea outputArea;
   JScrollPane scroller;

   // set up GUI and print out perfect numbers
   public void init()
   {
      outputArea = new JTextArea( 17, 40 );
      scroller = new JScrollPane( outputArea );

      String outputString = "";

      for ( int number = 2; number <= 1000; number++ ) {
         String result = perfect( number );

         if ( result != "0" )
            outputString += "\n" + number + "  is perfect."
               + "\n\tFactors: " + result;
      }

      outputArea.setText( outputString );
      Container container = getContentPane();
      container.add( scroller );

   } // end method init

   // returns a string of factors if parameter is a
   // perfect number, or a string containing 0 if it isn't.
   public String perfect( int value )
   {
      int factorSum = 1;
      String factors = "1 ";

      for ( int test = 2; test <= value / 2; test++ ) {

         if ( value % test == 0 ) {
            factorSum += test;
            factors += test + " ";
         }
      }

      if ( factorSum == value )
         return factors;

      return "0";

   } // end method perfect
```

Fig. S6.9 Solution to Exercise 6.25. (Part 2 of 3.)

```

} // end class PerfectNumber
```

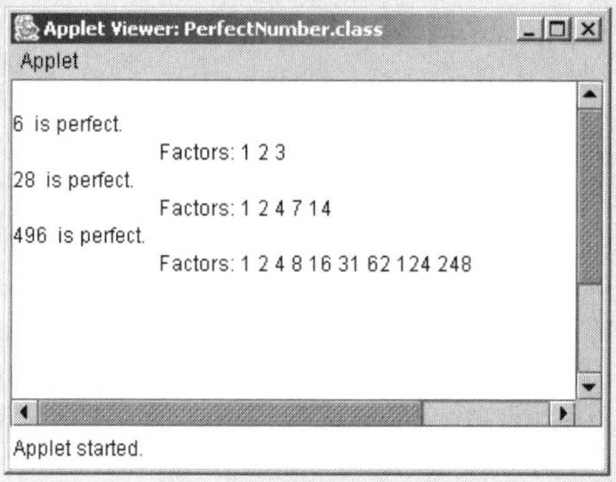

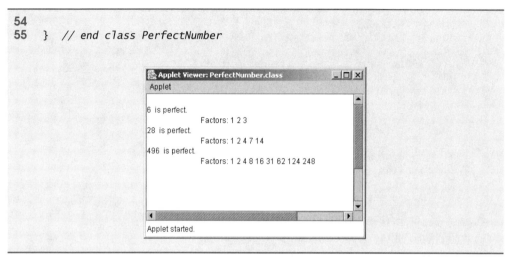

Fig. S6.9 Solution to Exercise 6.25. (Part 3 of 3.)

6.27 Write a method that takes an integer value and returns the number with its digits reversed. For example, given the number 7631, the method should return 1367. Incorporate the method into an applet that reads a value from the user. Display the result of the method in the status bar.

ANS:

```
// Exercise 6.27 Solution: Reverse.java
// Program takes a four digit number
// and prints out its digits reversed.

import java.awt.*;
import java.awt.event.*;
import javax.swing.*;

public class Reverse extends JApplet implements ActionListener {
   final int SIZE = 5;
   JLabel prompt;
   JTextField input;

   // obtain value from user
   public void init()
   {
      prompt = new JLabel( "Enter an integer: " );
      input = new JTextField( SIZE );
      input.addActionListener( this );
      Container container = getContentPane();
      container.setLayout( new FlowLayout() );
      container.add( prompt );
      container.add( input );
   }

```

Fig. S6.10 Solution to Exercise 6.27. (Part 1 of 2.)

```
   // perform action associated with pressing enter
   public void actionPerformed( ActionEvent e )
   {
      int number = Integer.parseInt( input.getText() );

      reverseDigits( number );
   }

   // print parameter number with digits reversed
   public void reverseDigits( int number )
   {
      int oldPlace, newPlace = 1, temp, value;
      String reverseNumber = "";

      // create largest required devisor
      for ( value = 1; value <= number; value *= 10 );
      value /= 10;

      oldPlace = value;

      for ( int count = value; count > 0; count /= 10 ) {
         temp = number / oldPlace;
         reverseNumber =  temp + reverseNumber;
         number %= oldPlace;
         oldPlace /= 10;
         newPlace *= 10;
      }

      showStatus( reverseNumber );
   }

} // end class Reverse
```

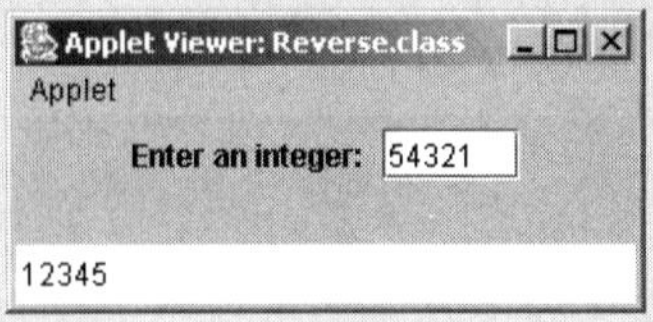

Fig. S6.10 Solution to Exercise 6.27. (Part 2 of 2.)

6.29 Write a method `qualityPoints` that inputs a student's average and returns 4 if the student's average is 90–100, 3 if the average is 80–89, 2 if the average is 70–79, 1 if the average is 60–69 and 0 if the average is lower than 60. Incorporate the method into an applet that reads a value from the user. Display the result of the method in the status bar.

ANS:

```
// Exercise 6.29 Solution: Average.java
// Program displays a number
```

Fig. S6.11 Solution to Exercise 6.29. (Part 1 of 3.)

```
// representing the student's average.

import java.awt.event.*;
import java.awt.*;
import javax.swing.*;

public class Average extends JApplet implements ActionListener {
   JTextField inputField;
   JLabel prompt;

   // set up GUI components
   public void init()
   {
      prompt = new JLabel( "Enter average:" );
      inputField = new JTextField( 4 );
      inputField.addActionListener( this );

      Container container = getContentPane();
      container.setLayout( new FlowLayout() );
      container.add( prompt );
      container.add( inputField );

   } // end method init

   // call method qualityPoints if user input is within range
   public void actionPerformed( ActionEvent actionEvent )
   {
      int inputNumber = Integer.parseInt( inputField.getText() );

      if ( inputNumber >= 0 && inputNumber <= 100 )
         showStatus( "Point is: " + qualityPoints( inputNumber ) );
      else
         showStatus( "Invalid input." );

   } // end method actionPerformed

   // return single digit value of grade
   public int qualityPoints( int grade )
   {
      if ( grade >= 90 )
         return 4;

      else if ( grade >= 80 )
         return 3;

      else if ( grade >= 70 )
         return 2;

      else if ( grade >= 60 )
         return 1;
```

Fig. S6.11 Solution to Exercise 6.29. (Part 2 of 3.)

```
      else
         return 0;

   } // end method qualityPoints

} // end class Average
```

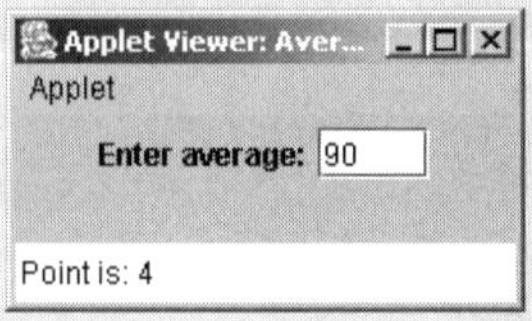

Fig. S6.11 Solution to Exercise 6.29. (Part 3 of 3.)

6.30 Write an applet that simulates coin tossing. Let the program toss a coin each time the user presses the "`Toss`" button. Count the number of times each side of the coin appears. Display the results. The program should call a separate method `flip` that takes no arguments and returns `false` for tails and `true` for heads. [*Note*: If the program realistically simulates coin tossing, each side of the coin should appear approximately half the time.]

ANS:

```
// Exercise 6.30 Solution: Coin.java
// Program simulates tossing a coin.

import java.awt.*;
import java.awt.event.*;
import javax.swing.*;

public class Coin extends JApplet implements ActionListener {
   JButton button;
   int heads, tails;

   // set up GUI components
   public void init()
   {
      heads = 0;
      tails = 0;

      button = new JButton( "Toss" );
      button.addActionListener( this );
      Container container = getContentPane();
      container.add( button );
   }

   // display result of tossing coin
   public void actionPerformed( ActionEvent e )
   {
```

Fig. S6.12 Solution to Exercise 6.30. (Part 1 of 2.)

```
      if ( flip() == true )
         heads++;
      else
         tails++;

      showStatus( "Heads: " + heads + "    Tails: " + tails );
   }

   // simulate flipping
   public boolean flip()
   {
      if ( ( int ) ( Math.random() * 2 ) == 1 )
         return true;
      else
         return false;
   }

} // end class Coin
```

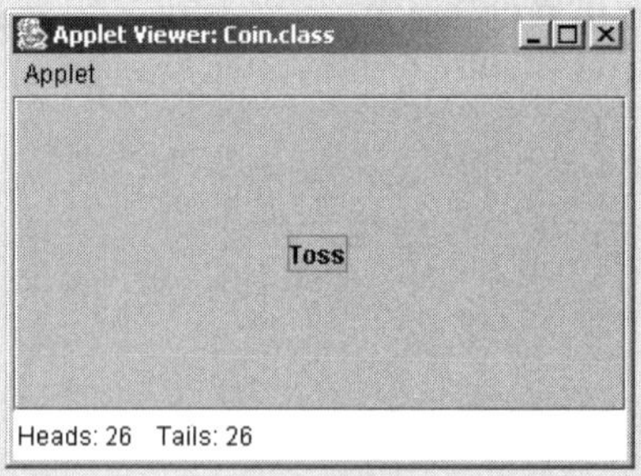

Fig. S6.12 Solution to Exercise 6.30. (Part 2 of 2.)

6.36 Write a recursive method `power( base, exponent )` that, when called, returns

$$base^{exponent}$$

For example, `power( 3, 4 )` = `3 * 3 * 3 * 3`. Assume that `exponent` is an integer greater than or equal to 1. (*Hint*: The recursion step should use the relationship

$$base^{exponent} = base \cdot base^{exponent - 1}$$

and the terminating condition occurs when `exponent` is equal to `1`, because

$$base^{1} = base$$

Incorporate this method into an applet that enables the user to enter the `base` and `exponent`.)

ANS:

```
// Exercise 6.36 Solution: Exponential.java
// Program calculates value of exponent.

```

Fig. S6.13 Solution to Exercise 6.36. (Part 1 of 3.)

```
import java.awt.event.*;
import java.awt.*;
import javax.swing.*;

public class Exponential extends JApplet implements ActionListener {
   JTextField baseInput, exponentInput;
   JLabel basePrompt, exponentPrompt;

   // set up GUI components
   public void init()
   {
      basePrompt = new JLabel( "Enter base: " );
      exponentPrompt = new JLabel( "Enter exponent: " );
      baseInput = new JTextField( 4 );
      exponentInput = new JTextField( 4 );
      exponentInput.addActionListener( this );

      Container container = getContentPane();
      container.setLayout( new FlowLayout() );
      container.add( basePrompt );
      container.add( baseInput );
      container.add( exponentPrompt );
      container.add( exponentInput );
   }

   // call method power passing user input
   public void actionPerformed( ActionEvent actionEvent )
   {
      int base = Integer.parseInt( baseInput.getText() );
      int exponent = Integer.parseInt( exponentInput.getText() );

      if ( exponent > 0 ) {
         int result = power( base, exponent );
         showStatus( "Value is " + result );
      }
      else
         showStatus( "Invalid Exponent." );
   }

   // recursively calculate value of exponent.
   public int power( int base, int exponent )
   {
      if ( exponent == 1 )
         return base;
      else
         return base * power( base, exponent - 1 );
   }

} // end class Exponential
```

Fig. S6.13 Solution to Exercise 6.36. (Part 2 of 3.)

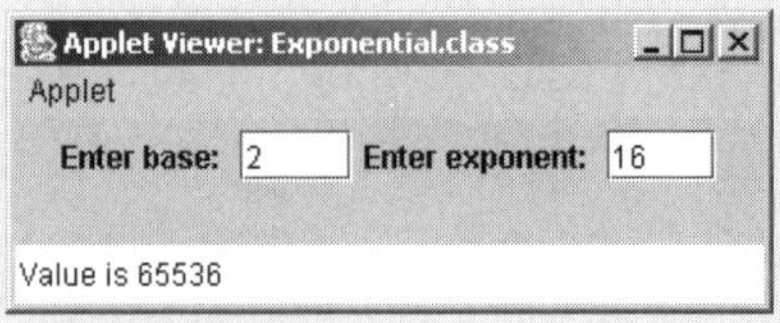

Fig. S6.13 Solution to Exercise 6.36. (Part 3 of 3.)

6.40 The greatest common divisor of integers `x` and `y` is the largest integer that evenly divides into both `x` and `y`. Write a recursive method `gcd` that returns the greatest common divisor of `x` and `y`. The `gcd` of `x` and `y` is defined recursively as follows: If `y` is equal to `0`, then `gcd( x, y )` is `x`; otherwise, `gcd( x, y )` is `gcd( y, x % y )`, where `%` is the remainder operator. Use this method to replace the one you wrote in the applet of Exercise 6.19.

ANS:

```java
// Exercise 6.40 Solution: Divisor.java
// Program recursively finds the greatest
// common divisor of two numbers.

import java.awt.event.*;
import java.awt.*;
import javax.swing.*;

public class Divisor extends JApplet implements ActionListener {
   JTextField inputField1, inputField2;
   JLabel label1, label2;

   // set up GUI components
   public void init()
   {
      label1 = new JLabel( "Enter first number:" );
      label2 = new JLabel( "Enter second number:" );
      inputField1 = new JTextField( 4 );
      inputField2 = new JTextField( 4 );
      inputField2.addActionListener( this );

      Container container = getContentPane();
      container.setLayout( new FlowLayout() );
      container.add( label1 );
      container.add( inputField1 );
      container.add( label2 );
      container.add( inputField2 );
   }

   // display greatest common divisor of user input numbers
   public void actionPerformed( ActionEvent actionEvent )
   {
      int input1, input2;

```

Fig. S6.14 Solution to Exercise 6.40. (Part 1 of 2.)

```
         input1 = Integer.parseInt( inputField1.getText() );
         input2 = Integer.parseInt( inputField2.getText() );
         showStatus( "GCD is: " + gcd( input1, input2 ) );
      }

      // recursively calculate greatest common divisor
      public int gcd( int x, int y )
      {
         if ( y == 0 )
            return x;
         else
            return gcd( y, x % y );
      }

   } // end class Divisor
```

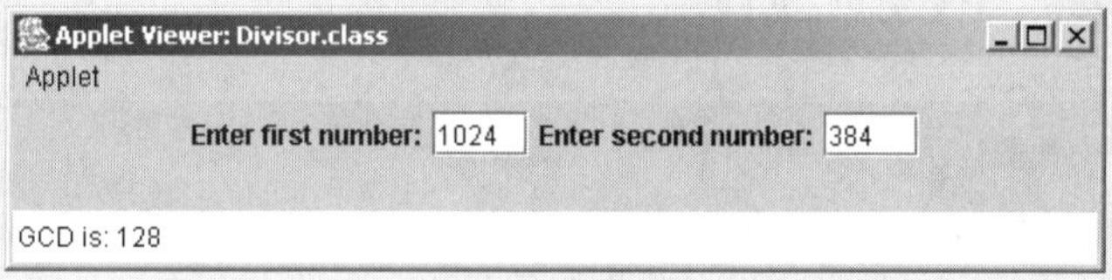

Fig. S6.14 Solution to Exercise 6.40. (Part 2 of 2.)

6.42 Write method `distance`, to calculate the distance between two points (*x1*, *y1*) and (*x2*, *y2*). All numbers and return values should be of type `double`. Incorporate this method into an applet that enables the user to enter the coordinates of the points.

ANS:

```
// Exercise 6.42 Solution: Points.java
// Program calculates the distance between two points.

import java.awt.*;
import java.awt.event.*;
import javax.swing.*;

public class Points extends JApplet implements ActionListener {
   JTextField x1Input, x2Input, y1Input, y2Input;
   JLabel labelX1, labelY1, labelX2, labelY2;

   // set up GUI components
   public void init()
   {
      labelX1 = new JLabel( "Enter X1: " );
      labelY1 = new JLabel( "Enter Y1: " );
      labelX2 = new JLabel( "Enter X2: " );
      labelY2 = new JLabel( "Enter Y2: " );
      x1Input = new JTextField( 4 );
      x2Input = new JTextField( 4 );
      y1Input = new JTextField( 4 );
```

Fig. S6.15 Solution to Exercise 6.42. (Part 1 of 2.)

```java
      y2Input = new JTextField( 4 );
      y2Input.addActionListener( this );

      Container container = getContentPane();
      container.setLayout( new FlowLayout() );
      container.add( labelX1 );
      container.add( x1Input );
      container.add( labelY1 );
      container.add( y1Input );
      container.add( labelX2 );
      container.add( x2Input );
      container.add( labelY2 );
      container.add( y2Input );
   }

   // display distance between user input points
   public void actionPerformed( ActionEvent e )
   {
      double x1, y1, x2, y2;

      // read in two points
      x1 = Double.parseDouble( x1Input.getText() );
      y1 = Double.parseDouble( y1Input.getText() );
      x2 = Double.parseDouble( x2Input.getText() );
      y2 = Double.parseDouble( y2Input.getText() );

      double theDistance = distance( x1, y1, x2, y2 );
      showStatus( "Distance is " + theDistance );
   }

   // calculate distance between two points
   public double distance( double x1, double y1, double x2, double y2 )
   {
      return Math.sqrt( Math.pow( ( x1 - x2 ), 2 ) +
         Math.pow( ( y1 - y2 ), 2 ) );
   }

} // end class Points
```

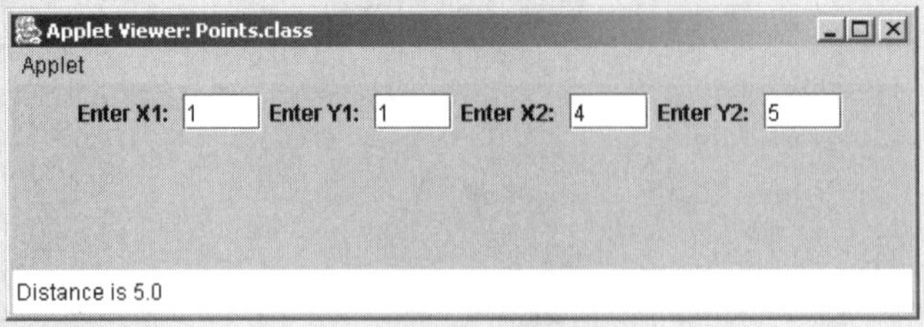

Fig. S6.15 Solution to Exercise 6.42. (Part 2 of 2.)

7

Arrays

Solutions to Selected Exercises

7.6 Fill in the blanks in each of the following statements:

a) Java stores lists of values in __________.

ANS: *arrays.*

b) The elements of an array are related by the fact that they __________.

ANS: *have the same name and type.*

c) When referring to an array element, the position number contained within brackets is called a(n) __________.

ANS: *subscript*

d) The names of the four elements of one-dimensional array `p` are __________, __________, __________ and __________.

ANS: `p[ 0 ]`, `p[ 1 ]`, `p[ 2 ]`, *and* `p[ 3 ]`

e) Naming an array, stating its type and specifying the number of dimensions in the array is called __________ the array.

ANS: *declaring and instantiating*

f) The process of placing the elements of an array into either ascending or descending order is called __________.

ANS: *sorting*

g) In a two-dimensional array, the first index identifies the __________ of an element and the second index identifies the __________ of an element.

ANS: *row, column*

h) An *m*-by-*n* array contains __________ rows, __________ columns and __________ elements.

ANS: `m, n, m * n`

i) The name of the element in row 3 and column 5 of array `d` is __________.

ANS: `d[ 3 ][ 5 ]`

7.9 Consider a two-by-three integer array `t`.

a) Write a statement that declares and creates `t`.

ANS: `int t[][] = new int[ 2 ][ 3 ];`

b) How many rows does `t` have?

ANS: *two*

c) How many columns does `t` have?

ANS: *three*

d) How many elements does `t` have?

ANS: *six*

e) Write the names of all the elements in the second row of `t`.

ANS: `t[ 1 ][ 0 ], t[ 1 ][ 1 ], t[ 1 ][ 2 ]`

f) Write the names of all the elements in the third column of `t`.

ANS: `t[ 0 ][ 2 ], t[ 1 ][ 2 ]`

g) Write a single statement that sets the element of `t` in row 1 and column 2 to zero.

ANS: `t[ 0 ][ 1 ] = 0;`

h) Write a series of statements that initializes each element of `t` to zero. Do not use a repetition statement.

ANS:
```
t[ 0 ][ 0 ] = 0;
t[ 0 ][ 1 ] = 0;
t[ 0 ][ 2 ] = 0;
t[ 1 ][ 0 ] = 0;
t[ 1 ][ 1 ] = 0;
t[ 1 ][ 2 ] = 0;
```

i) Write a nested `for` statement that initializes each element of `t` to zero.

ANS:
```
for ( int j = 0; j < t.length; j++ )
   for ( int k = 0; k < t[ j ].length; k++ )
      t[ j ][ k ] = 0;
```

j) Write a nested `for` statement that inputs the values for the elements of `t` from the user.

ANS:
```
for ( int r = 0; r < t.length; r++ )
   for ( int c = 0; c < t[ r ].length; c++ )
      t[ r ][ c ] = System.in.read();
```

k) Write a series of statements that determines and prints the smallest value in `t`.

ANS:
```
// assume small is declared and initialized
for ( int x = 0; x < t.length; x++ )
   for ( int y = 0; y < t[ x ].length; y++ )
      if ( t[ x ][ y ] < small )
         small = t[ x ][ y ];
```

l) Write a statement that displays the elements of the first row of `t`.

ANS:
```
System.out.println( t[ 0 ][ 0 ] + " " + t[ 0 ][ 1 ] + " " +
   t[ 0 ][ 2 ] );
```

m) Write a statement that totals the elements of the third column of `t`.

ANS: `total = t[ 0 ][ 2 ] + t[ 1 ][ 2 ];`

n) Write a series of statements that prints the contents of `t` in neat, tabular format. List the column indices as headings across the top, and list the row indices at the left of each row.

ANS:
```
System.out.println( "   0     1     2" );
for ( int e = 0; e < t.length; e++ ) {
   System.out.print( e + "  " );

   for ( int r = 0; r < t[ e ].length; r++ )
      System.out.print( t[ e ][ r ] + "     " );

   System.out.println();
}
```

7.10 Use a one-dimensional array to solve the following problem: A company pays its salespeople on a commission basis. The salespeople receive $200 per week plus 9% of their gross sales for that week. For example, a salesperson who grosses $5000 in sales in a week receives $200 plus 9% of $5000, or a total of $650. Write an applet (using an array of counters) that determines how many of the salespeople earned salaries in each of the following ranges (assume that each salesperson's salary is truncated to an integer amount):

a) $200–299
b) $300–399
c) $400–499
d) $500–599
e) $600–699
f) $700–799
g) $800–899
h) $900–999
i) $1000 and over

ANS:

```java
// Exercise 7.10 Solution: Sales.java
// Program calculates the amount of pay for a salesperson and counts the
// number of salespeople that earned salaries in given ranges.
import java.awt.*;
import java.awt.event.*;
import javax.swing.*;

public class Sales extends JApplet implements ActionListener {
   JTextField inputField;
   JTextArea outputArea;
   JLabel prompt;
   int total[];

   // set up GUI components
   public void init()
   {
      total = new int[ 9 ];

      for ( int counter = 0; counter < total.length; counter++ )
         total[ counter ] = 0;

      prompt = new JLabel( "Enter sales amount:" );
```

Fig. S7.1 Solution to Exercise 7.10. (Part 1 of 3.)

```java
      inputField = new JTextField( 5 );
      outputArea = new JTextArea();
      inputField.addActionListener( this );

      Container container = getContentPane();
      container.setLayout( new FlowLayout() );
      container.add( prompt );
      container.add( inputField );
      container.add( outputArea );

   } // end method init

   // calculate which range salary is in
   public void actionPerformed( ActionEvent actionEvent )
   {
      double dollars = Double.parseDouble( inputField.getText() );
      double salary = dollars * 0.09 + 200;
      int range = ( int ) ( salary / 100 );

      if ( range > 9 )
         range = 10;

      ++total[ range - 2 ];
      inputField.setText( "" );

      // print chart in JTextArea
      String output = "Range\t\tNumber";

      for ( int range2 = 0; range2 < total.length - 1; range2++ )
         output += "\n$" + (200 + 100 * range2) + "-$" +
            (299 + 100 * range2) + "\t\t" + total[ range2 ] ;

      output += "\n$1000 and over\t\t" + total[ total.length - 1 ];

      outputArea.setText( output );

   } // end method actionPerformed

} // end class Sales
```

Fig. S7.1 Solution to Exercise 7.10. (Part 2 of 3.)

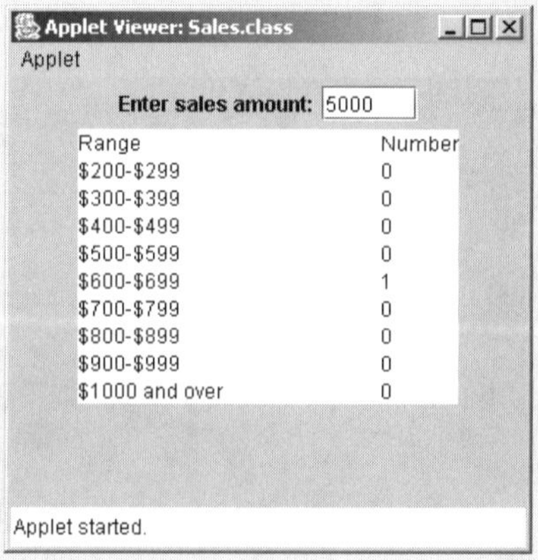

Fig. S7.1 Solution to Exercise 7.10. (Part 3 of 3.)

The applet should use the GUI techniques introduced in Chapter 6. Display the results in a `JTextArea`. Use `JTextArea` method `setText` to update the results after each value is input by the user.

7.15 Write an applet to simulate the rolling of two dice. The program should use `Math.random` once to roll the first die and again to roll the second die. The sum of the two values should then be calculated. Each die can show an integer value from 1 to 6, so the sum of the values will vary from 2 to 12, with 7 being the most frequent sum and 2 and 12 being the least frequent sums. Figure 7 shows the 36 possible combinations of the two dice. Your program should roll the dice 36,000 times. Use a one-dimensional array to tally the numbers of times each possible sum appears. Display the results in a `JTextArea` in tabular format. Also, determine whether the totals are reasonable (i.e., there are six ways to roll a 7, so approximately one-sixth of the rolls should be 7). The applet should use the GUI techniques introduced in Chapter 6. Provide a `JButton` to allow the user of the applet to roll the dice another 36,000 times. The applet should reset the elements of the one-dimensional array to zero before rolling the dice again.

	1	2	3	4	5	6
1	2	3	4	5	6	7
2	3	4	5	6	7	8
3	4	5	6	7	8	9
4	5	6	7	8	9	10
5	6	7	8	9	10	11
6	7	8	9	10	11	12

Fig. S7.2 The 36 possible sums of two dice.

ANS:

```
// Exercise 7.15 Solution: Roll36.java
// Program simulates rolling two six-sided dice 36,000 times.
import java.awt.*;
import java.awt.event.*;
import javax.swing.*;

public class Roll36 extends JApplet implements ActionListener {
   int total[];
   int totalRolls;
   JTextArea outputArea;
   JButton button;

   // set up GUI components, initialize array and roll dice
   public void init()
   {
      button = new JButton("Roll 36000 times");
      outputArea = new JTextArea();
      button.addActionListener( this );

      Container container = getContentPane();
      container.setLayout( new FlowLayout() );
      container.add( outputArea );
      container.add( button );

      totalRolls = 0;
      total = new int[ 13 ];

      for ( int index = 0; index < total.length; index++ )
         total[ index ] = 0;

      rollDice();

   } // end method init

   // simulate rolling of dice 36000 times
   public void rollDice()
   {
      int face1, face2;

      for ( int roll = 1; roll <= 36000; roll++ ) {
         face1 = ( int ) ( 1 + Math.random() * 6 );
         face2 = ( int ) ( 1 + Math.random() * 6 );
         total[ face1 + face2 ]++;
      }

      totalRolls += 36000;

      // print table on text area
      String output = "Sum\tFrequency\tPercentage";
```

Fig. S7.3 Solution to Exercise 7.15. (Part 1 of 2.)

```

        // ignore subscripts 0 and 1
        for ( int k = 2; k < total.length; k++ ) {

           int percent = total[ k ] / ( totalRolls / 100 );
           output += "\n" + k + "\t" + total[ k ] + "\t" + percent + "%";
        }

        outputArea.setText( output );

     } // end method roll2Dice

     // roll dice again
     public void actionPerformed( ActionEvent actionEvent )
     {
       for ( int i=0; i < total.length; i++ )
        total[ i ] = 0;

       totalRolls = 0;
        rollDice();

     } // end method actionPerformed

  } // end class Roll36
```

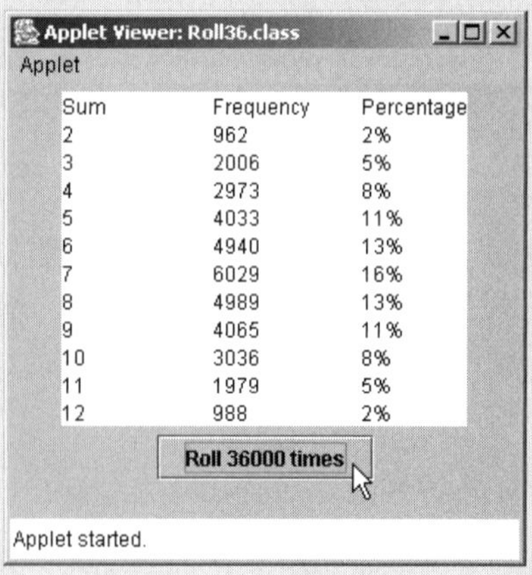

Fig. S7.3 Solution to Exercise 7.15. (Part 2 of 2.)

7.16 What does the following program do?

```
  // Exercise 7.16: WhatDoesThisDo.java
  import java.awt.*;
  import javax.swing.*;

  public class WhatDoesThisDo extends JApplet {
     int result;
```

```

    public void init()
    {
       int array[] = { 1, 2, 3, 4, 5, 6, 7, 8, 9, 10 };

       result = whatIsThis( array, array.length );

       Container container = getContentPane();
       JTextArea output = new JTextArea();
       output.setText( "Result is: " + result );
       container.add( output );
    }

    public int whatIsThis( int array2[], int length )
    {
       if ( length == 1 )
          return array2[ 0 ];
       else
          return array2[ length - 1 ] + whatIsThis( array2, length - 1 );
    }

 } // end class WhatDoesThisDo
```

ANS:

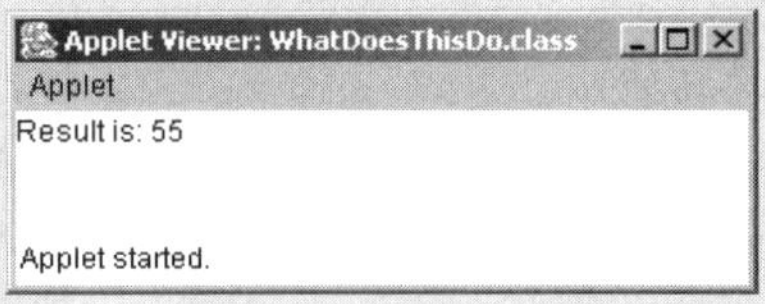

Fig. S7.4 Solution to Exercise 7.16.

7.18 (*Airline Reservations System*) A small airline has just purchased a computer for its new automated reservations system. You have been asked to program the new system. You are to write an applet to assign seats on each flight of the airline's only plane (capacity: 10 seats).

Your program should display the following alternatives: `Please type 1 for First Class` and `Please type 2 for Economy`. If the user types 1, your program should assign a seat in the first-class section (seats 1–5). If the person types 2, your program should assign a seat in the economy section (seats 6–10). Your program should then print a boarding pass indicating the person's seat number and whether it is in the first-class or economy section of the plane.

Use a one-dimensional array of primitive type `boolean` to represent the seating chart of the plane. Initialize all the elements of the array to `false` to indicate that all seats are empty. As each seat is assigned, set the corresponding elements of the array to `true` to indicate that the seat is no longer available.

Your program should never assign a seat that has already been assigned. When the economy section is full, your program should ask the person if it is acceptable to be placed in the first-class section (and vice versa). If yes, make the appropriate seat assignment. If no, print the message `"Next flight leaves in 3 hours."`

ANS:

```
// Exercise 7.18 Solution: Plane.java
// Program reserves airline seats.
import java.awt.*;
import java.awt.event.*;
import javax.swing.*;

public class Plane extends JApplet implements ActionListener {
   JTextField input;
   JLabel prompt;
   JButton yesButton, noButton;
   int section, firstClass, economyClass;
   boolean seats[];
   boolean questionPosed = false;

   // set up GUI components and initialize instance variables
   public void init()
   {
      prompt = new JLabel( "Please type 1 for First Class. " +
         "Please type 2 for Economy." );
      input = new JTextField( 4 );
      yesButton = new JButton( "Yes" );
      noButton = new JButton( "No" );

      input.addActionListener( this );
      yesButton.addActionListener( this );
      noButton.addActionListener( this );

      Container container = getContentPane();
      container.setLayout( new FlowLayout() );
      container.add( prompt );
      container.add( input );
      container.add( yesButton );
      container.add( noButton );

      // initialize values
      firstClass = 0;
      economyClass = 5;
      seats = new boolean[ 10 ];
      for ( int index = 0; index < seats.length; index++ )
         seats[ index ] = false;

   } // end method init

   // perform appropriate action
   public void actionPerformed( ActionEvent actionEvent )
   {
      // input field
      if ( actionEvent.getSource() == input ) {
         section = Integer.parseInt( input.getText() );
```

Fig. S7.5 Solution to Exercise 7.18. (Part 1 of 3.)

```
         String output = "";
         questionPosed = false;

         // first class
         if ( section == 1 ) {

            // if firstClass isn't full, reserve a seat
            if ( firstClass < 5 ) {
               seats[ firstClass ] = true;
               output = "First Class. Seat #" + ++firstClass;
            }

            // if it is full, offer a seat in economy class
            else if ( firstClass >= 5 && economyClass < 10 ) {
               output = "First Class is full. Economy Class?";
               questionPosed = true;
            }

            else
               output = "Flight is full. Try next flight.";
         }

         // economy class
         else if ( section == 2 ) {

            // if non-smoking isn't full, reserve a seat
            if ( economyClass < 10 ) {
               seats[ economyClass ] = true;
               output = "Economy Class. Seat #" + ++economyClass;
            }

            // if it is full, offer a seat in smoking
            else if ( economyClass == 10 && firstClass < 5 ) {
               output = "Economy class is full. First Class?";
               questionPosed = true;
            }

            else
               output = "Flight is full. Try next flight.";
         }

         else
            output = "Invalid input.";

         showStatus( output );
      }

      // yes button
      else if ( actionEvent.getSource() == yesButton ) {

```

Fig. S7.5 Solution to Exercise 7.18. (Part 2 of 3.)

```
         if ( questionPosed ) {

            if ( section == 1 ) {
               seats[ economyClass ] = true;
               showStatus( "Economy Class. Seat #" + ++economyClass );
            }

            else {  // section is 2
               seats[ firstClass ] = true;
               showStatus( "First Class. Seat #" + ++firstClass );
            }

            questionPosed = false;
         }
      }

      // no button
      else if ( actionEvent.getSource() == noButton ) {

         if ( questionPosed )
            showStatus( "Next flight leaves in 3 hours." );

         questionPosed = false;
      }

   }  // end method actionPerformed

}  // end class Plane
```

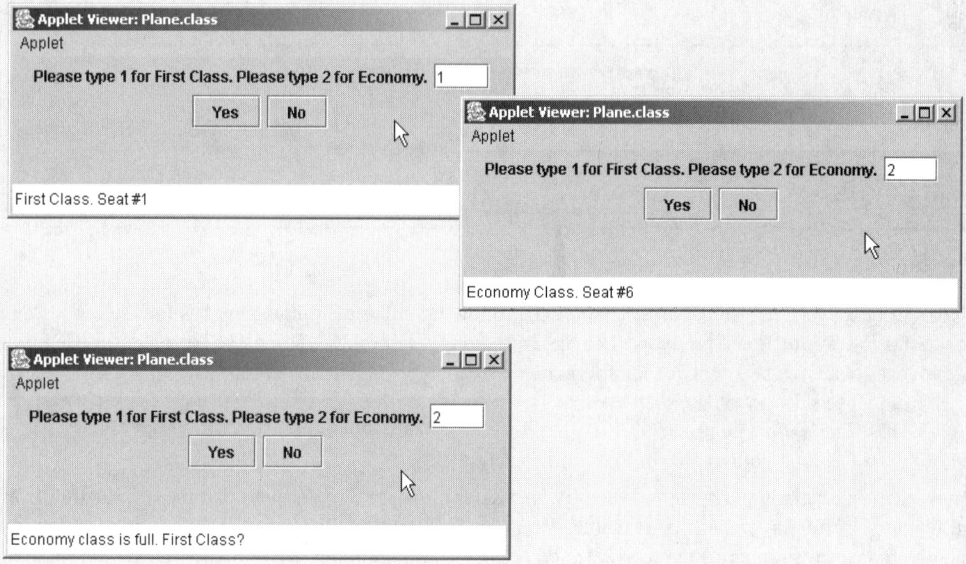

Fig. S7.5 Solution to Exercise 7.18. (Part 3 of 3.)

7.19 What does the following program do?

```java
// Exercise 7.19: WhatDoesThisDo2.java
import java.awt.*;
import javax.swing.*;

public class WhatDoesThisDo2 extends JApplet {

   public void init()
   {
      int array[] = { 1, 2, 3, 4, 5, 6, 7, 8, 9, 10 };
      JTextArea outputArea = new JTextArea();

      someFunction( array, 0, outputArea );

      Container container = getContentPane();
      container.add( outputArea );
   }

   public void someFunction( int array2[], int x, JTextArea out )
   {
      if ( x < array2.length ) {
         someFunction( array2, x + 1, out );
         out.append( array2[ x ] + "  " );
      }
   }
}
```

ANS:

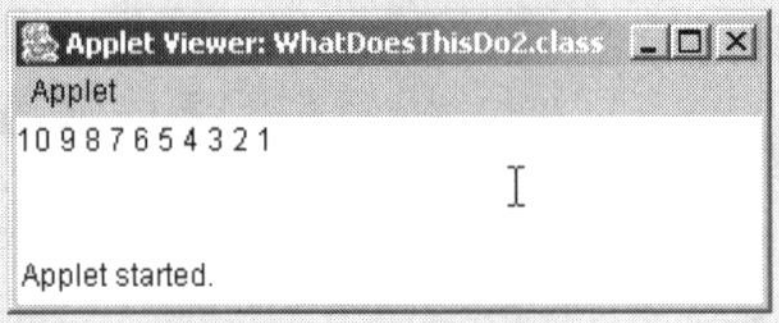

Fig. S7.6 Solution to Exercise 7.19.

7.20 Use a two-dimensional array to solve the following problem: A company has four salespeople (1 to 4) who sell five different products (1 to 5). Once a day, each salesperson passes in a slip for each type of product sold. Each slip contains the following:

a) The salesperson number
b) The product number
c) The total dollar value of that product sold that day

Thus, each salesperson passes in between 0 and 5 sales slips per day. Assume that the information from all of the slips for last month is available. Write an applet that will read all this information for last month's sales and summarize the total sales by salesperson by product. All totals should be stored in the two-dimensional array `sales`. After processing all the information for last month, display the results in tabular format, with each column representing a particular salesperson and each row representing a particular product. Cross-total each row to get the total sales of each product for last month; cross-total each column to get the total sales by salesperson for last month. Your tabular printout should include these cross-totals to the right of the totaled rows and to the bottom of the totaled columns. Display the results in a JTextArea.

ANS:

```
// Exercise 7.20 Solution: Sales2.java
// Program totals sales for salespeople and products.
import java.awt.*;
import java.awt.event.*;
import javax.swing.*;

public class Sales2 extends JApplet implements ActionListener {
   JLabel prompt1, prompt2, prompt3;
   JTextField input1, input2, input3;
   JTextArea outputArea;
   double sales[][];

   // set up GUI components
   public void init()
   {
      prompt1 = new JLabel( "Enter sales person number: " );
      prompt2 = new JLabel( "Enter product number: " );
      prompt3 = new JLabel( "Enter sales amount: " );

      // sales array holds data on number of each product sold
      // by each salesman
      sales = new double[ 5 ][ 4 ];

      input1 = new JTextField( 5 );
      input2 = new JTextField( 5 );
      input3 = new JTextField( 5 );
      input3.addActionListener( this );
      outputArea = new JTextArea();
      outputArea.setEditable( false );

      // add all components to GUI
      Container container = getContentPane();
      container.setLayout( new FlowLayout() );
      container.add( prompt1 );
      container.add( input1 );
      container.add( prompt2 );
      container.add( input2 );
      container.add( prompt3 );
      container.add( input3 );
      container.add( outputArea );

   } // end method init
```

Fig. S7.7 Solution to Exercise 7.20. (Part 1 of 3.)

```

   // obtain user input
   public void actionPerformed( ActionEvent actionEvent )
   {
      // read in sales of a product by a person
      int person = Integer.parseInt( input1.getText() );
      int product = Integer.parseInt( input2.getText() );
      double d = Double.parseDouble( input3.getText() );

      // error-check the input
      if ( person >= 1 && person < 5 &&
         product >= 1 && product < 6 && d >= 0 )

         sales[ product - 1 ][ person - 1 ] += d;

      else
         showStatus( "Invalid input!" );

      // display the updated table
      double salesPersonTotal[] = new double[ 4 ];

      for ( int column = 0; column < 4; column++ )
         salesPersonTotal[ column ] = 0;

      String output = "Product\tSalesperson 1\tSalesperson 2" +
            "\tSalesperson 3\tSalesperson 4\tTotal";

      // for each column of each row, print the appropriate
      // value representing a person's sales of a product
      for ( int row = 0; row < 5; row++ ) {

         double productTotal = 0.0;
         output += "\n" + ( row + 1 );

         for ( int column = 0; column < 4; column++ ) {
            output += "\t" + sales[ row ][ column ];
            productTotal += sales[ row ][ column ];
            salesPersonTotal[ column ] += sales[ row ][ column ];
         }

         output += "\t" + productTotal;
      }

      output += "\nTotal";

      for ( int column = 0; column < 4; column++ )
         output += "\t" + salesPersonTotal[ column ];

      outputArea.setText( output );

```

Fig. S7.7 Solution to Exercise 7.20. (Part 2 of 3.)

```
    } // end method actionPerformed

} // end class Sales2
```

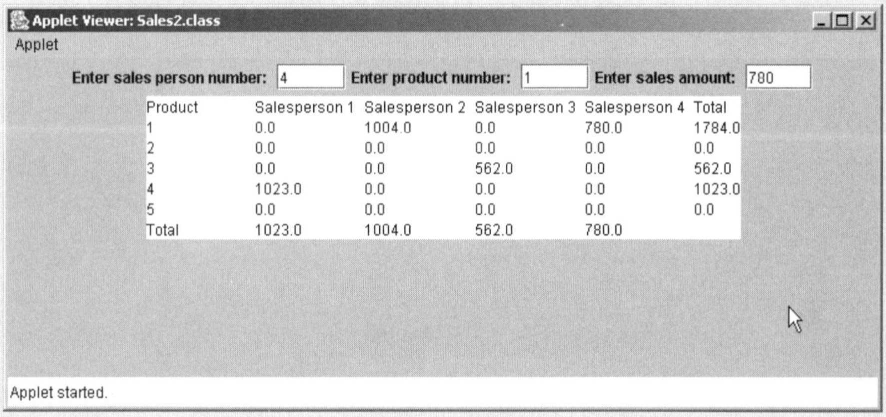

Fig. S7.7 Solution to Exercise 7.20. (Part 3 of 3.)

7.27 (*The Sieve of Eratosthenes*) A prime number is any integer that is evenly divisible only by itself and one. The Sieve of Eratosthenes is a method of finding prime numbers. It operates as follows:

a) Create a primitive type `boolean` array with all elements initialized to `true`. Array elements with prime indices will remain `true`. All other array elements will eventually be set to `false`.
b) Starting with array index 2, determine whether a given element is `true`. If so, loop through the remainder of the array and set to `false` every element whose index is a multiple of the index for the element with value `true`. Then continue the process with the next element with value `true`. For array index 2, all elements beyond element 2 in the array that have indices which are multiples of 2 (indices 4, 6, 8, 10, etc.) will be set to `false`; for array index 3, all elements beyond element 3 in the array that have indices which are multiples of 3 (indices 6, 9, 12, 15, etc.) will be set to `false`; and so on.

When this process is complete, the array elements that are still `true` indicate that the index is a prime number. These indices can be displayed. Write a program that uses an array of 1000 elements to determine and print the prime numbers between 2 and 999. Ignore elements 0 and 1 of the array.

ANS:

```
// Exercise 7.27 Solution: Sieve.java
// Sieve of Eratosthenes
import java.awt.*;
import javax.swing.*;

public class Sieve {

   public static void main( String args[] )
   {
      int count = 0;
```

Fig. S7.8 Solution to Exercise 7.27. (Part 1 of 3.)

```
      String result = "";
      JTextArea output = new JTextArea( 10, 15 );
      JScrollPane scroller = new JScrollPane( output );

      int array[] = new int[ 1000 ];

      // initialize all array values to 1
      for ( int index = 0; index < array.length; index++ )
         array[ index ] = 1;

      // starting at the third value, cycle through the array and put 0
      // as the value of any greater number that is a multiple
      for ( int i = 2; i < array.length; i++ )

         if ( array[ i ] == 1 )

            for ( int j = i + 1; j < array.length; j++ )

               if ( j % i == 0 )
                  array[ j ] = 0;

      // cycle through the array one last time to print all primes
      for ( int index = 2; index < array.length; index++ )

         if ( array[ index ] == 1 ) {
            result += index + " is prime.\n";
            ++count;
         }

      result += "\n" + count + " primes found.";

      output.setText( result );

      JOptionPane.showMessageDialog( null, scroller, "Sieve",
         JOptionPane.INFORMATION_MESSAGE );

      System.exit( 0 );

   } // end method main

} // end class Sieve
```

Fig. S7.8 Solution to Exercise 7.27. (Part 2 of 3.)

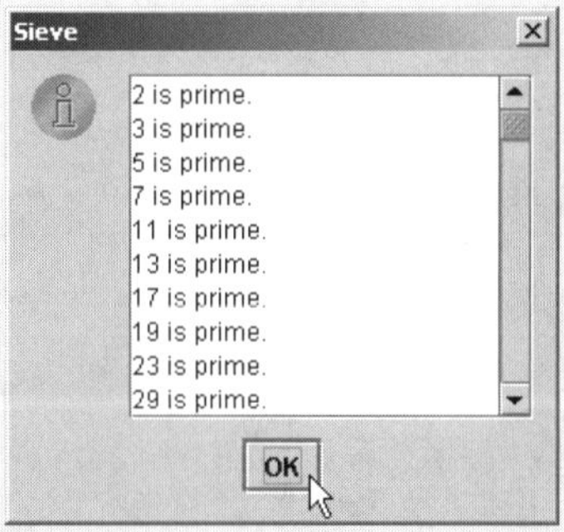

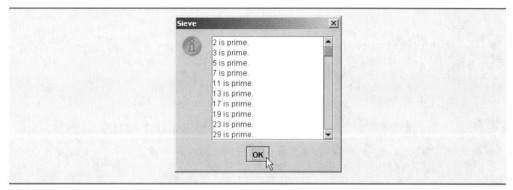

Fig. S7.8 Solution to Exercise 7.27. (Part 3 of 3.)

Solutions to Selected Recursion Exercises

7.32 (*Palindromes*) A palindrome is a string that is spelled the same way forward and backward. Some examples of palindromes are "radar," "able was i ere i saw elba" and (if blanks are ignored) "a man a plan a canal panama." Write a recursive method `testPalindrome` that returns `boolean` value `true` if the string stored in the array is a palindrome and `false` otherwise. The method should ignore spaces and punctuation in the string. [*Hint:* Use `String` method `toCharArray`, which takes no arguments, to get a `char` array containing the characters in the `String`. Then pass the array to method `testPalindrome`.]

ANS:

```java
// Exercise 7.32 Solution: Palindrome.java
// Program tests for a palindrome.
import java.awt.*;
import java.awt.event.*;
import javax.swing.*;

public class Palindrome extends JApplet implements ActionListener {

   JLabel prompt;
   JTextField input;

   // set up GUI components
   public void init()
   {
      prompt = new JLabel( "Enter a string:" );
      input = new JTextField( 20 );
      input.addActionListener( this );
      Container container = getContentPane();
      container.setLayout( new FlowLayout() );
      container.add( prompt );
      container.add( input);

   } // end method init
```

Fig. S7.9 Solution to Exercise 7.32. (Part 1 of 3.)

```

   // obtain user input and call method testPalindrome
   public void actionPerformed( ActionEvent actionEvent )
   {
      String string = actionEvent.getActionCommand();
      char[] copy = new char[ string.length() + 1 ];
      int counter = 0;

      for ( int index = 0; index < string.length(); index++ ) {

         // method charAt returns a character at
         // the specified subscript of a String
         char character = string.charAt( index );

         copy[ counter++ ] = character;
      }

      if ( testPalindrome( copy, 0, counter - 1 ) == 1 )
         showStatus( "Palindrome" );

      else
         showStatus( "Not a palindrome" );

   } // end method actionPerformed

   // recursively test if array is palindrome
   public int testPalindrome( char array[], int left, int right )
   {
      while ( array[ left ] == ' ' || array[ left ] == '.' ||
              array[ left ] == ';' || array[ left ] == ':' ||
             array[ left ] == '?' || array[ left ] == '!' ||
              array[ left ] == '-' || array[ left ] == ',' )

         left++;

      while ( array[ right ] == ' ' || array[ right ] == '.' ||
              array[ right ] == ';' || array[ right ] == ':' ||
              array[ right ] == '?' || array[ right ] == '!' ||
              array[ right ] == '-' || array[ right ] == ',' )

         right--;

      if ( left == right || left > right )
         return 1;

      else if ( array[ left ] != array[ right ] )
         return 0;

      else
         return testPalindrome( array, left + 1, right - 1 );
```

Fig. S7.9 Solution to Exercise 7.32. (Part 2 of 3.)

```

    } // end method testPalindrome

} // end class Palindrome
```

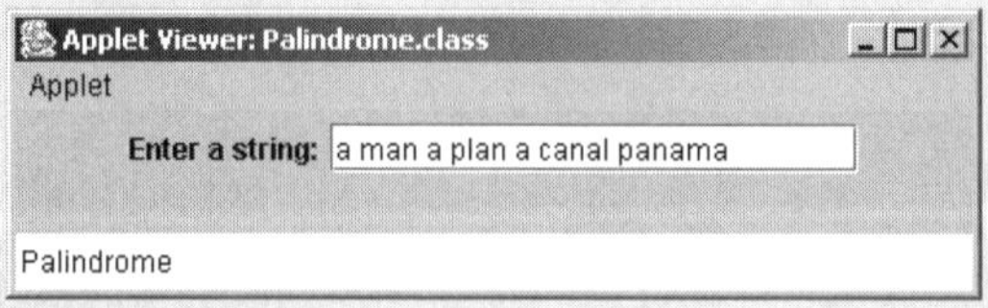

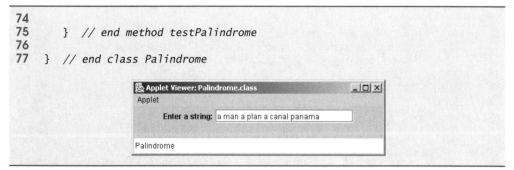

Fig. S7.9 Solution to Exercise 7.32. (Part 3 of 3.)

7.33 *(Linear Search)* Modify Fig. 7.11 to use recursive method `linearSearch` to perform a linear search of the array. The method should receive an integer array, the array's length and the search key as arguments. If the search key is found, return its index in the array; otherwise, return `-1`.

ANS:

```java
// Exercise 7.33 Solution: LinearSearch.java
// Program recursively performs linear search of an array.
import java.awt.*;
import java.awt.event.*;
import javax.swing.*;

public class LinearSearch extends JApplet implements ActionListener {

   int array[];
   JLabel enterLabel, resultLabel;
   JTextField enterField, resultField;

   // set up GUI components and initialize array
   public void init()
   {
      enterLabel = new JLabel( "Enter integer search key" );
      enterField = new JTextField( 10 );
      enterField.addActionListener( this );
      resultLabel = new JLabel( "Result" );
      resultField = new JTextField( 20 );
      resultField.setEditable( false );

      Container container = getContentPane();
      container.setLayout( new FlowLayout() );
      container.add( enterLabel );
      container.add( enterField );
      container.add( resultLabel );
      container.add( resultField );

      array = new int[ 100 ];
```

Fig. S7.10 Solution for Exercise 7.33. (Part 1 of 2.)

```java

      // initialize array with even numbers 0 to 198
      for ( int counter = 0; counter < array.length; counter++ )
         array[ counter ] = 2 * counter;

   } // end method init

   // obtain user input and call method linearSearch
   public void actionPerformed( ActionEvent actionEvent )
   {
      String stringKey = actionEvent.getActionCommand();
      int intKey = Integer.parseInt( stringKey );
      int element = linearSearch( array, array.length, intKey );

      if ( element != -1 )
         resultField.setText( "Found value in element " + element );

      else
         resultField.setText( "Value not found" );

   } // end method actionPerformed

   // recursively search for key within parameter array
   public int linearSearch( int array2[], int size, int intKey )
   {
      if ( size == 0 )
         return -1;

      else if ( array2[ --size ] == intKey )
         return size;

      else
         return linearSearch( array2, size, intKey );

   } // end method linearSearch

} // end class LinearSearch
```

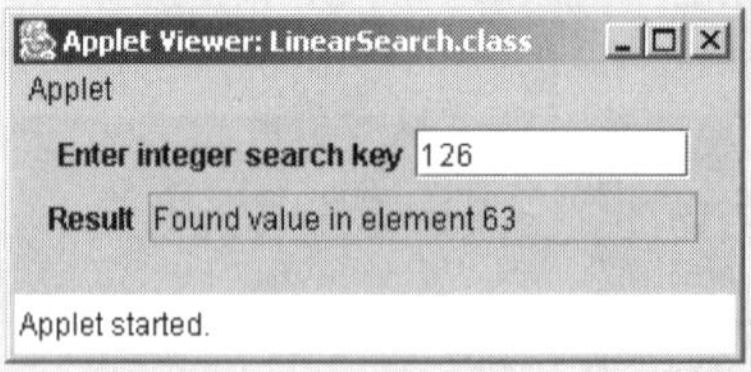

Fig. S7.10 Solution for Exercise 7.33. (Part 2 of 2.)

7.36 (*Print an array*) Write a recursive method `printArray` that takes an array of `int` values and the length of the array as arguments and returns nothing. The method should stop processing and return when it receives an array of length zero.

ANS:

```
// Exercise 7.36 Solution: Print.java
// Program prints a string.
import java.awt.*;
import javax.swing.*;

public class Print extends JApplet {
   int x;
   String result;
   JTextArea output;

   //initializes values
   public void init()
   {
      output = new JTextArea( 40, 40 );
      Container container = getContentPane();
      container.add( output );

      x = 0;
      result = "";
      int array[] = { 8, 22, 88, 34, 84, 21, 94 };

      printArray( array, array.length );
      output.append( result );

   } // end method init

   // recursively print array
   public void printArray( int array2[], int size )
   {
      if ( size == 0 )
         return;

      else {

         result += array2[ 0 ] + " ";

         int array3[] = new int[ --size ];

         for ( int counter = 0; counter < size; counter++ )
            array3[ counter ] = array2[ counter + 1 ];

         printArray( array3, size );
      }

   } // end method printArray

} // end class Print
```

Fig. S7.11 Solution for Exercise 7.36. (Part 1 of 2.)

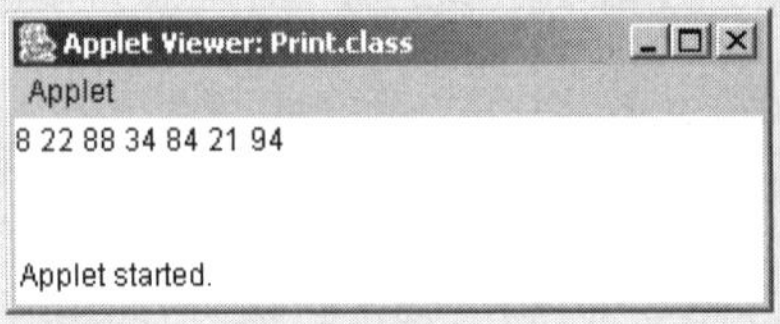

Fig. S7.11 Solution for Exercise 7.36. (Part 2 of 2.)

7.38 (*Find the minimum value in an array*) Write a recursive method `recursiveMinimum` that takes an integer array and the array's length as arguments and returns the smallest element of the array. The method should stop processing and return when it receives an array of one element.

ANS:

```
// Exercise 7.38 Solution: Minimum.java
// Program finds the minimum value in an array.
import java.awt.*;
import javax.swing.*;

public class Minimum extends JApplet {
   final int MAX = 100;
   int smallest;

   // initialize instance variable
   public void init()
   {
      smallest = MAX;
   }

   // initialize array and draw array values
   public void paint( Graphics g )
   {
      super.paint( g );
      int array[] = { 22, 88, 8, 94, 78, 84, 96, 73, 34 };
      int x = 0;

      for ( int counter = 0; counter < array.length; counter++ )
         g.drawString( "" + array[ counter ], x += 20, 40 );

      showStatus( "The smallest value in the array is: " +
         recursiveMinimum( array, array.length ) );

   } // end method paint

   // recursively find minimum value in array
   public int recursiveMinimum( int array2[], int size )
   {
      if ( size > 0 ) {

         if ( array2[ --size ] < smallest )
```

Fig. S7.12 Solution to Exercise 7.38. (Part 1 of 2.)

```
            smallest = array2[ size ];

         recursiveMinimum( array2, size );
      }

      return smallest;

   } // end method recursiveMinimum

} // end class Minimum
```

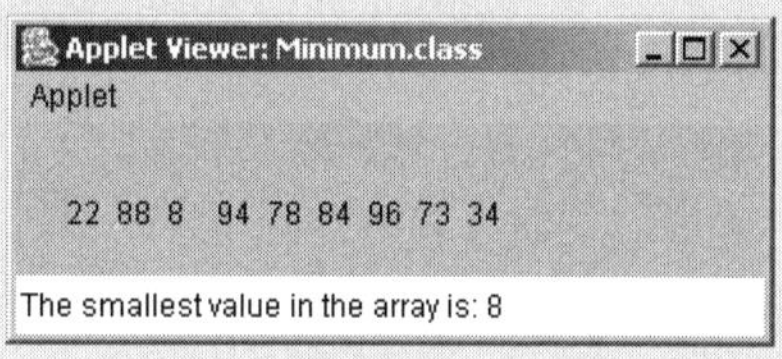

Fig. S7.12 Solution to Exercise 7.38. (Part 2 of 2.)

7.40 (*Maze Traversal*) The following grid of #s and dots (`.`) is a two-dimensional array representation of a maze. The #s represent the walls of the maze, and the dots represent squares in the possible paths through the maze. Moves can be made only to a location in the array that contains a dot.

```
# # # # # # # # # # # #
# . . . # . . . . . . #
. . # . # . # # # # . #
# # # . # . . . . # . #
# . . . . # # # . # . .
# # # # . # . # . # . #
# . . # . # . # . # . #
# # . # . # . # . # . #
# . . . . . . . . # . #
# # # # # # . # # # . #
# . . . . . . # . . . #
# # # # # # # # # # # #
```

There is a simple algorithm for walking through a maze that guarantees finding the exit (assuming there is an exit). If there is not an exit, you will arrive at the starting location again. Place your right hand on the wall to your right and begin walking forward. Never remove your hand from the wall. If the maze turns to the right, follow the wall to the right. As long as you do not remove your hand from the wall, eventually you will arrive at the exit of the maze. There may be a shorter path than the one you have taken, but you are guaranteed to get out of the maze if you follow the algorithm.

Write recursive method `mazeTraverse` to walk through this maze. The method should receive as arguments a 12-by-12 character array representing the maze and the starting location of the maze. As `mazeTraverse` attempts to locate the exit, it should place the character `X` in each square in the path. The method should display the maze after each move so the user can watch as the maze is solved.

ANS:

```
// Exercise 7.40 Solution: Maze.java
// Program traverses a maze.
import java.awt.*;
import javax.swing.*;

public class Maze extends JApplet {
   final int RIGHT = 1, LEFT = 3, UP = 2, DOWN = 0;
   final int Y_START = 2, X_START = 0;
   int move;
   char maze[][] =
      { { '#', '#', '#', '#', '#', '#', '#', '#', '#', '#', '#', '#' },
        { '#', '.', '.', '.', '#', '.', '.', '.', '.', '.', '.', '#' },
        { '.', '.', '#', '.', '#', '.', '#', '#', '#', '#', '.', '#' },
        { '#', '#', '#', '.', '#', '.', '.', '.', '.', '#', '.', '#' },
        { '#', '.', '.', '.', '.', '#', '#', '#', '.', '#', '.', '.' },
        { '#', '#', '#', '#', '.', '#', '.', '#', '.', '#', '.', '#' },
        { '#', '.', '.', '#', '.', '#', '.', '#', '.', '#', '.', '#' },
        { '#', '#', '.', '#', '.', '#', '.', '#', '.', '#', '.', '#' },
        { '#', '.', '.', '.', '.', '.', '.', '.', '.', '#', '.', '#' },
        { '#', '#', '#', '#', '#', '#', '.', '#', '#', '#', '.', '#' },
        { '#', '.', '.', '.', '.', '.', '.', '#', '.', '.', '.', '#' },
        { '#', '#', '#', '#', '#', '#', '#', '#', '#', '#', '#', '#' } };

   // initialize applet
   public void init()
   {
      move = 0;
   }

   // traverse maze recursively
   public void mazeTraversal( char maze2[][], int y, int x,
      int direction )
   {
      maze2[ y ][ x ] = 'x'; // place marker in maze
      move++;
      repaint();

     // if returned to starting location
      if ( y == Y_START && x == X_START && move > 1 ) {
         JOptionPane.showMessageDialog( null,
            "Returned to starting location!", "Maze Solver",
            JOptionPane.INFORMATION_MESSAGE );
         return;
      }

      // if maze exited
      else if ( mazeExited( y, x ) && move > 1 ) {
         JOptionPane.showMessageDialog( null, "Maze sucCessfully exited!",
            "Maze Solver", JOptionPane.INFORMATION_MESSAGE );
```

Fig. S7.13 Solution to Exercise 7.40. (Part 1 of 4.)

```
        }

        // make next move
        else {
           JOptionPane.showMessageDialog( null, "Next move?",
              "Maze Solver", JOptionPane.INFORMATION_MESSAGE );

           // determine where next move should be made
           for ( int move = direction, count = 0; count < 4;
              ++count, ++move, move %= 4 )

              // checks to see if the space to the right is free. If  so,
              // moves there and continues maze traversal. If not,  breaks
              // out of switch and tries new value of move in for loop.
              switch ( move ) {

                 case DOWN:

                    if ( validMove( y + 1, x ) ) {   // move down
                       mazeTraversal( maze2, y + 1, x, LEFT );
                       return;
                    }

                    break;

                 case RIGHT:

                    if ( validMove( y, x + 1 ) ) {   // move right
                       mazeTraversal( maze2, y, x + 1, DOWN );
                       return;
                    }

                    break;

                 case UP:

                    if ( validMove( y - 1, x ) ) {   // move up
                       mazeTraversal( maze2, y - 1, x, RIGHT );
                       return;
                    }

                    break;

                 case LEFT:

                    if ( validMove( y, x - 1 ) ) { // move left
                       mazeTraversal( maze2, y, x - 1, UP );
                       return;
                    }

```

Fig. S7.13 Solution to Exercise 7.40. (Part 2 of 4.)

```
         } // end switch statement

         // if no valid moves available
         JOptionPane.showMessageDialog( null, "Can't move!" ,
            "Maze Solver", JOptionPane.INFORMATION_MESSAGE );

      } // end else

   } // end method mazeTraversal

   // check if move is valid
   public boolean validMove( int row, int column )
   {
      return ( row >= 0 && row <= 11 && column >= 0 &&
         column <= 11 && maze[ row ][ column ] != '#' );
   }

   // check if location is on edge of maze
   public boolean mazeExited( int row, int column )
   {
      return ( row == 0 || row == 11 ||
         column == 0 || column == 11 );
   }

   // draw maze
   public void paint( Graphics g )
   {
      super.paint( g );
      int x = 5, y = 30;

      for ( int row = 0; row < maze.length; row++ ) {

         for ( int column = 0; column < maze[ row ].length; column++ )
            g.drawString( "" + maze[ row ][ column ], x += 20, y );

         y += 10;
         x = 5;
      }

      if ( move == 0 )
         mazeTraversal( maze, Y_START, X_START, RIGHT );

   } // end method paint

} // end class Maze
```

Fig. S7.13 Solution to Exercise 7.40. (Part 3 of 4.)

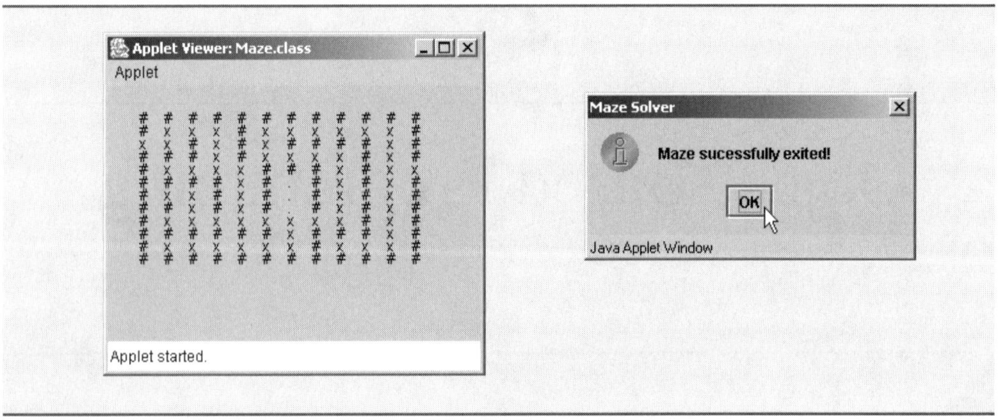
Applet Viewer: Maze.class
Applet
Applet started.
Maze Solver
Maze sucessfully exited!
OK
Java Applet Window

Fig. S7.13 Solution to Exercise 7.40. (Part 4 of 4.)

8

Object-Based Programming

Solutions to Selected Exercises

8.3 Create a class called `Rational` for performing arithmetic with fractions. Write a program to test your class. Use integer variables to represent the `private` instance variables of the class—the `numerator` and the `denominator`. Provide a constructor that enables an object of this class to be initialized when it is declared. The constructor should store the fraction in reduced form—the fraction

```
2/4
```

is equivalent to `1/2` and would be stored in the object as 1 in the `numerator` and 2 in the `denominator`. Provide a no-argument constructor with default values in case no initializers are provided. Provide `public` methods that perform each of the following operations:

a) Add two `Rational` numbers: The result of the addition should be stored in reduced form.
b) Subtract two `Rational` numbers: The result of the subtraction should be stored in reduced form.
c) Multiply two `Rational` numbers: The result of the multiplication should be stored in reduced form.
d) Divide two `Rational` numbers: The result of the division should be stored in reduced form.
e) Print `Rational` numbers in the form `a/b`, where `a` is the `numerator` and `b` is the `denominator`.
f) Print `Rational` numbers in floating-point format. (Consider providing formatting capabilities that enable the user of the class to specify the number of digits of precision to the right of the decimal point.)

ANS:

```java
// Exercise 8.3 Solution: RationalTest.java
// Program tests class Rational.
import java.awt.*;
import java.awt.event.*;
import javax.swing.*;

public class RationalTest extends JApplet implements ActionListener {
```

Fig. S8.1 Solution to Exercise 8.3: RationalTest.java. (Part 1 of 4.)

```
    private JLabel numeratorlabel1, numeratorlabel2,
       denominatorlabel1, denominatorlabel2, digitsLabel;
    private JTextField numeratorField1, numeratorField2,
       denominatorField1, denominatorField2, digitsField;
    private JButton add, subtract, multiply, divide;

    // set up GUI components
    public void init()
    {
       // text fields for user input
       numeratorlabel1 = new JLabel( "Enter numerator 1:" );
       numeratorlabel2 = new JLabel( "Enter numerator 2:" );
       denominatorlabel1 = new JLabel( "Enter denominator 1:" );
       denominatorlabel2 = new JLabel( "Enter denominator 2:" );
       digitsLabel = new JLabel( "Enter precision:" );

       numeratorField1 = new JTextField( 5 );
       numeratorField2 = new JTextField( 5 );
       denominatorField1 = new JTextField( 5 );
       denominatorField2 = new JTextField( 5 );
       digitsField = new JTextField( 5 );

       // buttons to manipulate the data
       add = new JButton( "Add" );
       subtract = new JButton( "Subtract" );
       multiply = new JButton( "Multiply" );
       divide = new JButton( "Divide" );

       add.addActionListener( this );
       subtract.addActionListener( this );
       multiply.addActionListener( this );
       divide.addActionListener( this );

       Container container = getContentPane();
       container.setLayout(new FlowLayout());

       // add all components to GUI
       container.add( numeratorlabel1 );
       container.add( numeratorField1 );
       container.add( denominatorlabel1 );
       container.add( denominatorField1 );
       container.add( numeratorlabel2 );
       container.add( numeratorField2 );
       container.add( denominatorlabel2 );
       container.add( denominatorField2 );
       container.add( digitsLabel );
       container.add( digitsField );
       container.add( add );
       container.add( subtract );
```

Fig. S8.1 Solution to Exercise 8.3: RationalTest.java. (Part 2 of 4.)

```java
      container.add( multiply );
      container.add( divide );

   } // end method init

   // perform calculations
   public void actionPerformed( ActionEvent actionEvent )
   {
      // read in the two rational numbers as data
      Rational rational1, rational2, result;
      rational1 = new Rational(
         Integer.parseInt( numeratorField1.getText() ),
         Integer.parseInt( denominatorField1.getText() ) );
      rational2 = new Rational(
         Integer.parseInt( numeratorField2.getText() ),
         Integer.parseInt( denominatorField2.getText() ) );

      // read in digits precision
      int digits = Integer.parseInt( digitsField.getText() );

      // recognize and perform the appropriate action on the data,
      // then output the result as a floating point number
      if ( actionEvent.getSource() == add ) {
         result = rational1.sum( rational2 );
         showStatus( "a + b = " + result.toRationalString() +
            " = " + result.toFloatString( digits ) );
      }

      else if ( actionEvent.getSource() == subtract ) {
         result = rational1.subtract( rational2 );
         showStatus( "a - b = " + result.toRationalString() +
            " = " + result.toFloatString( digits ) );
      }

      else if ( actionEvent.getSource() == multiply ) {
         result = rational1.multiply( rational2 );
         showStatus( "a * b = " + result.toRationalString() +
            " = " + result.toFloatString( digits ) );
      }

      else if ( actionEvent.getSource() == divide ) {
         result = rational1.divide( rational2 );
         showStatus( "a / b = " + result.toRationalString() +
            " = " + result.toFloatString( digits ) );
      }

   } // end method actionPerformed

} // end class RationalTest
```

Fig. S8.1 Solution to Exercise 8.3: RationalTest.java. (Part 3 of 4.)

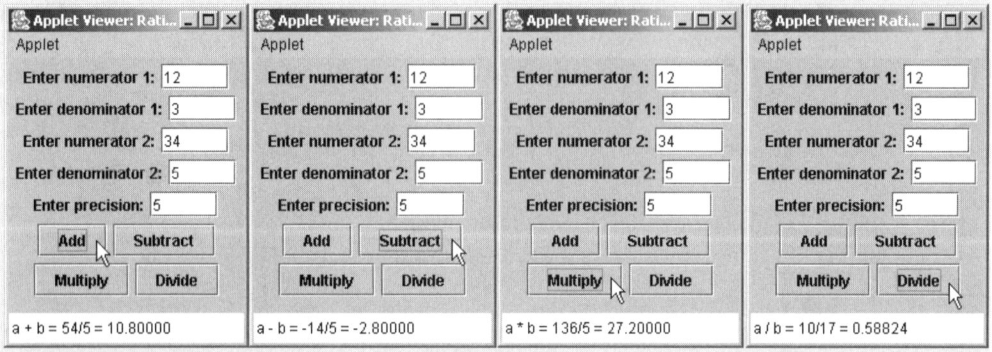

Fig. S8.1 Solution to Exercise 8.3: RationalTest.java. (Part 4 of 4.)

```java
// Exercise 8.3 Solution: Rational.java
// Rational class definition.
import java.text.DecimalFormat;

public class Rational {
   private int numerator, denominator;

   // no-argument constructor
   public Rational()
   {
      numerator = 1;
      denominator = 1;
   }

   // initialize numerator part to n and denominator part to d
   public Rational( int theNumerator, int theDenominator )
   {
      numerator = theNumerator;
      denominator = theDenominator;
      reduce();
   }

   // add two Rational numbers
   public Rational sum( Rational right )
   {
      int resultDenominator = denominator * right.denominator;
      int resultNumerator = numerator * right.denominator +
         right.numerator * denominator;

      return new Rational( resultNumerator, resultDenominator );
   }

   // subtract two Rational numbers
   public Rational subtract( Rational right )
```

Fig. S8.2 Solution to Exercise 8.3: Rational.java. (Part 1 of 3.)

```
   {
      int resultDenominator = denominator * right.denominator;
      int resultNumerator = numerator * right.denominator -
         right.numerator * denominator;

      return new Rational( resultNumerator, resultDenominator );
   }

   // multiply two Rational numbers
   public Rational multiply( Rational right )
   {
      return new Rational( numerator * right.numerator,
         denominator * right.denominator );
   }

   // divide two Rational numbers
   public Rational divide( Rational right )
   {
      return new Rational( numerator * right.denominator,
         denominator * right.numerator );
   }

   // reduce the fraction
   private void reduce()
   {
      int gcd = 0;
      int smaller;

      if ( numerator < denominator )
         smaller = numerator;
      else
         smaller = denominator;

      for ( int divisor = smaller; divisor >= 2; divisor-- ) {

         if ( numerator % divisor == 0 && denominator % divisor == 0 ) {
            gcd = divisor;
            break;
         }
      }

      if ( gcd != 0 ) {
         numerator /= gcd;
         denominator /= gcd;
      }
   }

   // return String representation of a Rational number
   public String toRationalString()
   {
```

Fig. S8.2 Solution to Exercise 8.3: Rational.java. (Part 2 of 3.)

```
      return numerator + "/" + denominator;
   }

   // return floating-point String representation of
   // a Rational number
   public String toFloatString( int digits )
   {
      String format = "0.";

      // get format string
      for ( int i = 0; i < digits; i++ )
         format += "0";

      DecimalFormat twoDigits = new DecimalFormat( format );

      return twoDigits.format(
         ( double )numerator / denominator ).toString();
   }

} // end class Rational
```

Fig. S8.2 Solution to Exercise 8.3: Rational.java. (Part 3 of 3.)

8.5 Modify class Date of Fig. 8.9 to perform error-checking on the initializer values for instance variables month, day and year (currently it validates only the month and day). Also, provide a method nextDay to increment the day by one. The Date object should always remain in a consistent state. Write a program that tests the nextDay method in a loop that prints the date during each iteration of the loop to illustrate that the nextDay method works correctly. Test the following cases:

a) incrementing into the next month.
b) incrementing into the next year.

ANS:

```
// Exercise 8.5 Solution: DateTest
// Program tests Date class.

public class DateTest {

   // method main begins execution of Java application
   public static void main( String args[] )
   {
      System.out.println( "Checking increment" );
      Date testDate = new Date( 11, 27, 1988 );

      // test incrementing of day, month and year
      for ( int counter = 0; counter < 40; counter++ ) {
         testDate.nextDay();
         System.out.println( "Incremented Date:" +
            testDate.toDateString() );
      }
```

Fig. S8.3 Solution to Exercise 8.5: DateTest. (Part 1 of 2.)

```
   }

} // end class DateTest
```

```
Checking increment
Date object constructor for date 11/27/1988
Incremented Date:11/28/1988
Incremented Date:11/29/1988
Incremented Date:11/30/1988
Day 31 invalid. Set to day 1.
Incremented Date:12/1/1988
Incremented Date:12/2/1988
...
Incremented Date:12/30/1988
Incremented Date:12/31/1988
Day 32 invalid. Set to day 1.
Incremented Date:1/1/1989
Incremented Date:1/2/1989
Incremented Date:1/3/1989
Incremented Date:1/4/1989
Incremented Date:1/5/1989
Incremented Date:1/6/1989
```

Fig. S8.3 Solution to Exercise 8.5: DateTest. (Part 2 of 2.)

```
// Exercise 8.5 Solution: Date.java
// Date class definition.

public class Date {
   private int month;  // 1-12
   private int day;    // 1-31 based on month
   private int year;   // any year

   // constructor: confirm proper value for month;
   // call method function checkDay to confirm proper value for day.
   public Date( int theMonth, int theDay, int theYear )
   {
      if ( theMonth > 0 && theMonth <= 12 )  // validate month
         month = theMonth;
      else {
         month = 1;
         System.out.println( "Month " + theMonth +
            " invalid. Set to month 1." );
      }

      if ( theYear > 0 )                     // validate year
         year = theYear;
      else {
         year = 1;
         System.out.println( "Year " + theYear +
            " invalid. Set to Year 1." );
      }
```

Fig. S8.4 Solution to Exercise 8.5: Date.java. (Part 1 of 3.)

```
      day = checkDay ( theDay );                // validate day

      System.out.println(
         "Date object constructor for date " + toDateString() );
   }

   // utility method to confirm proper day value
   // based on month and year.
   public int checkDay( int testDay )
   {
      int daysPerMonth[] =
         { 0, 31, 28, 31, 30, 31, 30, 31, 31, 30, 31, 30, 31 };

      // check if day in range for month
      if ( testDay > 0 && testDay <= daysPerMonth[ month ] )
         return testDay;

      // check for leap year
      if ( month == 2 && testDay == 29 && ( year % 400 == 0 ||
         ( year % 4 == 0 && year % 100 != 0 ) ) )
         return testDay;

      System.out.println( "Day " + testDay + " invalid. Set to day 1." );

      return 1;   // leave object in consistent state
   }

   // increment the day and check if doing so will change the month
   public void nextDay()
   {
      int testDay = day + 1;

      if ( checkDay( testDay ) == testDay )
         day = testDay;
      else {
         day = 1;
         nextMonth();
      }
   }

   // increment the month and check if doing so will change the year
   public void nextMonth()
   {
      if ( 12 == month )
        year++;

      month = month % 12 + 1;
   }
```

Fig. S8.4 Solution to Exercise 8.5: Date.java. (Part 2 of 3.)

```
    // create a String of the form month/day/year
    public String toDateString()
    {
       return month + "/" + day + "/" + year;
    }

} // end class Date
```

Fig. S8.4 Solution to Exercise 8.5: Date.java. (Part 3 of 3.)

8.8 Create a class `Rectangle`. The class has attributes `length` and `width`, each of which defaults to 1. It has methods that calculate the `perimeter` and the `area` of the rectangle. It has *set* and *get* methods for both `length` and `width`. The *set* methods should verify that `length` and `width` are each floating-point numbers larger than 0.0 and less than 20.0. Write a program to test class `Rectangle`.

ANS:

```
// Exercise 8.8 Solution: RectangleTest.java
// Program tests class Rectangle.
import java.awt.*;
import java.awt.event.*;
import javax.swing.*;

public class RectangleTest extends JApplet implements ActionListener {
   private JLabel prompt1, prompt2;
   private JTextField inputField1, inputField2;
   private JLabel outputLabel;
   private JTextArea outputArea;
   private Rectangle rectangle;

   // set up GUI components and instantiate new Rectangle
   public void init()
   {
      prompt1 = new JLabel( "Length:" );
      prompt2 = new JLabel( "Width:" );
      inputField1 = new JTextField( 10 );
      inputField2 = new JTextField( 10 );
      inputField2.addActionListener( this );

      outputLabel = new JLabel( "Test Output" );
      outputArea = new JTextArea( 4, 10 );
      outputArea.setEditable( false );

      // add components to GUI
      Container container = getContentPane();
      container.setLayout( new FlowLayout() );
      container.add( prompt1 );
      container.add( inputField1 );
      container.add( prompt2 );
      container.add( inputField2 );
```

Fig. S8.5 Solution to Exercise 8.8: RectangleTest.java. (Part 1 of 2.)

```
         container.add( outputLabel );
         container.add( outputArea );

         // create a new Rectangle with no initial values
         rectangle = new Rectangle();
      }

      // create rectangle with user input
      public void actionPerformed( ActionEvent actionEvent )
      {
         double double1, double2;

         double1 = Double.parseDouble( inputField1.getText() );
         double2 = Double.parseDouble( inputField2.getText() );

         rectangle.setLength( double1 );
         rectangle.setWidth( double2 );

         // see the results of the test
         outputArea.setText( rectangle.toRectangleString() );
      }

   } // end class RectangleTest
```

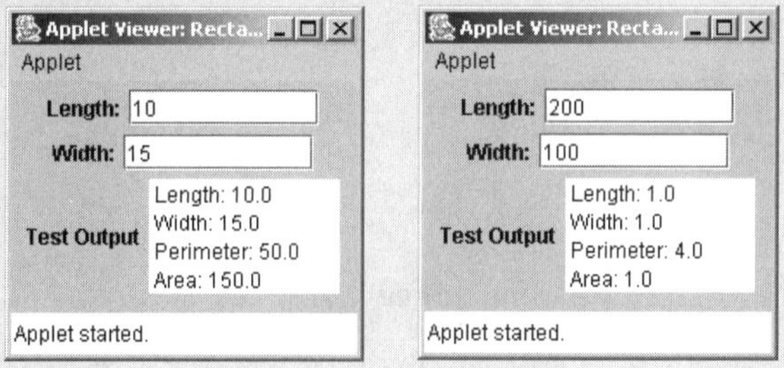

Fig. S8.5 Solution to Exercise 8.8: RectangleTest.java. (Part 2 of 2.)

```
// Exercise 8.8 Solution: Rectangle.java
// Definition of class Rectangle

public class Rectangle {
   private double length, width;

   // constructor without paramters
   public Rectangle()
   {
      setLength( 1.0 );
      setWidth( 1.0 );
   }

```

Fig. S8.6 Solution to Exercise 8.8: Rectangle.java. (Part 1 of 3.)

```java
   // constructor with length and width supplied
   public Rectangle( double theLength, double theWidth )
   {
      setLength( theLength );
      setWidth( theWidth );
   }

   // validate and set length
   public void setLength( double theLength )
   {
      length = ( theLength > 0.0 && theLength < 20.0 ? theLength : 1.0 );
   }

   // validate and set width
   public void setWidth( double theWidth )
   {
      width = ( theWidth > 0 && theWidth < 20.0 ? theWidth : 1.0 );
   }

   // get value of length
   public double getLength()
   {
      return length;
   }

   // get value of width
   public double getWidth()
   {
      return width;
   }

   // calculate rectangle's perimeter
   public double perimeter()
   {
      return 2 * length + 2 * width;
   }

   // calculate rectangle's area
   public double area()
   {
      return length * width;
   }

   // convert to String
   public String toRectangleString ()
   {
       return ( " Length: " + length + "\n" + " Width: " + width  + "\n" +
          " Perimeter: " + perimeter() + "\n" + " Area: " + area() );

   }
```

Fig. S8.6 Solution to Exercise 8.8: Rectangle.java. (Part 2 of 3.)

```java

} // end class Rectangle
```

Fig. S8.6 Solution to Exercise 8.8: Rectangle.java. (Part 3 of 3.)

8.9 Create a more sophisticated `Rectangle` class than the one you created in Exercise 8.8. This class stores only the Cartesian coordinates of the four corners of the rectangle. The constructor calls a *set* method that accepts four sets of coordinates and verifies that each of these is in the first quadrant with no single *x*- or *y*-coordinate larger than 20.0. The *set* method also verifies that the supplied coordinates specify a rectangle. Provide methods to calculate the `length`, `width`, `perimeter` and `area`. The length is the larger of the two dimensions. Include a predicate method `isSquare` which determines whether the rectangle is a square. Write a program to test class `Rectangle`.

ANS:

```java
// Exercise 8.9 Solution: RectangleTest.java
// Program tests class Rectangle.
import java.awt.*;
import java.awt.event.*;
import javax.swing.*;

public class RectangleTest extends JApplet implements ActionListener {
   private JLabel x1Prompt, y1Prompt, x2Prompt, y2Prompt,
      x3Prompt, y3Prompt, x4Prompt, y4Prompt;
   private JTextField directions, x1Field, y1Field, x2Field,
      y2Field, x3Field, y3Field, x4Field, y4Field;
   private JLabel outputLabel;
   private JTextArea outputArea;

   // set up GUI components and instantiate new Rectangle
   public void init()
   {
      x1Prompt = new JLabel( "x1:" );
      y1Prompt = new JLabel( "y1:" );
      x2Prompt = new JLabel( "x2:" );
      y2Prompt = new JLabel( "y2:" );
      x3Prompt = new JLabel( "x3:" );
      y3Prompt = new JLabel( "y3:" );
      x4Prompt = new JLabel( "x4:" );
      y4Prompt = new JLabel( "y4:" );

      directions = new JTextField(
         "Enter rectangle's coordinates in clockwise order.");
      directions.setEditable( false );

      // text fields for the four points' x and y values
      x1Field = new JTextField( 10 );
      y1Field = new JTextField( 10 );
      x2Field = new JTextField( 10 );
      y2Field = new JTextField( 10 );
```

Fig. S8.7 Solution to Exercise 8.9: RectangleTest.java. (Part 1 of 3.)

```java
      x3Field = new JTextField( 10 );
      y3Field = new JTextField( 10 );
      x4Field = new JTextField( 10 );
      y4Field = new JTextField( 10 );
      y4Field.addActionListener( this );

      // output area for rectangle information
      outputLabel = new JLabel( "Test Output" );
      outputArea = new JTextArea( 4, 10 );
      outputArea.setEditable( false );

      // add components to GUI
      Container container = getContentPane();
      container.setLayout( new FlowLayout() );
      container.add( directions );
      container.add( x1Prompt );
      container.add( x1Field );
      container.add( y1Prompt );
      container.add( y1Field );
      container.add( x2Prompt );
      container.add( x2Field );
      container.add( y2Prompt );
      container.add( y2Field );
      container.add( x3Prompt );
      container.add( x3Field );
      container.add( y3Prompt );
      container.add( y3Field );
      container.add( x4Prompt );
      container.add( x4Field );
      container.add( y4Prompt );
      container.add( y4Field );
      container.add( outputLabel );
      container.add( outputArea );

   } // end method init

   // create rectangle with user input
   public void actionPerformed( ActionEvent actionEvent )
   {
      double x1, x2, x3, x4, y1, y2, y3, y4;

      x1 = Double.parseDouble( x1Field.getText() );
      x2 = Double.parseDouble( x2Field.getText() );
      x3 = Double.parseDouble( x3Field.getText() );
      x4 = Double.parseDouble( x4Field.getText() );
      y1 = Double.parseDouble( y1Field.getText() );
      y2 = Double.parseDouble( y2Field.getText() );
      y3 = Double.parseDouble( y3Field.getText() );
      y4 = Double.parseDouble( y4Field.getText() );

```

Fig. S8.7 Solution to Exercise 8.9: RectangleTest.java. (Part 2 of 3.)

```
      // create a new shape with the points and determine whether
      // it is actually a rectangle.
      Rectangle rectangle =
         new Rectangle( x1, y1, x2, y2, x3, y3, x4, y4 );

      if ( rectangle.isRectangle() )
         outputArea.setText( rectangle.toRectangleString() );

      else
         outputArea.setText( "");

   } // end method actionPerformed

} // end class RectangleTest
```

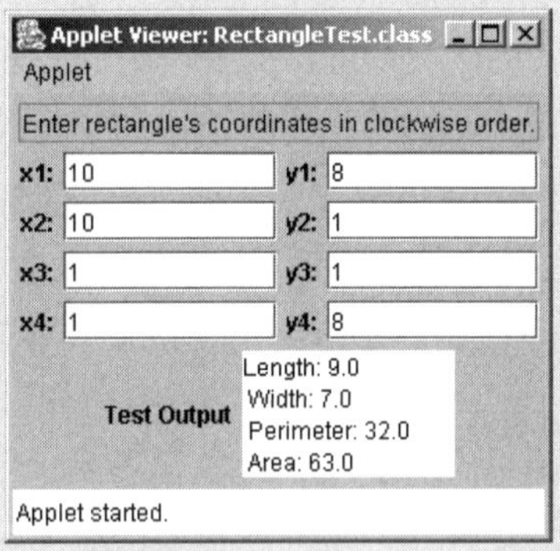

Fig. S8.7 Solution to Exercise 8.9: RectangleTest.java. (Part 3 of 3.)

```
// Exercise 8.9 Solution: Rectangle.java
// Definition of class Rectangle
import javax.swing.JOptionPane;

public class Rectangle {
   private double x1, x2, x3, x4, y1, y2, y3, y4;

   // no-argument constructor
   public Rectangle()
   {
      setCoordinates( 1, 1, 1, 1, 1, 1, 1, 1 );
   }

   // constructor
   public Rectangle( double x1, double y1, double x2,
      double y2, double x3, double y3, double x4, double y4 )
   {
      setCoordinates( x1, y1, x2, y2, x3, y3, x4, y4 );
   }
```

Fig. S8.8 Solution to Exercise 8.9: Rectangle.java. (Part 1 of 4.)

```java

   // check if coordinates are valid
   public void setCoordinates( double xInput1, double yInput1,
      double xInput2, double yInput2, double xInput3,
      double yInput3, double xInput4, double yInput4 )
   {
      x1 = ( xInput1 >= 0.0 && xInput1 <= 20.0 ? xInput1 : 1 );
      x2 = ( xInput2 >= 0.0 && xInput2 <= 20.0 ? xInput2 : 1 );
      x3 = ( xInput3 >= 0.0 && xInput3 <= 20.0 ? xInput3 : 1 );
      x4 = ( xInput4 >= 0.0 && xInput4 <= 20.0 ? xInput4 : 1 );
      y1 = ( yInput1 >= 0.0 && yInput1 <= 20.0 ? yInput1 : 1 );
      y2 = ( yInput2 >= 0.0 && yInput2 <= 20.0 ? yInput2 : 1 );
      y3 = ( yInput3 >= 0.0 && yInput3 <= 20.0 ? yInput3 : 1 );
      y4 = ( yInput4 >= 0.0 && yInput4 <= 20.0 ? yInput4 : 1 );

      if ( !isRectangle() )
         JOptionPane.showMessageDialog( null, "This is not a rectangle.",
            "Information", JOptionPane.INFORMATION_MESSAGE );
   }

   // calculate distance between two points
   public double distance( double x1, double y1, double x2, double y2 )
   {
      double distance;

      // calculate vertical lines
      if ( x1 == x2 )
         distance = y1 - y2 ;

      // calculate horizontal lines
      else if ( y1 == y2 )
         distance = x1 - x2 ;

      // calculate lines that aren't horizontal or vertical
      else
         distance = Math.sqrt( ( Math.pow( x1 - x2, 2 ) +
            Math.pow( y1 - y2, 2 ) ) );

      if ( distance < 0 )
         distance *= -1;

      return distance;
   }

   // check if coordinates specify a rectangle by determining if the
   // two diagonals are of the same length.
   public boolean isRectangle()
   {
      double side1 = distance( x1, y1, x2, y2 );
      double side2 = distance( x2, y2, x3, y3 );
```

Fig. S8.8 Solution to Exercise 8.9: Rectangle.java. (Part 2 of 4.)

```
      double side3 = distance( x3, y3, x4, y4 );

      if ( side1 * side1 + side2 * side2 ==
         side2 * side2 + side3 * side3 )
         return true;

      else
         return false;
   }

   // check if rectangle is a square
   public boolean isSquare()
   {
      return ( getLength() == getWidth() );
   }

   // get length of rectangle
   public double getLength()
   {
      double side1 = distance( x1, y1, x2, y2 );
      double side2 = distance( x2, y2, x3, y3 );

      return ( side1 > side2 ? side1 : side2 );
   }

   // get width of rectangle
   public double getWidth()
   {
      double side1 = distance( x1, y1, x2, y2 );
      double side2 = distance( x2, y2, x3, y3 );

      return ( side1 < side2 ? side1 : side2 );
   }

   // calculate perimeter
   public double perimeter()
   {
      return 2 * getLength() + 2 * getWidth();
   }

   // calculate area
   public double area()
   {
      return getLength() * getWidth();
   }

   // convert to String
   public String toRectangleString()
   {
      return ( "Length: " + getLength() + "\n" + " Width: " + getWidth() +
```

Fig. S8.8 Solution to Exercise 8.9: Rectangle.java. (Part 3 of 4.)

```
        "\n" + " Perimeter: " + perimeter() + "\n" + " Area: " +
        area() );
   }

} // end class Rectangle
```

Fig. S8.8 Solution to Exercise 8.9: Rectangle.java. (Part 4 of 4.)

8.13 What happens when a return type, even `void`, is specified for a constructor?

ANS: *It is treated as a method and is not considered to be a constructor.*

8.18 *(Drawing Program)* Create a drawing applet that randomly draws lines, rectangles and ovals. For this purpose, create a set of "smart" shape classes where objects of these classes know how to draw themselves if provided with a `Graphics` object that tells them where to draw (i.e., the applet's `Graphics` object allows a shape to draw on the applet's background). The class names should be `MyLine`, `MyRect` and `MyOval`.

The data for class `MyLine` should include *x1*, *y1*, *x2* and *y2* coordinates. Method `drawLine` of class `Graphics` will connect the two points supplied with a line. The data for classes `MyRect` and `MyOval` should include an upper-left *x*-coordinate value, an upper-left *y*-coordinate value, a *width* (must be nonnegative) and a *height* (must be nonnegative). All data in each class must be `private`.

In addition to the data, each class should declare at least the following `public` methods:

a) A constructor with no arguments that sets the coordinates to 0.
b) A constructor with arguments that sets the coordinates to the supplied values.
c) *Set* methods for each individual piece of data that allow the programmer to set any piece of data in a shape independently (e.g., if you have an instance variable `x1`, you should have a method `setX1`).
d) *Get* methods for each individual piece of data that allow the programmer to retrieve any piece of data in a shape independently (e.g., if you have an instance variable `x1`, you should have a method `getX1`).
e) A `draw` method with the first line

```
public void draw( Graphics g )
```

that will be called from the applet's `paint` method to draw a shape onto the screen.

If you would like to provide more methods for flexibility, please do so.

Begin by declaring class `MyLine` and an applet to test your classes. The applet should have a `MyLine` instance variable `line` that can refer to one `MyLine` object (created in the applet's `init` method with random coordinates). The applet's `paint` method should draw the shape with a statement like

```
line.draw( g );
```

where `line` is the `MyLine` reference and `g` is the `Graphics` object that the shape will use to draw itself on the applet.

Next, change the single `MyLine` reference into an array of `MyLine` references and hard code several `MyLine` objects into the program for drawing. The applet's `paint` method should walk through the array of `MyLine` objects and draw every one.

After the preceding part is working, you should declare the MyOval and MyRect classes and add objects of these classes into the MyRect and MyOval arrays. The applet's paint method should walk through each array and draw every shape. Create five shapes of each type.

Once the applet is running, select **Reload** from the appletviewer's **Applet** menu to reload the applet. This will cause the applet to choose new random numbers for the shapes and draw the shapes again.

ANS:

```java
// Exercise 8.18 Solution: TestDraw.java
// Program that tests classes MyLine, MyOval and MyRect
import java.awt.*;
import javax.swing.*;

public class TestDraw extends JApplet {
   private MyLine line[];
   private MyOval oval[];
   private MyRect rectangle[];

   // initialize arrays which hold five of each shape
   public void init()
   {
      line = new MyLine[ 5 ];
      oval = new MyOval[ 5 ];
      rectangle = new MyRect[ 5 ];

      for ( int count = 0; count < line.length; count++ ) {
         int x1 = (int) ( Math.random() * 400 );
         int y1 = (int) ( Math.random() * 400 );
         int x2 = (int) ( Math.random() * 400 );
         int y2 = (int) ( Math.random() * 400 );
         line[ count] = new MyLine( x1, y1, x2, y2 );
      }

      for ( int count = 0; count < oval.length; count++ ) {
         int x = (int) ( Math.random() * 400 );
         int y = (int) ( Math.random() * 400 );
         int theLength = (int) ( Math.random() * 400 );
         int theWidth = (int) ( Math.random() * 400 );
         oval[ count ] = new MyOval( x, y, theLength, theWidth );
      }

      for ( int count = 0; count < rectangle.length; count++ ) {
         int x = (int) ( Math.random() * 400 );
         int y = (int) ( Math.random() * 400 );
         int theLength = (int) ( Math.random() * 400 );
         int theWidth = (int) ( Math.random() * 400 );
         rectangle[ count ] = new MyRect( x, y, theLength, theWidth );
      }

```

Fig. S8.9 Solution to Exercise 8.18: TestDraw.java. (Part 1 of 2.)

```
   } // end method init

   // for each shape array, create shapes with random values,
   // then draw them.
   public void paint( Graphics g )
   {
      for ( int count = 0; count < line.length; count++ ) {
         line[ count ].draw( g );
      }

      for ( int count = 0; count < oval.length; count++ ) {
         oval[ count ].draw( g );
      }

      for ( int count = 0; count < rectangle.length; count++ ) {
         rectangle[ count ].draw( g );
      }

   } // end method paint

} // end method paint
```

Fig. S8.9 Solution to Exercise 8.18: TestDraw.java. (Part 2 of 2.)

```
// Exercise 8.18 Solution: MyLine.java
// Definition of class MyLine
import java.awt.Graphics;

public class MyLine {
   private int x1, x2, y1, y2;
```

Fig. S8.10 Solution to Exercise 8.18: MyLine.java. (Part 1 of 3.)

```java

   // constructor initializes private vars with
   // default values
   public MyLine()
   {
      x1 = 0;
      y1 = 0;
      x2 = 0;
      y2 = 0;
   }

   // constructor with input values
   public MyLine( int x1, int y1, int x2, int y2 )
   {
      setX1( x1 );
      setX2( x2 );
      setY1( y1 );
      setY2( y2 );
   }

   // accessor and mutator methods for each of the
   // four private variables:
   public void setX1( int x1 )
   {
     this.x1 = ( x1 >= 0 ? x1 : 0 );
   }

   public int getX1()
   {
     return x1;
   }

   public void setX2( int x2 )
   {
     this.x2 = ( x2 >= 0 ? x2 : 0 );
   }

   public int getX2()
   {
     return x2;
   }

   public void setY1( int y1 )
   {
     this.y1 = ( y1 >= 0 ? y1 : 0 );
   }

   public int getY1()
   {
     return y1;
```

Fig. S8.10 Solution to Exercise 8.18: MyLine.java. (Part 2 of 3.)

```java
    }

    public void setY2( int y2 )
    {
      this.y2 = ( y2 >= 0 ? y2 : 0 );
    }

    public int getY2()
    {
      return y2;
    }

    // Actually draws the line
    public void draw( Graphics g )
    {
       g.drawLine( x1, y1, x2, y2 );
    }

 } // end class MyLine
```

Fig. S8.10 Solution to Exercise 8.18: MyLine.java. (Part 3 of 3.)

```java
// Exercise 8.18 Solution: MyRect.java
// Definition of class MyRect
import java.awt.Graphics;

public class MyRect {
   private int length, width, upperLeftX, upperLeftY;

   // constructor initializes private vars with
   // default values
   public MyRect()
   {
      length =  0;
      width = 0;
      upperLeftX = 0;
      upperLeftY = 0;
   }

   // constructor
   public MyRect( int x, int y, int theLength, int theWidth )
   {
      setUpperLeftX( x );
      setUpperLeftY( y );
      setLength( theLength );
      setWidth( theWidth );
   }

   // accessor and mutator methods for each of the
```

Fig. S8.11 Solution to Exercise 8.18: MyRect.java. (Part 1 of 2.)

```
    // four private variables:
    public void setUpperLeftX( int x )
    {
      upperLeftX = x;
    }

    public int getUpperLeftX()
    {
      return upperLeftX;
    }

    public void setUpperLeftY( int y )
    {
      upperLeftY = y;
    }

    public int getUpperLeftY()
    {
      return upperLeftY;
    }

    public void setWidth( int theWidth )
    {
      width = ( theWidth >= 0 ? theWidth : 1 );
    }

    public int getWidth()
    {
      return width;
    }

    public void setLength( int theLength )
    {
      length = ( theLength >= 0.0 ? theLength : 1 );
    }

    public int getLength()
    {
      return length;
    }

    // Actually draws the rectangle
    public void draw( Graphics g )
    {
       g.drawRect( upperLeftX, upperLeftY, length, width );
    }

} // end class MyRect
```

Fig. S8.11 Solution to Exercise 8.18: MyRect.java. (Part 2 of 2.)

```java
// Exercise 8.18 Solution: MyOval.java
// Definition of class MyRect
import java.awt.Graphics;

public class MyOval {
   private int length, width, upperLeftX, upperLeftY;

   // constructor initializes private vars with
   // default values
   public MyOval()
   {
      length =  0;
      width = 0;
      upperLeftX = 0;
      upperLeftY = 0;
   }

   // constructor with input values
   public MyOval( int x, int y, int theLength, int theWidth )
   {
      setUpperLeftX( x );
      setUpperLeftY( y );
      setLength( theLength );
      setWidth( theWidth );
   }

   // accessor and mutator methods for each of the
   // four private variables:
   public void setUpperLeftX( int x )
   {
     upperLeftX = x;
   }

   public int getUpperLeftX()
   {
     return upperLeftX;
   }

   public void setUpperLeftY( int y )
   {
     upperLeftY = y;
   }

   public int getUpperLeftY()
   {
     return upperLeftY;
   }

   public void setWidth( int theWidth )
   {
```

Fig. S8.12 Solution to Exercise 8.18: MyOval.java. (Part 1 of 2.)

```
      width = ( theWidth >= 0 ? theWidth : 0 );
   }

   public int getWidth()
   {
      return width;
   }

   public void setLength( int theLength )
   {
      length = ( theLength >= 0 ? theLength : 0 );
   }

   public int getLength()
   {
      return length;
   }

   // Actually draws the oval
   public void draw( Graphics g )
   {
      g.drawOval( upperLeftX, upperLeftY, length, width );
   }

} // end class MyOval
```

Fig. S8.12 Solution to Exercise 8.18: MyOval.java. (Part 2 of 2.)

9

Object-Oriented Programming

Solutions to Selected Exercises

9.3 Many programs written with inheritance could be written with composition instead, and vice versa. Rewrite classes `Circle4` (Fig. 9.13) and `Cylinder` (Fig. 9.15) of the `Point3/Circle4/Cylinder` hierarchy to use composition rather than inheritance. After you do this, assess the relative merits of the two approaches for the `Point3`, `Circle4`, and `Cylinder` problems, as well as for object-oriented programs in general. Which approach is more natural? Why?

ANS: *For a relatively short program like this one, either approach is acceptable. But as programs become larger with more and more objects being instantiated, inheritance becomes preferable because it makes the program easier to modify and promotes the reuse of code.*

```java
// Exercise 9.3 solution: Circle4.java
// Definition of class Circle4.

public class Circle4 {
   private double radius;  // Circle4's radius
   private Point3 point;   // composition

   // no-argument constructor
   public Circle4()
   {
      point = new Point3( 0, 0 );
      setRadius( 0 );
   }

   // constructor
   public Circle4( int xValue, int yValue, double radiusValue )
   {
      // instantiate point object
      point = new Point3( xValue, yValue );
      setRadius( radiusValue );
   }

```

Fig. S9.1 Solution to Exercise 9.3: Circle4.java. (Part 1 of 3.)

```
   // set radius
   public void setRadius( double radiusValue )
   {
      radius = ( radiusValue < 0.0 ? 0.0 : radiusValue );
   }

   // return radius
   public double getRadius()
   {
      return radius;
   }

   // set x
   public void setX( int x )
   {
      point.setX( x );
   }

   // return x
   public int getX()
   {
      return point.getX();
   }

   // set y
   public void setY( int y )
   {
      point.setY( y );
   }

   // return y
   public int getY()
   {
      return point.getY();
   }

   // calculate and return diameter
   public double getDiameter()
   {
      return 2 * getRadius();
   }

   // calculate and return circumference
   public double getCircumference()
   {
      return Math.PI * getDiameter();
   }

   // calculate and return area
   public double getArea()
```

Fig. S9.1 Solution to Exercise 9.3: Circle4.java. (Part 2 of 3.)

```java
   {
      return Math.PI * getRadius() * getRadius();
   }

   // return String representation of Circle4 object
   public String toString()
   {
      return "Center = " + point.toString() + "; Radius = " + getRadius();
   }

} // end class Circle4
```

Fig. S9.1 Solution to Exercise 9.3: Circle4.java. (Part 3 of 3.)

```java
// Exercise 9.3 solution: Cylinder.java
// Cylinder class definition.

public class Cylinder {
   private double height;  // Cylinder's height
   private Circle4 circle;

   // no-argument constructor
   public Cylinder()
   {
      circle = new Circle4( 0, 0, 0 );
      setHeight( 0 );
   }

   // constructor
   public Cylinder( int xValue, int yValue, double radiusValue,
      double heightValue )
   {
      circle = new Circle4( xValue, yValue, radiusValue );
      setHeight( heightValue );
   }

   // set Cylinder's height
   public void setHeight( double heightValue )
   {
      height = ( heightValue < 0.0 ? 0.0 : heightValue );
   }

   // get Cylinder's height
   public double getHeight()
   {
      return height;
   }

   // set x
```

Fig. S9.2 Solution to Exercise 9.3: Cylinder.java. (Part 1 of 3.)

```
   public void setX( int x )
   {
      circle.setX( x );
   }

   // return x
   public int getX()
   {
      return circle.getX();
   }

   // set y
   public void setY( int y )
   {
      circle.setY( y );
   }

   // return y
   public int getY()
   {
      return circle.getY();
   }

   // set radius
   public void setRadius( double radiusValue )
   {
      circle.setRadius( radiusValue );
   }

   // return radius
   public double getRadius()
   {
      return circle.getRadius();
   }

   // return diameter
   public double getDiameter()
   {
      return circle.getDiameter();
   }

   // return circumference
   public double getCircumference()
   {
      return circle.getCircumference();
   }

   // calculate Cylinder area
   public double getArea()
   {
```

Fig. S9.2 Solution to Exercise 9.3: Cylinder.java. (Part 2 of 3.)

```
      return 2 * circle.getArea() +
         circle.getCircumference() * getHeight();
   }

   // calculate Cylinder volume
   public double getVolume()
   {
      return  circle.getArea() * getHeight();
   }

   // return String representation of Cylinder object
   public String toString()
   {
      return  circle.toString() + "; Height = " + getHeight();
   }

} // end class Cylinder
```

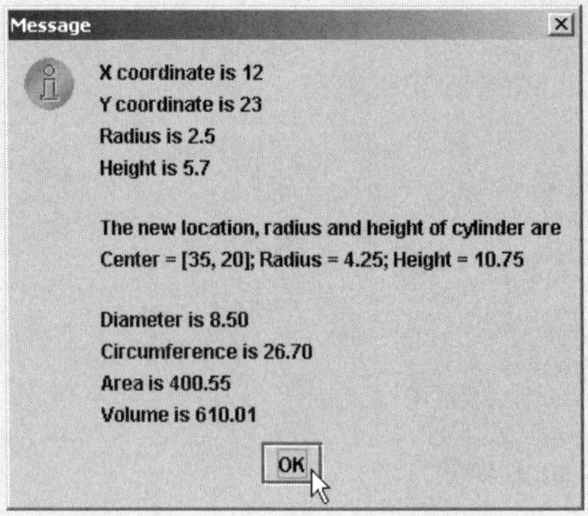

Fig. S9.2 Solution to Exercise 9.3: Cylinder.java. (Part 3 of 3.)

9.4 Some programmers prefer not to use `protected` access, because they believe it breaks the encapsulation of the superclass. Discuss the relative merits of using `protected` access vs. using `private` access in superclasses.

> **ANS:** *Inherited private data is hidden in the subclass and is accessible only through the public or protected methods of the superclass. Using protected access enables the subclass to manipulate the protected members without using the access methods of the superclass. If the superclass members are private, the methods of the superclass must be used to access the data. This may result in a decrease in performance due to the extra method calls.*

9.5 Rewrite the case study of Section 9.5 as a `Point–Square–Cube` hierarchy. Do this two ways—once via inheritance and once via composition.

ANS: *Composition Solution:*

```
// Exercise 9.5 solution: Point.java
// Point class definition represents an x-y coordinate pair.

public class Point {
   private int x;  // x part of coordinate pair
   private int y;  // y part of coordinate pair

   // no-argument constructor
   public Point()
   {
      // implicit call to Object constructor occurs here
   }

   // constructor
   public Point( int xValue, int yValue )
   {
      // implicit call to Object constructor occurs here
      x = xValue;  // no need for validation
      y = yValue;  // no need for validation
   }

   // set x in coordinate pair
   public void setX( int xValue )
   {
      x = xValue;  // no need for validation
   }

   // return x from coordinate pair
   public int getX()
   {
      return x;
   }

   // set y in coordinate pair
   public void setY( int yValue )
   {
      y = yValue;  // no need for validation
   }

   // return y from coordinate pair
   public int getY()
   {
      return y;
   }

   // return String representation of Point3 object
   public String toString()
   {
      return "[" + getX() + ", " + getY() + "]";
```

Fig. S9.3 Solution to Exercise 9.5: Point.java. (Part 1 of 2.)

```
    }

} // end class Point
```

Fig. S9.3 Solution to Exercise 9.5: Point.java. (Part 2 of 2.)

```
// Exercise 9.5 solution: Square.java
// Definition of class Square.

public class Square {
   private double sideLength;   // Square's side length
   private Point point;   // composition

   // no-argument constructor
   public Square()
   {
      point = new Point( 0, 0 );
      setSideLength( 0 );
   }

   // constructor
   public Square( int xValue, int yValue, double sidelength )
   {
      // instantiate point object
      point = new Point( xValue, yValue );
      setSideLength( sidelength );
   }

   // set sideLength
   public void setSideLength( double sidelength )
   {
      sideLength = ( sidelength < 0.0 ? 0.0 : sidelength );
   }

   // return sideLength
   public double getSideLength()
   {
      return sideLength;
   }

   // set x
   public void setX( int x )
   {
      point.setX( x );
   }

   // return x
   public int getX()
   {
```

Fig. S9.4 Solution to Exercise 9.5: Square.java. (Part 1 of 2.)

```
         return point.getX();
      }

      // set y
      public void setY( int y )
      {
         point.setY( y );
      }

      // return y
      public int getY()
      {
         return point.getY();
      }

      // calculate and return circumference
      public double getCircumference()
      {
         return 4 * getSideLength();
      }

      // calculate and return area
      public double getArea()
      {
         return getSideLength() * getSideLength();
      }

      // return String representation of Square object
      public String toString()
      {
         return "Up-left point = " + point.toString() + "; Side = " +
            getSideLength();
      }

   } // end class Square
```

Fig. S9.4 Solution to Exercise 9.5: Square.java. (Part 2 of 2.)

```
   // Exercise 9.5 solution: Cube.java
   // Cube class definition.

   public class Cube {
      private double depth;  // Cube's depth
      private Square square;

      // no-argument constructor
      public Cube()
      {
         square = new Square( 0, 0, 0 );
         depth = 0;
```

Fig. S9.5 Solution to Exercise 9.5: Cube.java. (Part 1 of 3.)

```java
   }

   // constructor
   public Cube( int xValue, int yValue, double sideValue )
   {
      square = new Square( xValue, yValue, sideValue );
      setDepth( sideValue );
   }

   // set Cube's depth
   public void setDepth( double depthValue )
   {
      depth = ( depthValue < 0.0 ? 0.0 : depthValue );
   }

   // get Cube's depth
   public double getDepth()
   {
      return depth;
   }

   // set x
   public void setX( int x )
   {
      square.setX( x );
   }

   // return x
   public int getX()
   {
      return square.getX();
   }

   // set y
   public void setY( int y )
   {
      square.setY( y );
   }

   // return y
   public int getY()
   {
      return square.getY();
   }

   // set side length
   public void setSideLength( double lengthValue )
   {
      square.setSideLength( lengthValue );
   }
```

Fig. S9.5 Solution to Exercise 9.5: Cube.java. (Part 2 of 3.)

```java

   // return side length
   public double getSideLength()
   {
      return square.getSideLength();
   }

   // calculate Cube area
   public double getArea()
   {
      return 6 * square.getArea();
   }

   // calculate Cube volume
   public double getVolume()
   {
      return square.getArea() * getDepth();
   }

   // return String representation of Cube object
   public String toString()
   {
      return square.toString() + "; Depth = " + getDepth();
   }

} // end class Cube
```

Fig. S9.5 Solution to Exercise 9.5: Cube.java. (Part 3 of 3.)

```java
// Exercise 9.5 solution: CubeTest.java
// Testing class Cube.
import java.text.DecimalFormat;
import javax.swing.JOptionPane;

public class CubeTest {

   public static void main( String[] args )
   {
      // create Cube object
      Cube cube = new Cube( 10, 20, 45.5 );

      // get Cube's initial x-y coordinates, side and depth
      String output = "X coordinate is " + cube.getX() +
         "\nY coordinate is " + cube.getY() + "\nRadius is " +
         cube.getSideLength() + "\nDepth is " + cube.getDepth();

      cube.setX( 35 );              // set new x-coordinate
      cube.setY( 15 );              // set new y-coordinate
      cube.setSideLength( 25.25 );   // set new side length
      cube.setDepth( 25.25 );   // set new depth
```

Fig. S9.6 Solution to Exercise 9.5: CubeTest.java. (Part 1 of 2.)

```java

      // get String representation of new cube value
      output += "\n\nThe new location, side and depth of cube are\n" +
         cube.toString();

      // format floating-point values with 2 digits of precision
      DecimalFormat twoDigits = new DecimalFormat( "0.00" );

      // get Cube's area
      output += "\nArea is " + twoDigits.format( cube.getArea() );

      // get Cube's volume
      output += "\nVolume is " + twoDigits.format( cube.getVolume() );

      JOptionPane.showMessageDialog( null, output ); // display output

      System.exit( 0 );

   } // end main

} // end class CubeTest
```

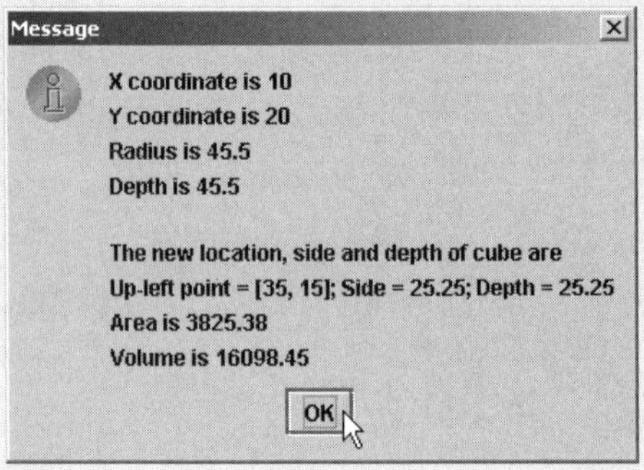

Fig. S9.6 Solution to Exercise 9.5: CubeTest.java. (Part 2 of 2.)

ANS: *Inheritance Solution: Classes* **Point** *and* **CubeTest** *are the same as in composition solution.*

```java
// Exercise 9.5 solution: Square.java
// Definition of class Square.

public class Square extends Point {
   private double sideLength;   // Square's side length

   // no-argument constructor
   public Square()
   {
```

Fig. S9.7 Solution to Exercise 9.5: Square.java. (Part 1 of 2.)

```java
      // implicit call to Point constructor occurs here
   }

   // constructor
   public Square( int xValue, int yValue, double sidelength )
   {
      // instantiate point object
      super( 0, 0 );
      setSideLength( sidelength );
   }

   // set sideLength
   public void setSideLength( double sidelength )
   {
      sideLength = ( sidelength < 0.0 ? 0.0 : sidelength );
   }

   // return sideLength
   public double getSideLength()
   {
      return sideLength;
   }

   // calculate and return circumference
   public double getCircumference()
   {
      return 4 * getSideLength();
   }

   // calculate and return area
   public double getArea()
   {
      return getSideLength() * getSideLength();
   }

   // return String representation of Square object
   public String toString()
   {
      return "Up-left point = " + super.toString() + "; Side = " +
         getSideLength();
   }

} // end class square
```

Fig. S9.7 Solution to Exercise 9.5: Square.java. (Part 2 of 2.)

```java
// Exercise 9.5 solution: Cube.java
// Cube class definition.

public class Cube extends Square{
```

Fig. S9.8 Solution to Exercise 9.5: Cube.java. (Part 1 of 2.)

```java
   private double depth;  // Cube's depth

   // no-argument constructor
   public Cube()
   {
      // implicit call to Square constructor occurs here
   }

   // constructor
   public Cube( int xValue, int yValue, double sideValue )
   {
      super( xValue, yValue, sideValue );
      setDepth( sideValue );
   }

   // set Cube's depth
   public void setDepth( double depthValue )
   {
      depth = ( depthValue < 0.0 ? 0.0 : depthValue );
   }

   // get Cube's depth
   public double getDepth()
   {
      return depth;
   }

   // calculate Cube area
   public double getArea()
   {
      return 6 * super.getArea();
   }

   // calculate Cube volume
   public double getVolume()
   {
      return  super.getArea() * getDepth();
   }

   // return String representation of Cube object
   public String toString()
   {
      return super.toString() + "; Depth = " + getDepth();
   }

} // end class Cube
```

Fig. S9.8 Solution to Exercise 9.5: Cube.java. (Part 2 of 2.)

10

Object-Oriented Programming: Polymorphism

Solutions to Selected Exercises

10.3 How is it that polymorphism enables you to program "in the general" rather than "in the specific"? Discuss the key advantages of programming "in the general."

ANS: *Polymorphism enables the programmer to concentrate on the processing of common operations that are applied to all data types in the system without going into the individual details of each data type. The general processing capabilities are separated from the internal details of each type.*

10.5 What are `abstract` methods? Describe a circumstance in which `abstract` methods would be appropriate.

ANS: *Abstract methods are methods with the same method header that are defined throughout a class hierarchy. Abstract methods do not provide implementations. At least the super class occurrence of the method is preceded by the keyword* **`abstract`**. *Abstract methods are used to enable generic processing of an entire class hierarchy of objects through a super class reference. For example, in a shape hierarchy, all shapes can be drawn. If all shapes are derived from a super class* **`Shape`** *which contains an* **`abstract`** *method, then generic processing of the hierarchy can be performed by calling every shape's* **`draw`** *generically through a super class* **`Shape`** *reference.*

10.7 Modify the payroll system of Fig. 10.12–Fig. 10.17 to include `private` instance variable `birthDate` (use class `Date`) in class `Employee`. Assume that payroll is processed once per month. Create an array of `Employee` variables to store references to the various employee objects. In a loop, calculate the payroll for each `Employee` (polymorphically), and add a $100.00 bonus to the person's payroll amount if the current month is the month in which the `Employee`'s birthday occurs.

ANS:

```
// Exercise 10.7 solution: PayrollSystemTest.java
// Employee hierarchy test program.
import java.text.DecimalFormat;
import javax.swing.JOptionPane;

public class PayrollSystemTest {

```

Fig. S10.1 Solution to Exercise 10.7: PayrollSystemTest.java. (Part 1 of 3.)

```
   public static void main( String[] args )
   {
      DecimalFormat twoDigits = new DecimalFormat( "0.00" );

      // create Employee array
      Employee employees[] = new Employee[ 4 ];

      // initialize array with Employees
      employees[ 0 ] = new SalariedEmployee( "John", "Smith",
         "111-11-1111", 6, 15, 1944, 800.00 );
      employees[ 1 ] = new CommissionEmployee( "Sue", "Jones",
         "222-22-2222", 9, 8, 1954, 10000, .06 );
      employees[ 2 ] = new BasePlusCommissionEmployee( "Bob", "Lewis",
         "333-33-3333", 3, 2, 1965, 5000, .04, 300 );
      employees[ 3 ] = new HourlyEmployee( "Karen", "Price",
         "444-44-4444", 12, 29, 1960, 16.75, 40 );

      String output = "";
      int currentMonth = Integer.parseInt(
         JOptionPane.showInputDialog( "Current month: " ) );

      // validate current month
      while ( !( currentMonth >= 0 && currentMonth <= 12 ) ) {
         currentMonth = Integer.parseInt(
            JOptionPane.showInputDialog( "Current month: " ) );
      }

      // generically process each element in array employees
      for ( int i = 0; i < employees.length; i++ ) {
         output += employees[ i ].toString();

         // determine whether element is a BasePlusCommissionEmployee
         if ( employees[ i ] instanceof BasePlusCommissionEmployee ) {

            // downcast Employee reference to
            // BasePlusCommissionEmployee reference
            BasePlusCommissionEmployee currentEmployee =
               ( BasePlusCommissionEmployee ) employees[ i ];

            double oldBaseSalary = currentEmployee.getBaseSalary();
            output += "\nold base salary: $" + oldBaseSalary;

            currentEmployee.setBaseSalary( 1.10 * oldBaseSalary );
            output += "\nnew base salary with 10% increase is: $" +
               currentEmployee.getBaseSalary();

         } // end if

         // if month of employee's birthday, add $100 to salary
         if ( currentMonth == employees[ i ].getBirthDate().getMonth() )
```

Fig. S10.1 Solution to Exercise 10.7: PayrollSystemTest.java. (Part 2 of 3.)

```
            output += "\nearned $" + employees[ i ].earnings() +
               " plus $100.00 birthday bonus\n";
         else
            output += "\nearned $" + employees[ i ].earnings() + "\n";

      } // end for

      // get type name of each object in employees array
      for ( int j = 0; j < employees.length; j++ )
         output += "\nEmployee " + j + " is a " +
            employees[ j ].getClass().getName();

      JOptionPane.showMessageDialog( null, output );  // display output
      System.exit( 0 );

   } // end main

} // end class PayrollSystemTest
```

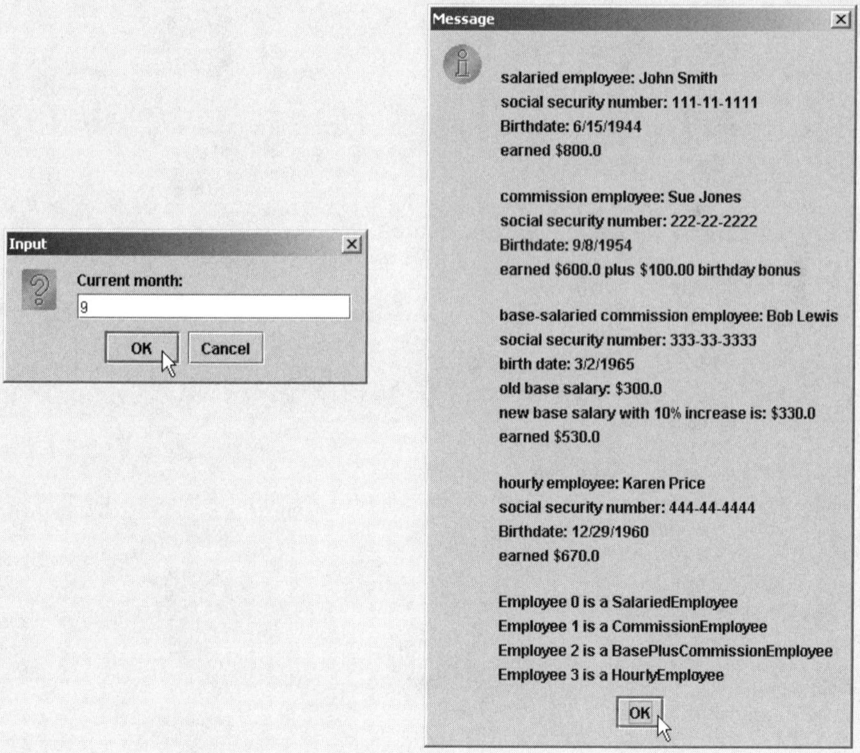

Fig. S10.1 Solution to Exercise 10.7: PayrollSystemTest.java. (Part 3 of 3.)

```java
// Exercise 10.7 solution: Date.java
// Date class definition.

public class Date {
   private int month;  // 1-12
   private int day;    // 1-31 based on month
   private int year;   // any year

   // constructor: call checkMonth to confirm proper value for month;
   // call checkDay to confirm proper value for day
   public Date( int theMonth, int theDay, int theYear )
   {
      month = checkMonth( theMonth ); // validate month
      year = theYear;                 // could validate year
      day = checkDay( theDay );       // validate day
   }

   // utility method to confirm proper month value
   private int checkMonth( int testMonth )
   {
      if ( testMonth > 0 && testMonth <= 12 )  // validate month
         return testMonth;

      else  // month is invalid
         return 1;  // maintain object in consistent state
   }

   // utility method to confirm proper day value based on month and year
   private int checkDay( int testDay )
   {
      int daysPerMonth[] =
         { 0, 31, 28, 31, 30, 31, 30, 31, 31, 30, 31, 30, 31 };

      // check if day in range for month
      if ( testDay > 0 && testDay <= daysPerMonth[ month ] )
         return testDay;

      // check for leap year
      if ( month == 2 && testDay == 29 && ( year % 400 == 0 ||
           ( year % 4 == 0 && year % 100 != 0 ) ) )
         return testDay;

      return 1;  // maintain object in consistent state

   } // end method checkDay

   // return month
   public int getMonth()
   {
      return month;
```

Fig. S10.2 Solution to Exercise 10.7: Date.java. (Part 1 of 2.)

```
   }

   // return a String of the form month/day/year
   public String toDateString()
   {
      return month + "/" + day + "/" + year;
   }

} // end class Date
```

Fig. S10.2 Solution to Exercise 10.7: Date.java. (Part 2 of 2.)

```
// Exercise 10.7 solution: Employee.java
// Employee abstract superclass.

public abstract class Employee {
   private String firstName;
   private String lastName;
   private String socialSecurityNumber;
   private Date birthDate;

   // constructor
   public Employee( String first, String last, String ssn,
      int month, int day, int year )
   {
      firstName = first;
      lastName = last;
      socialSecurityNumber = ssn;
      birthDate = new Date( month, day, year );
   }

   // set first name
   public void setFirstName( String first )
   {
      firstName = first;
   }

   // return first name
   public String getFirstName()
   {
      return firstName;
   }

   // set last name
   public void setLastName( String last )
   {
      lastName = last;
   }

```

Fig. S10.3 Solution to Exercise 10.7: Employee.java. (Part 1 of 2.)

```java
   // return last name
   public String getLastName()
   {
      return lastName;
   }

   // set social security number
   public void setSocialSecurityNumber( String number )
   {
      socialSecurityNumber = number;  // should validate
   }

   // return social security number
   public String getSocialSecurityNumber()
   {
      return socialSecurityNumber;
   }

   // set birth date
   public void setBirthDate( int month, int day, int year )
   {
      birthDate = new Date( month, day, year );
   }

   // return birth date
   public Date getBirthDate()
   {
      return birthDate;
   }

   // return String representation of Employee object
   public String toString()
   {
      return getFirstName() + " " + getLastName() +
         "\nsocial security number: " + getSocialSecurityNumber() +
         "\nBirthdate: " + birthDate.toDateString();
   }

   // abstract method overridden by subclasses
   public abstract double earnings();

} // end abstract class Employee
```

Fig. S10.3 Solution to Exercise 10.7: Employee.java. (Part 2 of 2.)

```java
// Exercise 10.7 solution: SalariedEmployee.java
// SalariedEmployee class derived from Employee.

public class SalariedEmployee extends Employee {
```

Fig. S10.4 Solution to Exercise 10.7: SalariedEmployee,java. (Part 1 of 2.)

```java
   private double weeklySalary;

   // constructor
   public SalariedEmployee( String first, String last, String
      socialSecurityNumber, int month, int day, int year, double salary )
   {
      super( first, last, socialSecurityNumber, month, day, year );
      setWeeklySalary( salary );
   }

   // set salaried employee's salary
   public void setWeeklySalary( double salary )
   {
      weeklySalary = salary < 0.0 ? 0.0 : salary;
   }

   // return salaried employee's salary
   public double getWeeklySalary()
   {
      return weeklySalary;
   }

   // calculate salaried employee's pay;
   // override abstract method earnings in Employee
   public double earnings()
   {
      return getWeeklySalary();
   }

   // return String representation of SalariedEmployee object
   public String toString()
   {
      return "\nsalaried employee: " + super.toString();
   }

} // end class SalariedEmployee
```

Fig. S10.4 Solution to Exercise 10.7: SalariedEmployee.java. (Part 2 of 2.)

```java
// Exercise 10.7 solution: HourlyEmployee.java
// HourlyEmployee class derived from Employee.

public class HourlyEmployee extends Employee {
   private double wage;   // wage per hour
   private double hours;  // hours worked for week

   // constructor
   public HourlyEmployee( String first, String last,
      String socialSecurityNumber, int month, int day, int year,
```

Fig. S10.5 Solution to Exercise 10.7: HourlyEmployee.java. (Part 1 of 2.)

```
         double hourlyWage, double hoursWorked )
      {
         super( first, last, socialSecurityNumber, month, day, year );
         setWage( hourlyWage );
         setHours( hoursWorked );
      }

      // set hourly employee's wage
      public void setWage( double wageAmount )
      {
         wage = wageAmount < 0.0 ? 0.0 : wageAmount;
      }

      // return wage
      public double getWage()
      {
         return wage;
      }

      // set hourly employee's hours worked
      public void setHours( double hoursWorked )
      {
         hours = ( hoursWorked >= 0.0 && hoursWorked <= 168.0 ) ?
            hoursWorked : 0.0;
      }

      // return hours worked
      public double getHours()
      {
         return hours;
      }

      // calculate hourly employee's pay;
      // override abstract method earnings in Employee
      public double earnings()
      {
         if ( hours <= 40 )  // no overtime
            return wage * hours;
         else
            return 40 * wage + ( hours - 40 ) * wage * 1.5;
      }

      // return String representation of HourlyEmployee object
      public String toString()
      {
         return "\nhourly employee: " + super.toString();
      }

   } // end class HourlyEmployee
```

Fig. S10.5 Solution to Exercise 10.7: HourlyEmployee.java. (Part 2 of 2.)

```java
// Exercise 10.7 solution: CommissionEmployee.java
// CommissionEmployee class derived from Employee.

public class CommissionEmployee extends Employee {
   private double grossSales;      // gross weekly sales
   private double commissionRate;  // commission percentage

   // constructor
   public CommissionEmployee( String first, String last,
      String socialSecurityNumber, int month, int day, int year,
      double grossWeeklySales, double percent )
   {
      super( first, last, socialSecurityNumber, month, day, year );
      setGrossSales( grossWeeklySales );
      setCommissionRate( percent );
   }

   // set commission employee's rate
   public void setCommissionRate( double rate )
   {
      commissionRate = ( rate > 0.0 && rate < 1.0 ) ? rate : 0.0;
   }

   // return commission employee's rate
   public double getCommissionRate()
   {
      return commissionRate;
   }

   // set commission employee's weekly base salary
   public void setGrossSales( double sales )
   {
      grossSales = sales < 0.0 ? 0.0 : sales;
   }

   // return commission employee's gross sales amount
   public double getGrossSales()
   {
      return grossSales;
   }

   // calculate commission employee's pay;
   // override abstract method earnings in Employee
   public double earnings()
   {
      return getCommissionRate() * getGrossSales();
   }

   // return String representation of CommissionEmployee object
   public String toString()
   {
```

Fig. S10.6 Solution to Exercise 10.7: CommissionEmployee.java. (Part 1 of 2.)

```java
        return "\ncommission employee: " + super.toString();
    }

} // end class CommissionEmployee
```

Fig. S10.6 Solution to Exercise 10.7: CommissionEmployee.java. (Part 2 of 2.)

```java
// Exercise 10.7 solution: BasePlusCommissionEmployee.java
// BasePlusCommissionEmployee class derived from CommissionEmployee.

public class BasePlusCommissionEmployee extends CommissionEmployee {
    private double baseSalary;  // base salary per week

    // constructor
    public BasePlusCommissionEmployee( String first, String last,
        String socialSecurityNumber, int month, int day, int year,
        double grossSalesAmount, double rate, double baseSalaryAmount )
    {
        super( first, last, socialSecurityNumber, month, day, year,
            grossSalesAmount, rate );
        setBaseSalary( baseSalaryAmount );
    }

    // set base-salaried commission employee's base salary
    public void setBaseSalary( double salary )
    {
        baseSalary = salary < 0.0 ? 0.0 : salary;
    }

    // return base-salaried commission employee's base salary
    public double getBaseSalary()
    {
        return baseSalary;
    }

    // calculate base-salaried commission employee's earnings;
    // override method earnings in CommissionEmployee
    public double earnings()
    {
        return getBaseSalary() + super.earnings();
    }

    // return String representation of BasePlusCommissionEmployee
    public String toString()
    {
        return "\nbase-salaried commission employee: " +
            super.getFirstName() + " " + super.getLastName() +
            "\nsocial security number: " + super.getSocialSecurityNumber() +
            "\nbirth date: " + super.getBirthDate().toDateString();
    }
```

Fig. S10.7 Solution to Exercise 10.7: BasePlusCommissionEmployee.java. (Part 1 of 2.)

```java

} // end class BasePlusCommissionEmployee
```

Fig. S10.7 Solution to Exercise 10.7: BasePlusCommissionEmployee.java. (Part 2 of 2.)

10.8 Implement the Shape hierarchy shown in Fig. 9.3. Each TwoDimensionalShape should contain method getArea to calculate the area of the two-dimensional shape. Each ThreeDimensionalShape should have methods getArea and getVolume to calculate the surface area and volume, respectively, of the three-dimensional shape, respectively. Create a program that uses an array of Shape references to objects of each concrete class in the hierarchy. The program should print the object to which each array element refers. Also, in the loop that processes all the shapes in the array, determine whether each shape is a TwoDimensionalShape or a ThreeDimensionalShape. If a shape is a TwoDimensionalShape, display its area. If a shape is a ThreeDimensionalShape, display its area and volume.

ANS:

```java
// Exercise 10.8 Solution: ShapeTest.java
// Program tests the Shape hierarchy.

public class ShapeTest {
   private Shape shapeArray[];
   private TwoDimensionalShape twoDArray[];
   private ThreeDimensionalShape threeDArray[];

   // create shapes
   public ShapeTest() {
      shapeArray = new Shape[ 4 ];
      twoDArray = new TwoDimensionalShape[ 2 ];
      threeDArray = new ThreeDimensionalShape[ 2 ];

      Circle circle = new Circle( 22, 88, 21 );
      shapeArray[ 0 ] = circle;
      twoDArray[ 0 ] = circle;

      Square square = new Square( 71, 96, 95 );
      shapeArray[ 1 ] = square;
      twoDArray[ 1 ] = square;

      Sphere sphere = new Sphere( 8, 89, 78 );
      shapeArray[ 2 ] = sphere;
      threeDArray[ 0 ] = sphere;

      Cube cube = new Cube( 79, 61, 73 );
      shapeArray[ 3 ] = cube;
      threeDArray[ 1 ] = cube;
   }

   // display shape info
   public void displayShapeInfo()
   {
```

Fig. S10.8 Solution to Exercise 10.8: ShapeTest.java. (Part 1 of 2.)

```
      // call method print on all shapes
      for ( int i = 0; i < shapeArray.length; i++ ) {
         System.out.print( shapeArray[ i ].getName() + ": " );
         shapeArray[ i ].print();
      }

      // print area of 2D shapes
      for ( int j = 0; j < twoDArray.length; j++ )
         System.out.println( twoDArray[ j ].getName() +
            "'s area is " + twoDArray[ j ].area() );

      // print area and volume of 3D shapes
      for ( int k = 0; k < threeDArray.length; k++ ) {
         System.out.println( threeDArray[ k ].getName() +
            "'s area is " + threeDArray[ k ].area() );
         System.out.println( threeDArray[ k ].getName() +
            "'s volume is " + threeDArray[ k ].volume() );
      }
   }

   // create ShapeTest object and display info
   public static void main( String args[] )
   {
      ShapeTest driver = new ShapeTest();
      driver.displayShapeInfo();
   }

} // end class ShapeTest
```

```
Circle: (22, 88) radius: 21
Square: (71, 96) side: 95
Sphere: (8, 89) radius: 78
Cube: (79, 61) side: 73
Circle's area is 1385
Square's area is 9025
Sphere's area is 76453
Sphere's volume is 1490849
Cube's area is 31974
Cube's volume is 389017
```

Fig. S10.8 Solution to Exercise 10.8: ShapeTest.java. (Part 2 of 2.)

```
// Exercise 10.8 Solution: Shape.java
// Definition of class Shape.

public abstract class Shape {
   private int x, y;    // coordinates of shape

```

Fig. S10.9 Solution to Exercise 10.8: Shape.java. (Part 1 of 2.)

```java
   // constructor
   public Shape( int x, int y )
   {
      this.x = x;
      this.y = y;
   }

   // set x coordinate
   public void setX( int x )
   {
      this.x = x;
   }

   // set y coordinate
   public void setY( int y )
   {
      this.y = y;
   }

   // get x coordinate
   public int getX()
   {
      return x;
   }

   // get y coordinate
   public int getY()
   {
      return y;
   }

   // abstract methods
   public abstract String getName();
   public abstract void print();

} // end class Shape
```

Fig. S10.9 Solution to Exercise 10.8: Shape.java. (Part 2 of 2.)

```java
// Exercise 10.8 Solution: TwoDimensionalShape.java
// Definition of class TwoDimensionalShape.

public abstract class TwoDimensionalShape extends Shape {
   private int dimension1, dimension2;

   // constructor
   public TwoDimensionalShape( int x, int y, int d1, int d2 )
   {
      super( x, y );
```

Fig. S10.10 Solution to Exercise 10.8: TwoDimensionalShape.java. (Part 1 of 2.)

```java
      dimension1 = d1;
      dimension2 = d2;
   }

   // set methods
   public void setDimension1( int d )
   {
      dimension1 = d;
   }

   public void setDimension2( int d )
   {
      dimension2 = d;
   }

   // get methods
   public int getDimension1()
   {
      return dimension1;
   }

   public int getDimension2()
   {
      return dimension2;
   }

   // abstract method
   public abstract int area();

} // end class TwoDimensionalShape
```

Fig. S10.10 Solution to Exercise 10.8: TwoDimensionalShape.java. (Part 2 of 2.)

```java
// Exercise 10.8 Solution: ThreeDimensionalShape.java
// Definition of class ThreeDimensionalShape.

public abstract class ThreeDimensionalShape extends Shape {
   private int dimension1, dimension2, dimension3;

   // constructor
   public ThreeDimensionalShape(
      int x, int y, int d1, int d2, int d3 )
   {
      super( x, y );
      dimension1 = d1;
      dimension2 = d2;
      dimension3 = d3;
   }

```

Fig. S10.11 Solution to Exercise 10.8: ThreeDimensionalShape.java. (Part 1 of 2.)

```java
    // set methods
    public void setDimension1( int d )
    {
       dimension1 = d;
    }

    public void setDimension2( int d )
    {
       dimension2 = d;
    }

    public void setDimension3( int d )
    {
       dimension3 = d;
    }

    // get methods
    public int getDimension1() {
       return dimension1;
    }

    public int getDimension2()
    {
       return dimension2;
    }

    public int getDimension3()
    {
       return dimension3;
    }

    // abstract methods
    public abstract int area();
    public abstract int volume();

 } // end class ThreeDimensionalShape
```

Fig. S10.11 Solution to Exercise 10.8: ThreeDimensionalShape.java. (Part 2 of 2.)

```java
 // Exercise 10.8 Solution: Circle.java
 // Definition of class Circle.

 public class Circle extends TwoDimensionalShape {

    // constructor
    public Circle( int x, int y, int radius )
    {
       super( x, y, radius, radius );
    }

```

Fig. S10.12 Solution to Exercise 10.8: Circle.java. (Part 1 of 2.)

```
    // overridden methods
    public String getName()
    {
       return "Circle";
    }

    public void print()
    {
       System.out.println( "(" + super.getX() + ", " + super.getY() +
          ") " + "radius: " + super.getDimension1() );
    }

    public int area()
    {
       return ( int )
          ( Math.PI * super.getDimension1() * super.getDimension1() );
    }

    // set method
    public void setRadius( int radius )
    {
       super.setDimension1( radius );
    }

    // get method
    public int getRadius()
    {
       return super.getDimension1();
    }

 } // end class Circle
```

Fig. S10.12 Solution to Exercise 10.8: Circle.java. (Part 2 of 2.)

```
// Exercise 10.8 Solution: Square.java
// Definition of class Square.

public class Square extends TwoDimensionalShape {

   // constructor
   public Square( int x, int y, int side )
   {
      super( x, y, side, side );
   }

   // overridden methods
   public String getName()
   {
      return "Square";
   }
```

Fig. S10.13 Solution to Exercise 10.8: Square.java. (Part 1 of 2.)

```java

   public void print()
   {
      System.out.println( "(" + super.getX() + ", " + super.getY() +
         ") " + "side: " + super.getDimension1() );
   }

   public int area()
   {
      return super.getDimension1() * super.getDimension1();
   }

   // set method
   public void setSide( int side )
   {
      super.setDimension1( side );
   }

   // get method
   public int getSide()
   {
      return super.getDimension1();
   }

} // end class Square
```

Fig. S10.13 Solution to Exercise 10.8: Square.java. (Part 2 of 2.)

```java
// Exercise 10.8 Solution: Sphere.java
// Definition of class Sphere.

public class Sphere extends ThreeDimensionalShape {

   // constructor
   public Sphere( int x, int y, int radius )
   {
      super( x, y, radius, radius, radius );
   }

   // overridden methods
   public String getName()
   {
      return "Sphere";
   }

   public int area()
   {
      return ( int ) ( 4 * Math.PI *
         super.getDimension1() * super.getDimension1() );
   }
```

Fig. S10.14 Solution to Exercise 10.8: Sphere.java. (Part 1 of 2.)

```java

   public int volume()
   {
      return ( int ) ( 4 / 3 * Math.PI * super.getDimension1() *
         super.getDimension1() * super.getDimension1() );
   }

   public void print()
   {
      System.out.println( "(" + super.getX() + ", " + super.getY() +
         ") " + "radius: " + super.getDimension1() );
   }

   // set method
   public void setRadius( int radius )
   {
      super.setDimension1( radius );
   }

   // get method
   public int getRadius()
   {
      return super.getDimension1();
   }

} // end class Sphere
```

Fig. S10.14 Solution to Exercise 10.8: Sphere.java. (Part 2 of 2.)

```java
// Exercise 10.8 Solution: Cube.java
// Definition of class Cube.

public class Cube extends ThreeDimensionalShape {

   // constructor
   public Cube( int x, int y, int side )
   {
      super( x, y, side, side, side );
   }

   // overridden methods
   public String getName()
   {
      return "Cube";
   }

   public int area()
   {
      return ( int )
         ( 6 * super.getDimension1() * super.getDimension1() );
```

Fig. S10.15 Solution to Exercise 10.8: Cube.java. (Part 1 of 2.)

```
    }

    public int volume()
    {
       return ( int ) ( super.getDimension1() *
          super.getDimension1() * super.getDimension1() );
    }

    public void print()
    {
       System.out.println( "(" + super.getX() + ", " + super.getY() +
          ") " + "side: " + super.getDimension1() );
    }

    // set method
    public void setSide( int side )
    {
       super.setDimension1( side );
    }

    // get method
    public int getSide()
    {
       return super.getDimension1();
    }

 } // end class Cube
```

Fig. S10.15 Solution to Exercise 10.8: Cube.java. (Part 2 of 2.)

11

Strings and Characters

Solutions to Selected Exercises

11.3 Modify the program in Fig. 11.19 so that the card-dealing method deals a five-card poker hand. Then write methods that determine whether the hand contains

a) a pair.
b) two pairs.
c) three of a kind (e.g., three jacks).
d) four of a kind (e.g., four aces).
e) a flush (i.e., all five cards of the same suit).
f) a straight (i.e., five cards of consecutive face values).
g) a full house (i.e., two cards of one face value and three cards of another face value).

ANS:

```java
// Exercise 11.3 Solution: Poker.java
// Program deals a five-card poker hand.
import java.awt.*;
import java.awt.event.*;
import javax.swing.*;

public class Poker extends JFrame {
   private Card deck[];
   private Card hand[];
   private int currentCard;
   private JButton dealButton, shuffleButton;
   private JTextArea displayCard, status;
   private int numbers[], triples, couples;
   private String faces[], suits[], output;

   // constructor
   public Poker()
   {
```

Fig. S11.1 Solution to Exercise 11.3. (Part 1 of 8.)

```java
      super( "Card Dealing Program" );

      String faceArray[] = { "Ace", "Deuce", "Three", "Four", "Five",
        "Six", "Seven", "Eight", "Nine", "Ten", "Jack", "Queen", "King" };
      String suitArray[] = { "Hearts", "Diamonds", "Clubs", "Spades" };

      faces = faceArray;
      suits = suitArray;

      numbers = new int[ 13 ];
      triples = 0;
      couples = 0;

      deck = new Card[ 52 ];
      hand = new Card[ 5 ];

      currentCard = -1;

      // initialize the deck array
      for ( int count = 0; count < deck.length; count++ )
         deck[ count ] =
            new Card( faces[ count % 13 ], suits[ count / 13 ] );

      Container container = getContentPane();
      container.setLayout( new FlowLayout() );

      dealButton = new JButton( "Deal hand" );
      dealButton.addActionListener(

         new ActionListener() {  // anonymous inner class

            // deal one hand of cards
            public void actionPerformed( ActionEvent e )
            {
               displayCard.setText( "" );    // clear text area
               output = "";
               triples = 0;
               couples = 0;

               // deal a round of cards
               for ( int count = 0; count < hand.length; count++ ) {
                  Card dealt = dealCard();

                  if ( dealt != null ) {
                     hand[ count ] = dealt;
                     displayCard.setText( displayCard.getText() +
                        hand[ count ].toString() + "\n" );
                  }

                  else {
```

Fig. S11.1 Solution to Exercise 11.3. (Part 2 of 8.)

```
                     displayCard.setText( "NOT ENOUGH CARDS TO DEAL" );
                     status.setText( "Shuffle cards to continue" );
                     return;
                  }
               }

               // calculate contents of the hand
               totalHand();
               pairs();
               twoPair();
               threeOfAKind();
               fullHouse();
               fourOfAKind();
               straight();
               flush();
            }

         } // end anonymous inner class

      ); // end call to addActionListener

      container.add( dealButton );

      shuffleButton = new JButton( "Shuffle cards" );
      shuffleButton.addActionListener(

         new ActionListener() {  // anonymous inner class

            // shuffle deck
            public void actionPerformed( ActionEvent e )
            {
               displayCard.setText( "SHUFFLING ..." );
               shuffle();
               displayCard.setText( "DECK IS SHUFFLED" );
            }

         } // end anonymous inner class

      ); // end call to addActionListener

      container.add( shuffleButton );

      displayCard = new JTextArea( 6, 20 );
      displayCard.setEditable( false );
      container.add( displayCard );

      status = new JTextArea( 2, 20 );
      status.setEditable( false );
      container.add( status );

```

Fig. S11.1 Solution to Exercise 11.3. (Part 3 of 8.)

```
      setSize( 275, 250 );  // set the window size
      show();               // show the window

   } // end Poker

   // shuffle deck of cards with one-pass algorithm
   public void shuffle()
   {
      currentCard = -1;

      // swap two cards as many times as there are cards in the deck
      for ( int first= 0; first< deck.length; first++ ) {
         int second =  ( int ) ( Math.random() * deck.length );
         Card temp = deck[ first];
         deck[ first] = deck[ second ];
         deck[ second ] = temp;
      }

      dealButton.setEnabled( true );
   }

   // deal one card
   public Card dealCard()
   {
      if ( ++currentCard < deck.length )
         return deck[ currentCard ];

      else {
         dealButton.setEnabled( false );

         return null;
      }
   }

   // tally the number of each face card in hand
   private void totalHand()
   {
      // initialize all elements of numbers[] to zero
      for ( int x = 0; x < faces.length; x++ )
         numbers[ x ] = 0;

      // compare each card in the hand to each element in the faces array
      for ( int h = 0; h < hand.length; h++ )

         for ( int f = 0; f < faces.length; f++ )

            if ( hand[ h ].getFace().equals( faces[ f ] ) )
               ++numbers[ f ];
   }

```

Fig. S11.1 Solution to Exercise 11.3. (Part 4 of 8.)

```
   // determine if hand contains pairs
   public void pairs()
   {
      for ( int k = 0; k < faces.length; k++ )

         if ( numbers[ k ] == 2 ) {
            output += ( "Pair of " + faces[ k ] + "'s  " );
            couples++;
         }

      status.setText( output );
   }

   // determine if hand contains a three of a kind
   public void threeOfAKind()
   {
      for ( int k = 0; k < faces.length; k++ )

         if ( numbers[ k ] == 3 ) {
            output += ( "Three " + faces[ k ] + "'s" );
            triples++;
            break;
         }

      status.setText( output );
   }

   // determine if hand contains a four of a kind
   public void fourOfAKind()
   {
      for ( int k = 0; k < faces.length; k++ )

         if ( numbers[ k ] == 4 )
            output += ( "Four " + faces[ k ] + "'s" );

      status.setText( output );
   }

   // determine if hand contains a flush
   public void flush()
   {
      String theSuit = hand[ 0 ].getSuit();

      for ( int s = 1; s < hand.length; s++ )

         if ( hand[ s ].getSuit().compareTo( theSuit ) != 0 )
            return;   // not a flush

      output += ( "Flush in " + theSuit );
      status.setText( output );
```

Fig. S11.1 Solution to Exercise 11.3. (Part 5 of 8.)

```
   }

   // determine if hand contains a straight
   public void straight()
   {
      int locations[] = new int[ 5 ], z = 0;

      for ( int y = 0; y < numbers.length; y++ )

         if ( numbers[ y ] == 1 )
            locations[ z++ ] = y;

      bubbleSort( locations );

      int faceValue = locations[ 0 ];

      for ( int m = 1; m < locations.length; m++ ) {

         if ( faceValue != locations[ m ] - 1 )
            return;   // not a straight

         else
            faceValue = locations[ m ];
      }

      output += "Straight ";
      status.setText( output );
   }

   // sort hand in ascending order
   private void bubbleSort( int values[] )
   {
      for ( int pass = 1; pass < values.length; pass++ )

         for ( int comp = 0; comp < values.length - 1; comp++ )

            if ( values[ comp ] > values[ comp + 1 ] ) {
               int temp = values[ comp ];
               values[ comp ] = values[ comp + 1 ];
               values[ comp + 1 ] = values[ comp ];
            }
   }

   // determine if hand contains a full house
   public void fullHouse()
   {
      if ( couples == 1 && triples == 1 ) {
         output += "\nFull House!";
         status.setText( output );
      }
```

Fig. S11.1 Solution to Exercise 11.3. (Part 6 of 8.)

```java
    }

    // determine if hand contains two pairs
    public void twoPair()
    {
       if ( couples == 2 ) {
          output += "\nTwo Pair!";
          status.setText( output );
       }
    }

    // execute application
    public static void main( String args[] )
    {
       Poker application = new Poker();

       // set application to terminate on close
       application.setDefaultCloseOperation( JFrame.EXIT_ON_CLOSE );

    } // end method main


    // internal class to represent card
    class Card {
       private String face;
       private String suit;

       // constructor to initialize Card
       public Card( String f, String s )
       {
          face = f;
          suit = s;
       }

       // get suit
       protected String getSuit()
       {
          return suit;
       }

       // get face
       protected String getFace()
       {
          return face;
       }

       // return String representation of Card
       public String toString()
       {
          return face + " of " + suit;
```

Fig. S11.1 Solution to Exercise 11.3. (Part 7 of 8.)

```
      }

   } // end class Card

} // end class Poker
```

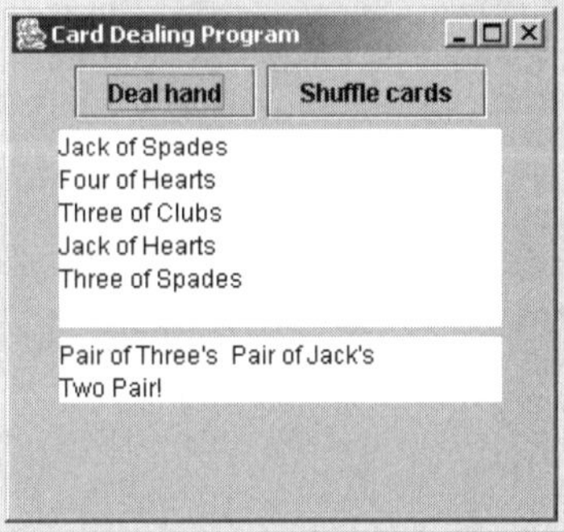

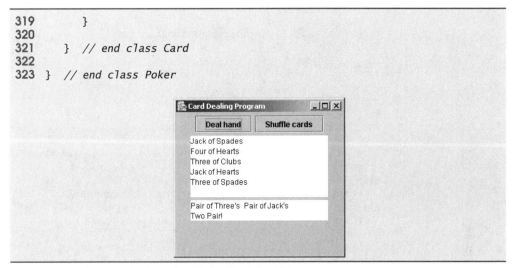

Fig. S11.1 Solution to Exercise 11.3. (Part 8 of 8.)

11.7 Write an application that uses `String` method `compareTo` to compare two strings input by the user. Output whether the first string is less than, equal to or greater than the second.

ANS:

```
// Exercise 11.7 Solution: CompareStrings.java
// Program compares two strings.
import java.awt.*;
import java.awt.event.*;
import javax.swing.*;

public class CompareStrings extends JFrame {
   private JLabel prompt1, prompt2;
   private JTextField inputField1, inputField2, outputField;

   // constructor
   public CompareStrings()
   {
      super( "Compare Strings" );

      // create GUI components
      prompt1 = new JLabel( "Enter first string:" );
      prompt2 = new JLabel( "Enter second string:" );
      inputField1 = new JTextField( 20 );
      inputField2 = new JTextField( 20 );
      outputField = new JTextField( 30 );
      outputField.setEditable( false );

      inputField2.addActionListener(
```

Fig. S11.2 Solution to Exercise 11.7. (Part 1 of 3.)

```

            new ActionListener() {  // anonymous inner class

               // compare Strings
               public void actionPerformed( ActionEvent e )
               {
                  String first = inputField1.getText();
                  String second = inputField2.getText();
                  int value = first.compareTo( second );

                  if ( value == 0 )
                     outputField.setText( first + " == " + second );
                  else if ( value > 0 )
                     outputField.setText( first + " > " + second );
                  else
                     outputField.setText( first + " < " + second );
               }

            } // end anonymous inner class

         ); // end call to addActionListener

         // add components to GUI
         Container container = getContentPane();
         container.setLayout( new FlowLayout() );
         container.add( prompt1 );
         container.add( inputField1 );
         container.add( prompt2 );
         container.add( inputField2 );
         container.add( outputField );

         setSize( 375, 150 );
         setVisible( true );

      } // end constructor

      // execute application
      public static void main( String args[] )
      {
         CompareStrings application = new CompareStrings();
         application.setDefaultCloseOperation( JFrame.EXIT_ON_CLOSE );
      }

   } // end class CompareStrings
```

Fig. S11.2 Solution to Exercise 11.7. (Part 2 of 3.)

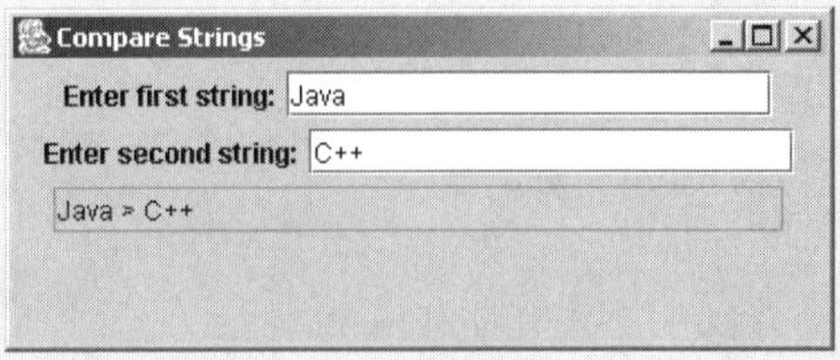

Fig. S11.2 Solution to Exercise 11.7. (Part 3 of 3.)

11.11 *(Pig Latin)* Write an application that encodes English language phrases into pig Latin. Pig Latin is a form of coded language. Many variations exist in the methods used to form pig Latin phrases. For simplicity, use the following algorithm:

To form a pig Latin phrase from an English language phrase, tokenize the phrase into words with an object of class `StringTokenizer`. To translate each English word into a pig Latin word, place the first letter of the English word at the end of the word and add the letters "ay." Thus, the word "jump" becomes "umpjay," the word "the" becomes "hetay," and the word "computer" becomes "omputercay." Blanks between words remain as blanks. Assume the following: The English phrase consists of words separated by blanks, there are no punctuation marks and all words have two or more letters. Method `printLatinWord` should display each word. Each token returned from `nextToken` is passed to method `printLatinWord` to print the pig Latin word. Enable the user to input the sentence. Keep a running display of all the converted sentences in a text area.

ANS:

```
// Exercise 11.11 Solution: PigLatin.java
// Program translates English to Pig Latin.
import java.awt.*;
import java.awt.event.*;
import java.util.*;
import javax.swing.*;

public class PigLatin extends JFrame {
   private JLabel prompt;
   private JTextField inputField;
   private JTextArea outputArea;
   private int count;

   // constructor
   public PigLatin()
   {
      super( "Pig Latin Generator" );
      prompt = new JLabel( "Enter English phrase:" );
      inputField = new JTextField( 30 );
      inputField.addActionListener(

         new ActionListener() {  // anonymous inner class

            // translate user input
```

Fig. S11.3 Solution to Exercise 11.11. (Part 1 of 3.)

```
            public void actionPerformed( ActionEvent event )
            {
               String inputString = event.getActionCommand().toString();
               StringTokenizer tokens =
                  new StringTokenizer( inputString );

               count = tokens.countTokens();

               while ( tokens.hasMoreTokens() ) {
                  count--;
                  printLatinWord( tokens.nextToken() );
               }
            }

         } // end anonymous inner class

      ); // end call to addActionListener

      outputArea = new JTextArea( 10, 30 );
      outputArea.setEditable( false );

      // add components to GUI
      Container container = getContentPane();
      container.setLayout( new FlowLayout() );
      container.add( prompt );
      container.add( inputField );
      container.add( outputArea );

      setSize( 500, 150 );
      setVisible( true );

   } // end constructor

   // translate English into Pig Latin
   private void printLatinWord( String token )
   {
      char letters[] = token.toCharArray();
      StringBuffer translation = new StringBuffer();

      translation.append( letters, 1, letters.length - 1 ) ;
      translation.append( Character.toLowerCase( letters[ 0 ] ) );
      translation.append( "ay" );

      outputArea.append( translation.toString() + " " );

      if ( count == 0 )
         outputArea.append( "\n" );

   } // end method printLatinWord

```

Fig. S11.3 Solution to Exercise 11.11. (Part 2 of 3.)

```
    public static void main( String args[] )
    {
       PigLatin application = new PigLatin();
       application.setDefaultCloseOperation( JFrame.EXIT_ON_CLOSE );
    }

} // end class PigLatin
```

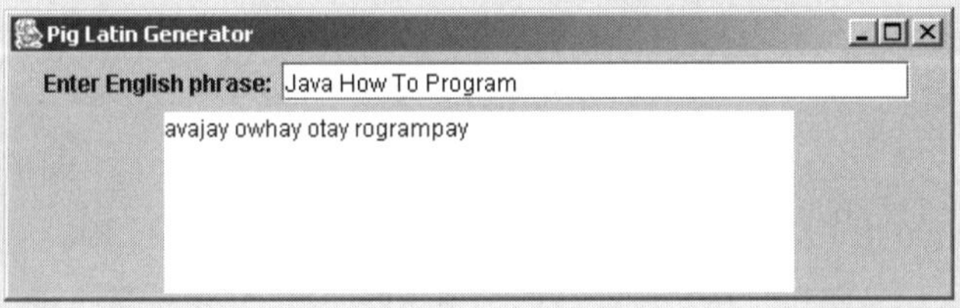

Fig. S11.3 Solution to Exercise 11.11. (Part 3 of 3.)

11.14 Use the string-comparison methods discussed in this chapter and the techniques for sorting arrays developed in Chapter 7 to write a program that alphabetizes a list of strings. Allow the user to enter the strings in a text field. Display the results in a text area.

ANS:

```
// Exercise 11.14 Solution: SortThem.java
// Program sorts strings.
import java.awt.*;
import java.awt.event.*;
import java.util.*;
import javax.swing.*;

public class SortThem extends JFrame {
   private JTextField inputField;
   private JLabel prompt;
   private JTextArea outputArea;
   private JScrollPane scroller;

   // sort Strings and set up GUI
   public SortThem()
   {
      super( "String Sorter" );
      inputField = new JTextField( 10 );
      inputField.addActionListener(

         new ActionListener() {  // anonymous inner class

            // sort Strings
            public void actionPerformed( ActionEvent e )
            {
               String newString = inputField.getText();
```

Fig. S11.4 Solution to Exercise 11.14. (Part 1 of 3.)

```
                  String oldString = outputArea.getText();
                  StringTokenizer tokenizer =
                     new StringTokenizer( oldString, "\n" );
                  int number = tokenizer.countTokens(), count = 0;
                  String tokens[] = new String[ number + 1 ];

                  inputField.setText( "" );
                  outputArea.setText( "" );

                  while ( tokenizer.hasMoreTokens() && count < number )
                     tokens[ count++ ] = tokenizer.nextToken();

                  tokens[ count ] = newString;
                  bubbleSort( tokens );

                  for ( int counter = 0; counter < tokens.length; counter++ )
                     outputArea.append( tokens[ counter ] + "\n" );
               }

            } // end anonymous inner class

         ); // end call to addActionListener

         // create GUI components...
         outputArea = new JTextArea( 10, 25 );
         scroller = new JScrollPane( outputArea );
         prompt = new JLabel( "Enter a String:" );

         // ...and add them to the GUI
         Container container = getContentPane();
         container.setLayout( new FlowLayout() );
         container.add( prompt );
         container.add( inputField );
         container.add( scroller );

         setSize( 300, 240 );
         setVisible( true );

      } // end constructor

      // sort using bubble sort algorithm
      private void bubbleSort( String strings[] )
      {
         for ( int pass = 1; pass < strings.length; pass++ )

            for ( int comparison = 0; comparison < strings.length - pass;
               comparison++ )

               // starting at the first element in the array, if any two
               // consecutive elements are not in ascending order switch them
```

Fig. S11.4 Solution to Exercise 11.14. (Part 2 of 3.)

```
            if ( strings[ comparison ].compareTo(
               strings[ comparison + 1 ] ) > 0 ) {
               String temp = strings[ comparison ];
               strings[ comparison ] = strings[ comparison + 1 ];
               strings[ comparison + 1 ] = temp;
            }
      }

      // execute application
      public static void main( String args[] )
      {
         SortThem application = new SortThem();
         application.setDefaultCloseOperation( JFrame.EXIT_ON_CLOSE );
      }

   } // end class SortThem
```

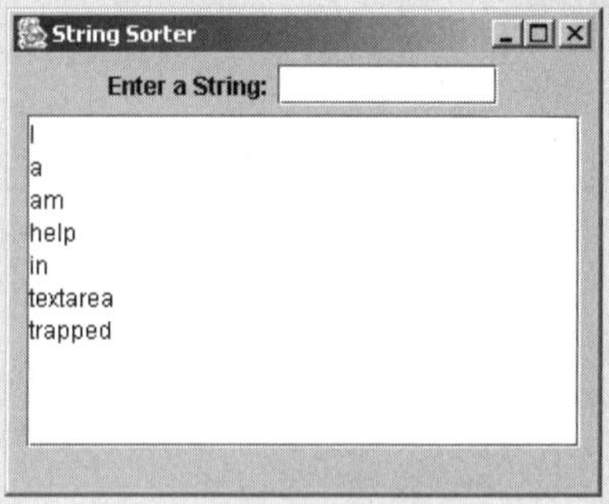

Fig. S11.4 Solution to Exercise 11.14. (Part 3 of 3.)

11.16 Write an application that inputs several lines of text and a search character and uses `String` method `indexOf` to determine the number of occurrences of the character in the text.

ANS:

```
// Exercise 11.16 Solution: Index.java
// Program outputs the number of times a search character was found.
import java.awt.*;
import java.awt.event.*;
import javax.swing.*;

public class Index extends JFrame {
   private JTextField inputKey;
   private JLabel promptArea, promptKey;
   private JTextArea inputArea;

   // constructor
   public Index()
   {
```

Fig. S11.5 Solution to Exercise 11.16. (Part 1 of 3.)

```
      super( "Character Finder" );

      inputKey = new JTextField( 4 );
      inputKey.addActionListener(

         new ActionListener() {  // anonymous inner class

            // search for input character
            public void actionPerformed( ActionEvent event )
            {
               int count = 0, current = 0;
               String inputKey = event.getActionCommand().toString();
               char key = inputKey.charAt( 0 );
               String inputString = inputArea.getText();
               current = inputString.indexOf( key, 0 );

               while ( current != -1 ) {
                  count++;
                  current = inputString.indexOf( key, current + 1 );
               }

               JOptionPane.showMessageDialog( null,
                  "Number of " + key + "'s: " + count, "Results",
                  JOptionPane.INFORMATION_MESSAGE );
            }

         }  // end anonymous inner class

      ); // end call to addActionListener

      promptArea = new JLabel( "Enter text to be searched" );
      promptKey = new JLabel( "Enter a character:" );
      inputArea = new JTextArea( 4, 20 );
      JScrollPane scrollPane = new JScrollPane( inputArea );

      // add components to GUI
      Container container = getContentPane();
      container.setLayout( new FlowLayout() );
      container.add( promptArea );
      container.add( scrollPane );
      container.add( promptKey );
      container.add( inputKey );

      setSize( 450, 150 );
      setVisible( true );

   }  // end constructor

   public static void main( String args[] )
   {
```

Fig. S11.5 Solution to Exercise 11.16. (Part 2 of 3.)

```java
        Index application = new Index();
        application.setDefaultCloseOperation( JFrame.EXIT_ON_CLOSE );
    }

} // end class Index
```

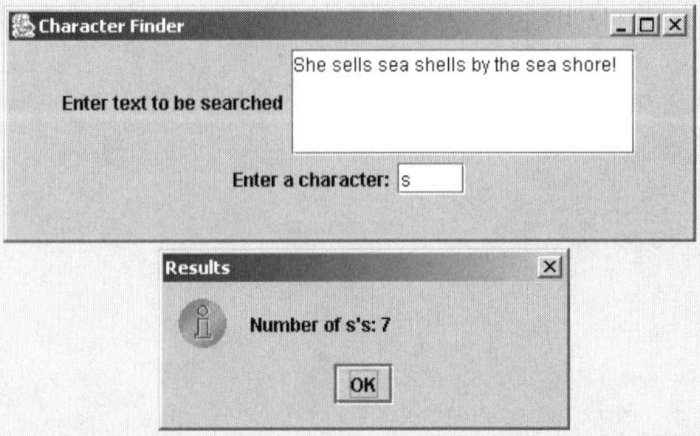

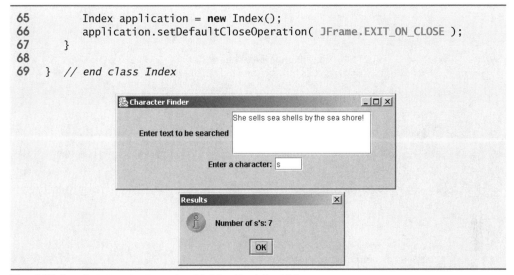

Fig. S11.5 Solution to Exercise 11.16. (Part 3 of 3.)

11.18 Write an application that reads a line of text, tokenizes the line using space characters as delimiters and outputs only those words beginning with the letter “b.” The results should appear in a text area.

ANS:

```java
// Exercise 11.18 Solution: FirstB.java
// Program outputs strings that begin with "b"
import java.awt.*;
import java.awt.event.*;
import java.util.*;
import javax.swing.*;

public class FirstB extends JFrame {
   private JTextField inputField;
   private JLabel prompt;
   private JTextArea display;

   // constructor
   public FirstB()
   {
      super( "FirstB" );
      inputField = new JTextField( 20 );
      inputField.addActionListener(

         new ActionListener() {  // anonymous inner class

            // search for Strings beginning with "b"
            public void actionPerformed( ActionEvent event )
            {
               String inputString = event.getActionCommand().toString();
```

Fig. S11.6 Solution to Exercise 11.18. (Part 1 of 2.)

```
               StringTokenizer tokens =
                  new StringTokenizer( inputString );

               while ( tokens.hasMoreTokens() ) {
                  String test = tokens.nextToken();

                  if( test.startsWith( "b" ) )
                     display.append( test + "\n" );
               }

               inputField.setText( "" );
            }

         } // end anonymous inner class

      ); // end call to addActionListener

      prompt = new JLabel( "Enter a string:" );
      display = new JTextArea( 4, 20 );
      display.setEditable( false );

      JScrollPane displayScrollPane = new JScrollPane( display );

      // add components to GUI
      Container container = getContentPane();
      container.setLayout( new FlowLayout() );
      container.add( prompt );
      container.add( inputField );
      container.add( displayScrollPane );

      setSize( 375, 150 );
      setVisible( true );

   } // end constructor

   public static void main( String args[] )
   {
      FirstB application = new FirstB();
      application.setDefaultCloseOperation( JFrame.EXIT_ON_CLOSE );
   }

} // end class FirstB
```

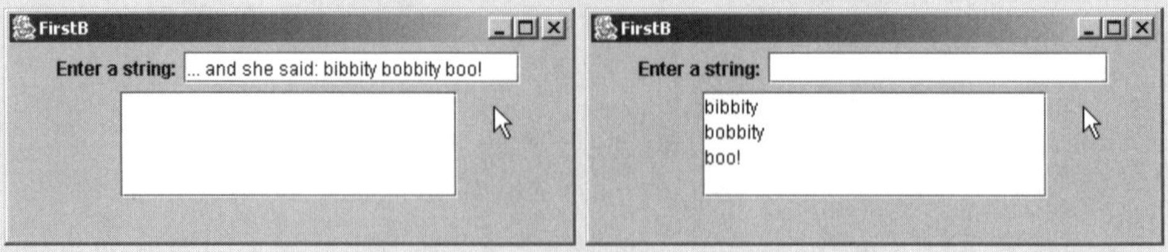

Fig. S11.6 Solution to Exercise 11.18. (Part 2 of 2.)

12

Graphics and Java2D

Solutions to Selected Exercises

12.4 Fill in the blanks in each of the following statements:

a) Class __________ of the Java2D API is used to draw ovals.

ANS: `Ellipse2D`.

b) Methods `draw` and `fill` of class `Graphics2D` require an object of type __________ as their argument.

ANS: `Shape`.

c) The three constants that specify font style are __________, __________ and __________.

ANS: `Font.PLAIN`, `Font.BOLD` *and* `Font.ITALIC`.

d) `Graphics2D` method __________ sets the painting color for Java2D shapes.

ANS: `setColor`.

12.5 State whether each of the following is *true* or *false*. If *false*, explain why.

a) The `drawPolygon` method automatically connects the endpoints of the polygon.

ANS: *True.*

b) The `drawLine` method draws a line between two points.

ANS: *True.*

c) The `fillArc` method uses degrees to specify the angle.

ANS: *True.*

d) In the Java coordinate system, *y* values increase from top to bottom.

ANS: *False. In the Java coordinate system, y values increase from top to bottom.*

e) The `Graphics` class inherits directly from class `Object`.

ANS: *True.*

f) The `Graphics` class is an `abstract` class.

ANS: *True.*

g) The `Font` class inherits directly from class `Graphics`.

ANS: *False. Class* `Font` *inherits directly from class* `Object`.

12.6 Write a program that draws a series of eight concentric circles. The circles should be separated by 10 pixels. Use the `drawOval` method of class `Graphics`.

ANS:

```java
// Exercise 12.6 Solution: Concentric.java
// Program draws concentric circles.
import java.awt.*;
import javax.swing.*;

public class Concentric extends JFrame {

   private int screenOffset = 150;

   // constructor sets window's title bar string and dimensions
   public Concentric()
   {
      super( "Concentric" );

      setSize( 500, 500 );
      setVisible( true );
   }

   // draw concentric ovals
   public void paint( Graphics g )
   {
      super.paint( g );

      for ( int i = 1; i <= 8; i++ ) {

         int origin = screenOffset + 80 - i * 10;
         g.drawOval( origin, origin, i * 20, i * 20);
      }
   }

   public static void main( String args[] )
   {
      Concentric application = new Concentric();
      application.setDefaultCloseOperation( JFrame.EXIT_ON_CLOSE );
   }

} // end class Concentric
```

Fig. S12.1 Solution to Exercise 12.6. (Part 1 of 2.)

Fig. S12.1 Solution to Exercise 12.6. (Part 2 of 2.)

12.12 Write a program that randomly draws characters in different font sizes and colors.

ANS:

```java
// Exercise 12.12 Solution: Draw.java
// Program randomly draws characters
import java.awt.*;
import java.awt.event.*;
import javax.swing.*;

public class Draw extends JFrame {
   private final int DELAY = 999999;

   // constructor sets window's title bar string and dimensions
   public Draw()
   {
      super( "Drawing Characters" );

      setSize( 380, 150 );
      setVisible( true );
   }

   // draw characters
   public void paint( Graphics g )
```

Fig. S12.2 Solution to Exercise 12.12. (Part 1 of 2.)

```
    {
       super.paint( g );

       int fontSize = ( int ) ( 10 + Math.random() * 63 );
       int x = ( int ) ( Math.random() * 380 );
       int y = ( int ) ( 50 + Math.random() * 95 );
       char letters[] = { 'V', 'O', 'L', 'S', '8', '7' };
       Font font = new Font( "Monospaced", Font.BOLD, fontSize );

       g.setColor( new Color( ( float ) Math.random(),
          ( float ) Math.random(), ( float ) Math.random() ) );
       g.setFont( font );
       g.drawChars( letters, ( int ) ( Math.random() * 6 ), 1, x, y );

       // adding delay is optional the body of the for loop is empty
       for ( int h = 1; h < DELAY; h++ ) ;

       repaint();
    }

    public static void main( String args[] )
    {
       Draw application = new Draw();
       application.setDefaultCloseOperation( JFrame.EXIT_ON_CLOSE );
    }

 } // end class Draw
```

Fig. S12.2 Solution to Exercise 12.12. (Part 2 of 2.)

12.15 Write a program that draws a 10-by-10 grid. Use the `drawRect` method.

ANS:

```
// Exercise 12.15 Solution: Grid.java
// Program draws a 10x10 grid using drawRect().
import java.awt.*;
import javax.swing.*;

public class Grid extends JFrame {

   // constructor sets window's title bar string and dimensions
   public Grid()
```

Fig. S12.3 Solution to Exercise 12.15. (Part 1 of 2.)

```
    {
       super( "Drawing a Grid" );

       setSize( 500, 500 );
       setVisible( true );
    }

    // draw grid
    public void paint( Graphics g )
    {
       super.paint( g );

       for ( int x = 30; x <= 300; x += 30 )
          for ( int y = 30; y <= 300; y += 30 )
             g.drawRect( x, y, 30, 30 );
    }

    public static void main( String args[] )
    {
       Grid application = new Grid();
       application.setDefaultCloseOperation( JFrame.EXIT_ON_CLOSE );
    }

 } // end class Grid
```

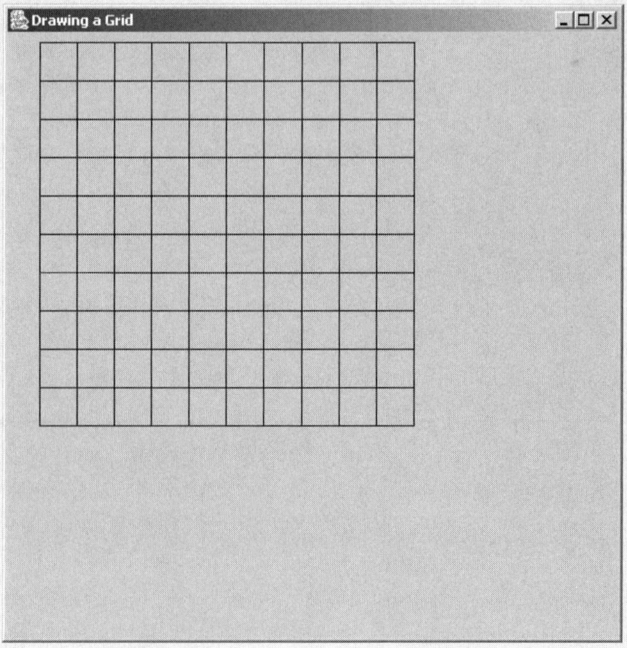

Fig. S12.3 Solution to Exercise 12.15. (Part 2 of 2.)

12.16 Modify your solution to Exercise 12.15 to draw the grid by using instances of class `Rectangle2D.Double` and method `draw` of class `Graphics2D`.

ANS:

```
// Exercise 12.16 Solution: Grid2.java
// Program draws 10x10 grid using draw().
import java.awt.*;
import java.awt.geom.*;
import javax.swing.*;

public class Grid2 extends JFrame {

   // constructor sets window's title bar string and dimensions
   public Grid2()
   {
      super( "Drawing grid" );

      setSize( 500, 500 );
      setVisible( true );
   }

   // draw grid
   public void paint( Graphics g )
   {
      super.paint( g );

      Graphics2D g2d = ( Graphics2D ) g;

      for ( int x = 30; x <= 300; x += 30 )
         for ( int y = 30; y <= 300; y += 30 )
            g2d.draw( new Rectangle2D.Double( x, y, 30, 30 ) );
   }

   public static void main( String args[] )
   {
      Grid2 application = new Grid2();
      application.setDefaultCloseOperation( JFrame.EXIT_ON_CLOSE );
   }

} // end class Grid2
```

Fig. S12.4 Solution to Exercise 12.16. (Part 1 of 2.)

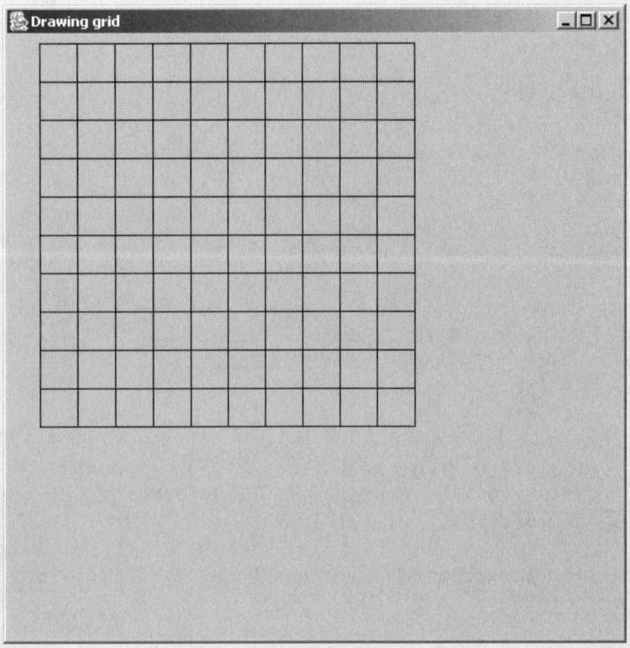

Fig. S12.4 Solution to Exercise 12.16. (Part 2 of 2.)

12.20 Write an application that simulates a screen saver. The application should randomly draw lines using method `drawLine` of class `Graphics`. After drawing 100 lines, the application should clear itself and start drawing lines again. To allow the program to draw continuously, place a call to `repaint` as the last line in method `paint`. Do you notice any problems with this on your system?

ANS:

```java
// Exercise 12.20 Solution: Saver1.java
// Program simulates a simple screen saver
import java.awt.*;
import java.awt.event.*;
import java.awt.geom.*;
import javax.swing.*;

public class Saver1 extends JFrame {
   private final int DELAY = 9999999;

   // constructor sets window's title bar string and dimensions
   public Saver1()
   {
      super( "Saver1" );

      setSize( 300, 300 );
      setVisible( true );
```

Fig. S12.5 Solution to Exercise 12.20. (Part 1 of 2.)

```java
   }

   // draw lines
   public void paint( Graphics g )
   {
      super.paint( g );

      int x, y, x1, y1;

      // draw 100 random lines
      for ( int i = 0; i < 100; i++ ) {

         x = ( int ) ( Math.random() * 300 );
         y = ( int ) ( Math.random() * 300 );
         x1 = ( int ) ( Math.random() * 300 );
         y1 = ( int ) ( Math.random() * 300 );

         g.setColor( new Color( ( float ) Math.random(),
            ( float ) Math.random(), ( float ) Math.random() ) );
         g.drawLine( x, y, x1, y1 );

         // slow the drawing down. the body of the for loop is empty
         for ( int q = 1; q < DELAY; q++ ) ;
      }

      repaint();

   } // end method paint

   public static void main( String args[] )
   {
      Saver1 application = new Saver1();
      application.setDefaultCloseOperation( JFrame.EXIT_ON_CLOSE );
   }

} // end class Saver1
```

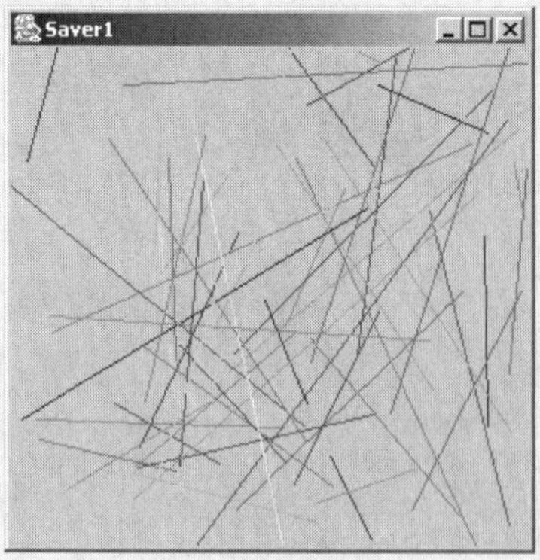

Fig. S12.5 Solution to Exercise 12.20. (Part 2 of 2.)

13

Graphical User Interface Components: Part 1

Solutions to Selected Exercises

13.4 Fill in the blanks in each of the following statements:

a) The `JTextField` class directly extends class __________.

ANS: `JTextComponent`.

b) List three layout managers from this chapter: __________, __________ and __________.

ANS: `FlowLayout`, `BorderLayout` *and* `GridLayout`.

c) `Container` method __________ attaches a GUI component to a container.

ANS: `add`.

d) Method __________ is called when a mouse button is released (without moving the mouse).

ANS: `mouseClicked`.

e) The __________ class is used to create a group of `JRadioButton`s.

ANS: `ButtonGroup`.

13.5 Determine whether each statement is *true* or *false*. If *false*, explain why.

a) Only one layout manager can be used per `Container`.

ANS: *True.*

b) GUI components can be added to a `Container` in any order in a `BorderLayout`.

ANS: *True.*

c) `JRadioButton`s provide a series of mutually exclusive options (i.e., only one can be `true` at a time).

ANS: *True.*

d) `Graphics` method `setFont` is used to set the font for text fields.

ANS: *False.* `Component` *method* `setFont` *is used.*

e) A `JList` displays a scrollbar if there are more items in the list than can be displayed.

ANS: *False. A* `JList` *never provides a scrollbar.*

f) A `Mouse` object has a method called `mouseDragged`.

ANS: *False. A* `Mouse` *object is not provided by Java.*

13.8 Create the following GUI. You do not have to provide any functionality.

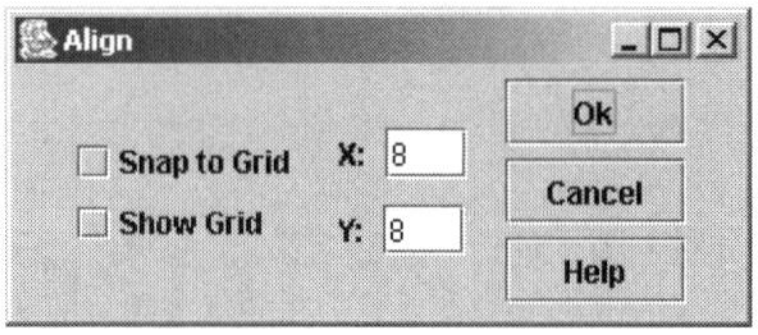

ANS:

```
// Exercise 13.8 Solution: Align.java
// Program creates a simple GUI.
import java.awt.*;
import javax.swing.*;

public class Align extends JFrame {
   private JButton okButton, cancelButton, helpButton;
   private JTextField xValue, yValue;
   private JCheckBox snapBox, showBox;
   private JLabel xLabel, yLabel;
   private JPanel checkPanel, buttonPanel, fieldPanel1,
      fieldPanel2, fieldPanel;

   // constructor sets up GUI
   public Align()
   {
      super( "Align" );

      // build checkPanel
      snapBox = new JCheckBox( "Snap to Grid" );
      showBox = new JCheckBox( "Show Grid" );
      checkPanel = new JPanel();
      checkPanel.setLayout( new GridLayout( 2 , 1 ) );
      checkPanel.add( snapBox );
      checkPanel.add( showBox );

      // build field panel1
      xLabel = new JLabel( "X: " );
      xValue = new JTextField( "8", 3 );
      fieldPanel1 = new JPanel();
      fieldPanel1.setLayout( new FlowLayout() );
      fieldPanel1.add( xLabel );
      fieldPanel1.add( xValue );

      // build field panel2
      yLabel = new JLabel( "Y: " );
      yValue = new JTextField( "8", 3 );
      fieldPanel2 = new JPanel();
      fieldPanel2.setLayout( new FlowLayout() );
      fieldPanel2.add( yLabel );
```

Fig. S13.1 Solution to Exercise 13.8. (Part 1 of 2.)

```
      fieldPanel2.add( yValue );

      // build field panel
      fieldPanel = new JPanel();
      fieldPanel.setLayout( new BorderLayout() );
      fieldPanel.add( fieldPanel1, BorderLayout.NORTH );
      fieldPanel.add( fieldPanel2, BorderLayout.SOUTH );

      // build button panel
      okButton = new JButton( "Ok" );
      cancelButton = new JButton( "Cancel" );
      helpButton = new JButton( "Help" );
      buttonPanel = new JPanel();
      buttonPanel.setLayout( new GridLayout( 3, 1, 10, 5 ) );
      buttonPanel.add( okButton );
      buttonPanel.add( cancelButton );
      buttonPanel.add( helpButton );

      // set layout for applet
      Container container = getContentPane();
      container.setLayout(
         new FlowLayout( FlowLayout.CENTER, 10, 5 ) );
      container.add( checkPanel );
      container.add( fieldPanel );
      container.add( buttonPanel );

      setSize( 300, 125 );
      setVisible( true );

   } // end Align constructor

   // execute application
   public static void main( String args[] )
   {
      Align application = new Align();
      application.setDefaultCloseOperation( JFrame.EXIT_ON_CLOSE );
   }

} // end class Align
```

Fig. S13.1 Solution to Exercise 13.8. (Part 2 of 2.)

13.9 Create the following GUI. You do not have to provide any functionality.

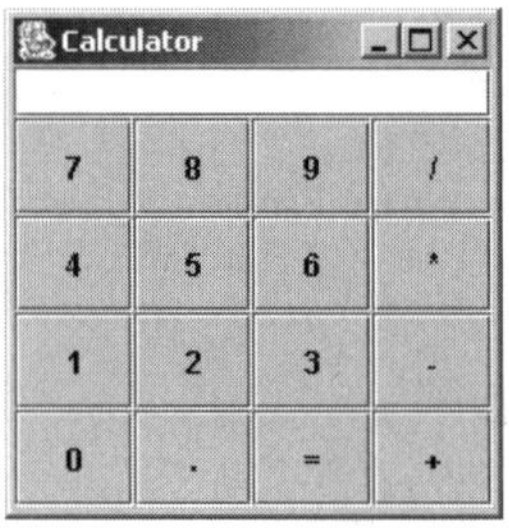

ANS:

```java
// Solution exercise 13.9: Calculator.java
// Program creates a GUI that resembles a calculator.
import java.awt.*;
import javax.swing.*;

public class Calculator extends JFrame {
   private JButton keys[];
   private JPanel keyPad;
   private JTextField lcd;

   // constructor sets up GUI
   public Calculator()
   {
      super( "Calculator" );

      lcd = new JTextField( 20 );
      lcd.setEditable( true );

      keys = new JButton[ 16 ];

      // initialize all non-digit key Buttons
      for ( int i = 0; i <= 9; i++ )
         keys[ i ] = new JButton( String.valueOf( i ) );

      // initialize all digit key Buttons
      keys[ 10 ] = new JButton( "/" );
      keys[ 11 ] = new JButton( "*" );
      keys[ 12 ] = new JButton( "-" );
      keys[ 13 ] = new JButton( "+" );
      keys[ 14 ] = new JButton( "=" );
      keys[ 15 ] = new JButton( "." );

      // set keyPad layout to grid layout
      keyPad = new JPanel();
      keyPad.setLayout( new GridLayout( 4, 4 ) );

      // add buttons to keyPad panel
      // 7, 8, 9, divide
```

Fig. S13.2 Solution to Exercise 13.9. (Part 1 of 2.)

```
      for ( int i = 7; i <= 10; i++ )
         keyPad.add( keys[ i ] );

      // 4, 5, 6
      for ( int i = 4; i <= 6; i++ )
         keyPad.add( keys[ i ] );

      // multiply
      keyPad.add( keys[ 11 ] );

      // 1, 2, 3
      for ( int i = 1; i <= 3; i++ )
         keyPad.add( keys[ i ] );

      // subtract
      keyPad.add( keys[ 12 ] );

      // 0
      keyPad.add( keys[ 0 ] );

      // ., =, add
      for ( int i = 15; i >= 13; i-- )
         keyPad.add( keys[ i ] );

      // add components to (default) border layout
      Container container = getContentPane();
      container.add( lcd, BorderLayout.NORTH );
      container.add( keyPad, BorderLayout.CENTER );

      setSize( 200, 200 );
      setVisible( true );

   } // end Calculator constructor

   // execute application
   public static void main( String args[] )
   {
      Calculator application = new Calculator();
      application.setDefaultCloseOperation( JFrame.EXIT_ON_CLOSE );
   }

} // end class Calculator
```

Fig. S13.2 Solution to Exercise 13.9. (Part 2 of 2.)

13.13 Enhance the temperature conversion program of Exercise 13.12 by adding the Kelvin temperature scale. The program should also allow the user to make conversions between any two scales. Use the following formula for the conversion between Kelvin and Celsius (in addition to the formula in Exercise 13.12):

$$Kelvin = Celsius + 273.15$$

ANS:

```java
// Exercise 13.13 Solution: Convert.java
// Program converts temperatures.
import java.awt.*;
import java.awt.event.*;
import javax.swing.*;

public class Convert extends JFrame {
   private JPanel convertFrom, convertTo;
   private JLabel label1, label2, label3, label4;
   private JTextField temperature1, temperature2;
   private ButtonGroup radioFrom, radioTo;
   private JRadioButton celciusBoxTo, fahrenheitBoxTo,
      kelvinBoxTo, celciusBoxFrom, fahrenheitBoxFrom, kelvinBoxFrom;

   // set up GUI
   public Convert()
   {
      super( "Temperature Conversion" );

      fahrenheitBoxFrom = new JRadioButton( "Fahrenheit", true );
      celciusBoxFrom = new JRadioButton( "Celcius", false );
      kelvinBoxFrom = new JRadioButton( "Kelvin",   false );
      radioFrom = new ButtonGroup();
      radioFrom.add( fahrenheitBoxFrom );
      radioFrom.add( celciusBoxFrom );
      radioFrom.add( kelvinBoxFrom );

      fahrenheitBoxTo = new JRadioButton( "Fahrenheit", false );
      celciusBoxTo = new JRadioButton( "Celcius", true );
      kelvinBoxTo = new JRadioButton( "Kelvin", false );
      radioTo = new ButtonGroup();
      radioTo.add( fahrenheitBoxTo );
      radioTo.add( celciusBoxTo );
      radioTo.add( kelvinBoxTo );

      convertFrom = new JPanel();
      convertFrom.setLayout( new GridLayout( 1, 3 ) );
      convertFrom.add( fahrenheitBoxFrom );
      convertFrom.add( celciusBoxFrom );
      convertFrom.add( kelvinBoxFrom );

      convertTo = new JPanel();
      convertTo.setLayout( new GridLayout( 1, 3 ) );
      convertTo.add( fahrenheitBoxTo );
      convertTo.add( celciusBoxTo );
      convertTo.add( kelvinBoxTo );

      label1 = new JLabel( "Convert from:" );
      label2 = new JLabel( "Convert to:" );
```

Fig. S13.3 Solution to Exercise 13.13. (Part 1 of 4.)

```
      label3 = new JLabel( "Enter Numeric Temperature: " );
      label4 = new JLabel( "Comparable Temperature is: " );

      temperature1 = new JTextField( 10 );
      temperature1.addActionListener(

         new ActionListener() {  // anonymous inner class

            // perform conversions
            public void actionPerformed( ActionEvent event )
            {
               int convertTemp, temp;

               temp = Integer.parseInt( ( ( JTextField )
                  event.getSource() ).getText() );

               // fahrenheit to celcius
               if ( fahrenheitBoxFrom.isSelected() &&
                  celciusBoxTo.isSelected() ) {
                  convertTemp = ( int ) ( 5.0f / 9.0f * ( temp - 32 ) );
                  temperature2.setText( String.valueOf( convertTemp ) );
               }

               // fahrenheit to kelvin
               else if ( fahrenheitBoxFrom.isSelected() &&
                  kelvinBoxTo.isSelected() ) {
                  convertTemp = ( int )
                     ( 5.0f / 9.0f * ( temp - 32 ) + 273 );
                  temperature2.setText( String.valueOf( convertTemp ) );
               }

               // celcius to fahrenheit
               else if ( celciusBoxFrom.isSelected() &&
                  fahrenheitBoxTo.isSelected() ) {
                  convertTemp = ( int ) ( 9.0f / 5.0f * temp + 32 );
                  temperature2.setText( String.valueOf( convertTemp ) );
               }

               // celcius to kelvin
               else if ( celciusBoxFrom.isSelected() &&
                  kelvinBoxTo.isSelected() ) {
                  convertTemp = temp + 273;
                  temperature2.setText( String.valueOf( convertTemp ) );
               }

               // kelvin to celcius
               else if ( kelvinBoxFrom.isSelected() &&
                  celciusBoxTo.isSelected() ) {
                  convertTemp = temp - 273;
                  temperature2.setText( String.valueOf( convertTemp ) );
```

Fig. S13.3 Solution to Exercise 13.13. (Part 2 of 4.)

```
               }

               // kelvin to fahrenheit
               else if ( kelvinBoxFrom.isSelected() &&
                  fahrenheitBoxTo.isSelected() ) {
                  convertTemp = ( int ) ( 5.0f /
                     9.0f * ( temp - 273 ) + 32  );
                  temperature2.setText( String.valueOf( convertTemp ) );
               }

            } // end method actionPerformed

         } // end anonymous inner class

      ); // end call to addActionListener

      temperature2 = new JTextField( 10 );
      temperature2.setEditable( false );

      // add components to GUI
      Container container = getContentPane();
      container.setLayout( new GridLayout( 8, 1 ) );
      container.add( label1 );
      container.add( convertFrom );
      container.add( label3 );
      container.add( temperature1 );
      container.add( label2 );
      container.add( convertTo );
      container.add( label4 );
      container.add( temperature2 );

      setSize( 250, 225 );
      setVisible( true );

   } // end constructor

   public static void main ( String args[] )
   {
      Convert application = new Convert();
      application.setDefaultCloseOperation( JFrame.EXIT_ON_CLOSE );
   }

} // end class Convert
```

Fig. S13.3 Solution to Exercise 13.13. (Part 3 of 4.)

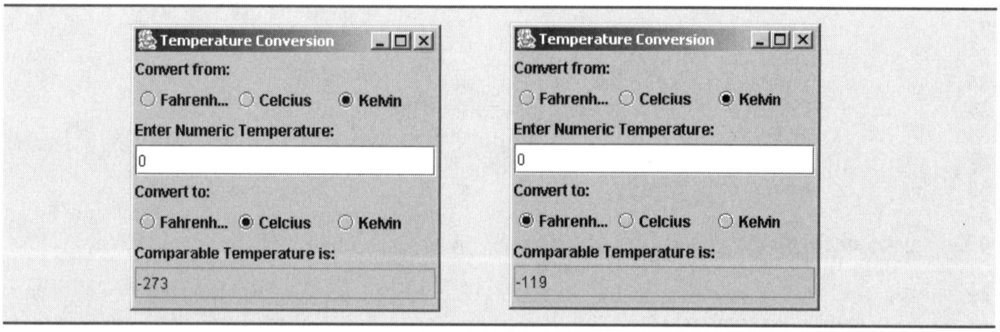

Fig. S13.3 Solution to Exercise 13.13. (Part 4 of 4.)

13.15 Modify the program of Exercise 13.14 to draw different shapes. The user should be allowed to choose from an oval, an arc, a line and a rectangle with rounded corners. Also display the mouse coordinates in the status bar.

ANS:

```java
// Exercise 13.15 Solution: DrawShape.java
// Program draws shapes with the mouse
import java.awt.*;
import java.awt.event.*;
import javax.swing.*;
import javax.swing.event.*;

public class DrawShape extends JFrame {
   private int topX, topY, width, height, shape, bottomX, bottomY;
   private JLabel status;
   private final int LINE = 1, OVAL = 2, ARC = 3, ROUND = 4, POLY = 5;
   private String shapeNames[] =
      { "Oval", "Arc", "Line", "Round Rect", "Polygon" };

   // constructor
   public DrawShape()
   {
      super( "Draw Shapes" );
      topX = 0;
      topY = 0;

      status = new JLabel();

      addMouseListener( new MouseHandler() );
      addMouseMotionListener( new MouseMotionHandler() );
      addKeyListener( new KeyHandler() );

      // add label to bottom of window via call to default layout
      Container container = getContentPane();
      container.add( status, BorderLayout.SOUTH );

```

Fig. S13.4 Solution to Exercise 13.15. (Part 1 of 4.)

```
      setSize( 300, 300 );
      setVisible( true );
      JOptionPane.showMessageDialog( null,
         "Press a key to choose the shape to draw\n" +
         "1 - line\n2 - oval\n3 - arc\n4 - rectangle\n5 - polygon\n" );

   } // end constructor

   // draw shape
   public void paint( Graphics g )
   {
      super.paint( g );

      if ( shape != LINE ) {
         topX = Math.min( topX, bottomX );
         topY = Math.min( topY, bottomY );
      }

      switch ( shape ) {

         case LINE:
            g.drawLine( topX, topY, bottomX, bottomY );
            break;

         case OVAL:
            g.drawOval( topX, topY, width, height );
            break;

         case ARC:
            g.drawArc( topX, topY, width, height, 0, 90 );
            break;

         case ROUND:
            g.drawRoundRect( topX, topY, width, height, 20, 10 );
            break;

         case POLY:
            int xValues[] =
               { topX + 10, topX, bottomX, topX - 20, topX - 10, topX };
            int yValues[] =
               { topY, topY + 10, bottomY, topY + 20, topY + 10, topY };
            g.drawPolygon( xValues, yValues, 6 );
            break;
      }

   } // end method paint

   public static void main( String args[] )
   {
      DrawShape application = new DrawShape();
```

Fig. S13.4 Solution to Exercise 13.15. (Part 2 of 4.)

```
      application.setDefaultCloseOperation( JFrame.EXIT_ON_CLOSE );
   }

   // inner class to handle mouse motion events
   private class MouseMotionHandler extends MouseMotionAdapter {

      public void mouseMoved( MouseEvent event )
      {
         status.setText(
            "( " + event.getX() + ", " + event.getY() + " )" );
      }
   }

   // inner class to handle mouse events
   private class MouseHandler extends MouseAdapter {

      public void mousePressed( MouseEvent event )
      {
         topX = event.getX();
         topY = event.getY();
      }

      public void mouseReleased( MouseEvent event )
      {
         bottomX = event.getX();
         bottomY = event.getY();
         width = Math.abs( topX - bottomX );
         height = Math.abs( topY - bottomY );

         repaint();
      }

   } // end private inner class MouseHandler

   // inner class to handle key events
   private class KeyHandler extends KeyAdapter {

      public void keyPressed( KeyEvent event )
      {
         shape = Integer.parseInt( String.valueOf( event.getKeyChar() ) );
      }

   } // end inner class KeyHandler

} // end class DrawShape
```

Fig. S13.4 Solution to Exercise 13.15. (Part 3 of 4.)

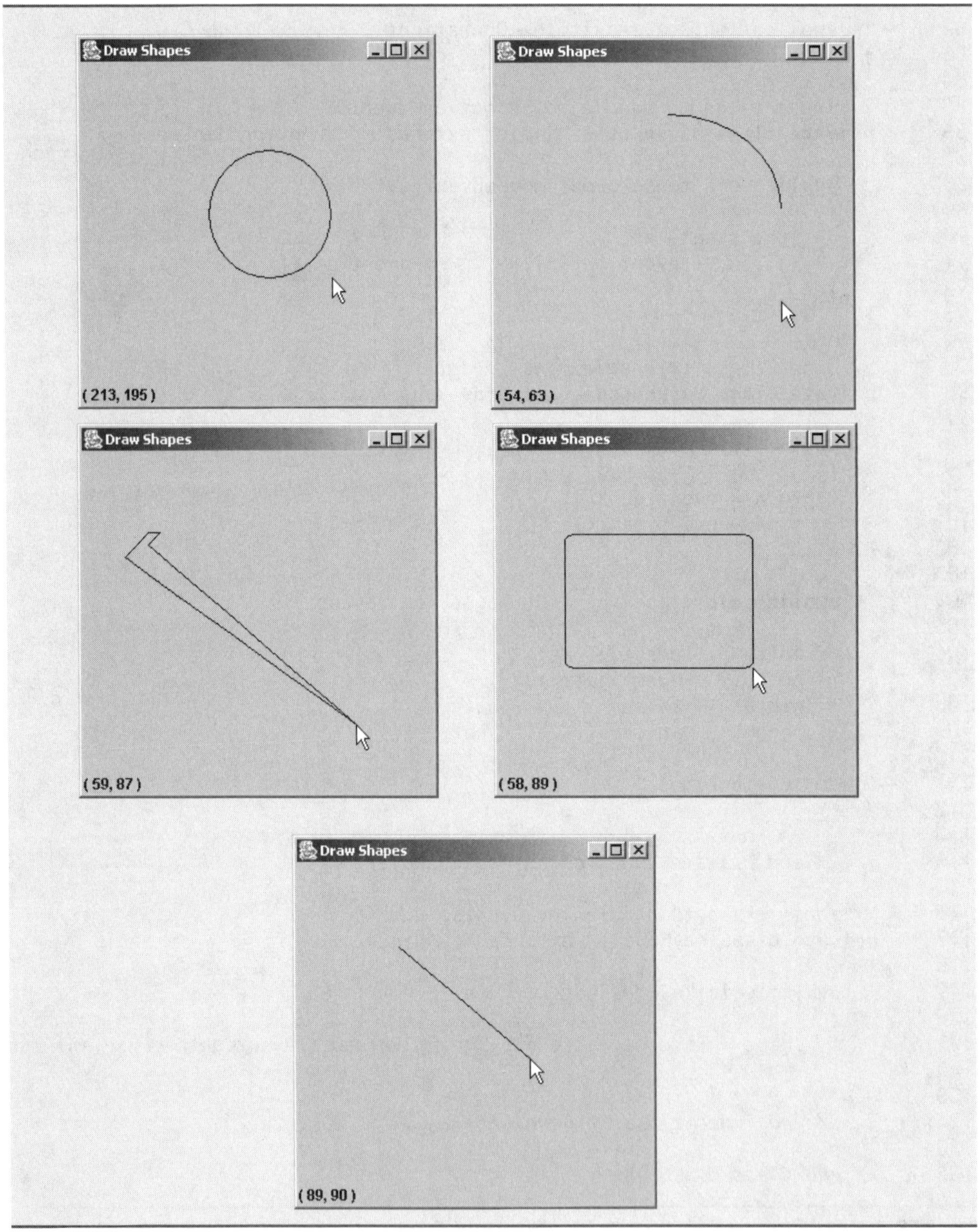
Draw Shapes
(213, 195)
Draw Shapes
(54, 63)
Draw Shapes
(59, 87)
Draw Shapes
(58, 89)
Draw Shapes
(89, 90)

Fig. S13.4 Solution to Exercise 13.15. (Part 4 of 4.)

13.23 Modify your solution to Exercise 13.17 to enable the user to select a font and a font size and type text into a `JTextField`. When the user presses *Enter,* the text should be displayed in the chosen font and size. Modify the program further to allow the user to specify the exact position at which the text should be displayed.

ANS:

```
// Exercise 13.23 Solution: Painter2.java
// Program paints shapes and text of different fonts and colors.
import java.awt.*;
import java.awt.event.*;
import javax.swing.*;
import javax.swing.event.*;

public class Painter2 extends JFrame {
   private int topX, topY, width, fontSize,
      height, bottomX, bottomY, shape;
   private boolean clear, textOn, filled;
   private Color drawingColor;
   private String font;
   private JTextField text;
   private JPanel panel1, panel2, panel3;
   private JRadioButton ovalBox, rectBox, lineBox;
   private ButtonGroup shapeGroup;
   private JCheckBox fillBox;
   private JComboBox colorList, fontList, sizeList;
   private JButton clearButton;
   private String colorNames[] = {"Black", "Green", "Blue",
      "Red", "Cyan" };
   private Color colors[] = { Color.black, Color.green, Color.blue,
      Color.red, Color.cyan };
   private String fontNames[] = { "Serif", "SansSerif", "Monospaced" };
   private String sizeNames[] =  {"9", "10", "22", "72" };
   private int sizes[] = { 9, 10, 22, 72 };
   private final int OVAL = 1, LINE = 2, RECT = 3;

   private ToolWindow tools;

   // Painter2 constructor
   public Painter2()
   {
      addMouseListener( new MouseHandler() );

      // set defaults for painting
      drawingColor = Color.black;
      shape = OVAL;
      font = "Serif";
      fontSize = 9;

      setSize( 300, 300 );
      setVisible( true );

```

Fig. S13.5 Solution to Exercise 13.23. (Part 1 of 7.)

```
      // create new ToolWindow
      tools = new ToolWindow();
   }

   // paint the new window.  super is not called so
   // that the previous images will not be erased.
   public void paint( Graphics g )
   {
      g.setColor( drawingColor );

      // draw text
      if ( textOn ) {
         g.setFont( new Font( font, Font.PLAIN, fontSize ) );
         g.drawString( text.getText(), topX, topY );
         textOn = false;
         return;
      }

      // set shape's top left coordinates
      if ( shape != LINE ) {
         topX = Math.min( topX, bottomX );
         topY = Math.min( topY, bottomY );
      }

      // draw filled shape
      if ( filled && shape != LINE )

         switch ( shape ) {

            case OVAL:
               g.fillOval( topX, topY,  width, height );
               break;

            case RECT:
               g.fillRect( topX, topY, width, height );
               break;
         }

      // draw unfilled shapes
      else

         switch ( shape ) {

            case OVAL:
               g.drawOval( topX, topY,  width, height );
               break;

            case LINE:
               g.drawLine( topX, topY, bottomX, bottomY );
               break;
```

Fig. S13.5 Solution to Exercise 13.23. (Part 2 of 7.)

```java

            case RECT:
               g.drawRect( topX, topY, width, height );
               break;
         }

      // clear background
      if ( clear == true ) {
         g.setColor( Color.white );
         g.fillRect( 0, 0, getSize().width, getSize().height );
         clear = false;
      }

   } // end method paint

   // inner class for window containing GUI
   private class ToolWindow extends JFrame {

      // ToolWindow constructor
      public ToolWindow()
      {
         // set up to edit text
         text = new JTextField( "Text", 20 );
         text.addActionListener(

            // anonymous inner class to handle text drawing
            new ActionListener () {

               public void actionPerformed( ActionEvent event )
               {
                  textOn = true;
                  repaint();
               }

            } // end anonymous inner class

         ); // end call to addActionListener

         // set up to choose font
         fontList = new JComboBox( fontNames );
         fontList.setMaximumRowCount( 3 );
         fontList.addItemListener(

            new ItemListener() { // anonymous inner class to select font

               // change font
               public void itemStateChanged( ItemEvent event )
               {
                  font = fontNames[ fontList.getSelectedIndex() ];
               }
```

Fig. S13.5 Solution to Exercise 13.23. (Part 3 of 7.)

```
      } // end anonymous inner class

   ); // end call to addItemListener

   // set up to choose font size
   sizeList = new JComboBox( sizeNames );
   sizeList.setMaximumRowCount( 3 );
   sizeList.addItemListener(

      // anonymous inner class to select font size
      new ItemListener() {

         // change font size
         public void itemStateChanged( ItemEvent event )
         {
            fontSize = sizes[ sizeList.getSelectedIndex() ];
         }

      } // end anonymous inner class

   ); // end call to addItemListener

   // set up to choose color
   colorList = new JComboBox( colorNames );
   colorList.setMaximumRowCount( 3 );
   colorList.addItemListener(

      new ItemListener() { // anonymous inner class to select color

         // change color
         public void itemStateChanged( ItemEvent event )
         {
            drawingColor = colors[ colorList.getSelectedIndex() ];
         }

      } // end anonymous inner class

   ); // end call to addItemListener

   // set up clear button
   clearButton = new JButton( "Clear" );
   clearButton.addActionListener( new ClearButtonHandler() );

   // set up to choose filled
   fillBox  = new JCheckBox( "filled" );
   FillBoxHandler fillHandle = new FillBoxHandler();
   fillBox.addItemListener( fillHandle );

   // set up to choose shapes
```

Fig. S13.5 Solution to Exercise 13.23. (Part 4 of 7.)

```
         ovalBox = new JRadioButton( "Oval", true );
         lineBox = new JRadioButton( "Line", false );
         rectBox = new JRadioButton( "Rectangle", false );
         RadioButtonHandler handler = new RadioButtonHandler();
         ovalBox.addItemListener( handler );
         lineBox.addItemListener( handler );
         rectBox.addItemListener( handler );
         shapeGroup = new ButtonGroup();
         shapeGroup.add( ovalBox );
         shapeGroup.add( lineBox );
         shapeGroup.add( rectBox );

         // set up GUI layout
         panel1 = new JPanel();
         panel2 = new JPanel();
         panel3 = new JPanel();

         panel1.setLayout( new GridLayout( 1, 3 ) );
         panel2.setLayout( new GridLayout( 1, 2 ) );
         panel3.setLayout( new GridLayout( 1, 3 ) );

         panel1.add( ovalBox );
         panel1.add( lineBox );
         panel1.add( rectBox );
         panel2.add( fillBox );
         panel2.add( clearButton );
         panel3.add( new JScrollPane ( colorList ) );
         panel3.add( new JScrollPane ( fontList ) );
         panel3.add( new JScrollPane ( sizeList ) );

         Container container = getContentPane();
         container.setLayout( new FlowLayout() );
         container.add( panel1 );
         container.add( panel2 );
         container.add( panel3 );
         container.add( text );

         setSize( 350, 200 );
         setLocation( 300, 0 );
         setVisible( true );

      } // end ToolWindow constructor

   } // end inner class ToolWindow

   // set coordinate and dimension values
   private class MouseHandler extends MouseAdapter {

      public void mousePressed( MouseEvent event )
      {
```

Fig. S13.5 Solution to Exercise 13.23. (Part 5 of 7.)

```
         topX = event.getX();
         topY = event.getY();
      }

      public void mouseReleased( MouseEvent event )
      {
         bottomX = event.getX();
         bottomY = event.getY();
         width = Math.abs( topX - bottomX );
         height = Math.abs( topY - bottomY );

         repaint();
      }

   } // end inner class MouseHandler

   // clear background
   private class ClearButtonHandler implements ActionListener {

      public void actionPerformed( ActionEvent event )
      {
         clear = true;
         repaint();
      }

   } // end inner class ClearButtonHandler

   // determine which type of shape to draw
   private class RadioButtonHandler implements ItemListener {

      public void itemStateChanged( ItemEvent event )
      {
         if ( event.getSource() == ovalBox )
            shape = OVAL;

         else if ( event.getSource() == lineBox )
            shape = LINE;

         else if ( event.getSource() == rectBox )
            shape = RECT;
      }

   } // end inner class RadioButtonHandler

   // determine if shape should be filled
   private class FillBoxHandler implements ItemListener {

      public void itemStateChanged( ItemEvent event )
      {
         if ( event.getStateChange() == ItemEvent.SELECTED )
```

Fig. S13.5 Solution to Exercise 13.23. (Part 6 of 7.)

```
            filled = true;

         else
            filled = false;
      }

   } // end inner class FillBoxHandler

   public static void main( String args[] )
   {
      Painter2 application = new Painter2();
      application.setDefaultCloseOperation( JFrame.EXIT_ON_CLOSE );
   }

} // end class Painter2
```

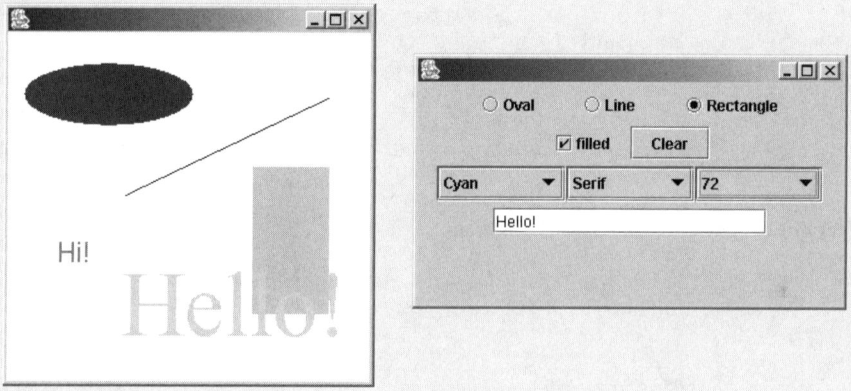

Fig. S13.5 Solution to Exercise 13.23. (Part 7 of 7.)

13.27 Write a program using methods from interface `MouseListener` that allows the user to press the mouse button, drag the mouse and release the mouse button. When the mouse is released, draw a rectangle with the appropriate upper-left corner, width and height. [*Hint*: The `mousePressed` method should capture the set of coordinates at which the user presses and holds the mouse button initially, and the `mouseReleased` method should capture the set of coordinates at which the user releases the mouse button. Both methods should store the appropriate coordinate values. All calculations of the width, height and upper-left corner should be performed by the `paint` method before the shape is drawn.]

ANS:

```
// Exercise 13.27 Solution: DrawRectangle.java
// Program draws a rectangle with the mouse.
import java.awt.*;
import java.awt.event.*;
import javax.swing.*;

public class DrawRectangle extends JFrame {
```

Fig. S13.6 Solution to Exercise 13.27. (Part 1 of 3.)

```
   private int topX, topY, width, height, bottomX, bottomY;

   // constructor
   public DrawRectangle()
   {
      super( "Draw" );
      addMouseListener( new MouseHandler() );
      setSize( 300, 200 );
      setVisible( true );
   }

   // draw rectangle
   public void paint( Graphics g )
   {
      super.paint( g );

      width = Math.abs( topX - bottomX );
      height = Math.abs( topY - bottomY );
      int upperX = Math.min( topX, bottomX );
      int upperY = Math.min( topY, bottomY );

      g.drawRect( upperX, upperY, width, height );
   }

   public static void main( String args[] )
   {
      DrawRectangle application = new DrawRectangle();
      application.setDefaultCloseOperation( JFrame.EXIT_ON_CLOSE );
   }

   // set coordinate values
   private class MouseHandler extends MouseAdapter {

      public void mouseReleased( MouseEvent event )
      {
         bottomX = event.getX();
         bottomY = event.getY();
         repaint();
      }

      public void mousePressed( MouseEvent event )
      {
         topX = event.getX();
         topY = event.getY();
      }

   } // end inner class MouseHandler

} // end class DrawRectangle
```

Fig. S13.6 Solution to Exercise 13.27. (Part 2 of 3.)

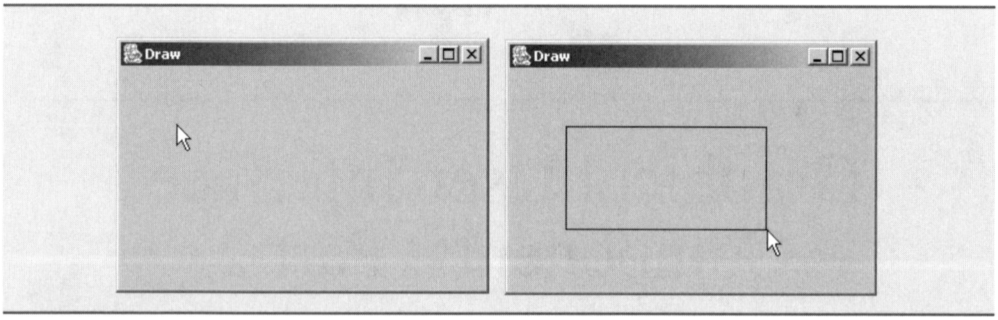

Fig. S13.6 Solution to Exercise 13.27. (Part 3 of 3.)

14

Graphical User Interface Components: Part 2

Solutions to Selected Exercises

14.4 Fill in the blanks in each of the following statements:

a) A dedicated drawing area can be declared as a subclass of _________.

ANS: `JPanel`

b) A `JMenuItem` that is a `JMenu` is called a(n) _________.

ANS: *submenu*

c) Both `JTextField`s and `JTextArea`s directly extend class _________.

ANS: `JTextComponent`

d) Method _________ attaches a `JMenuBar` to a `JFrame`.

ANS: `setJMenuBar`

e) Container class _________ has a default `BoxLayout`.

ANS: `Box`

f) A(n) _________ manages a set of child windows declared with class `JInternalFrame`.

ANS: `JDesktopPane`

14.5 State whether each of the following is *true* or *false*. If *false*, explain why.

a) Menus require a `JMenuBar` object so they can be attached to a `JFrame`.

ANS: *True*

b) A `JPanel` object is capable of receiving mouse events.

ANS: *True*

c) `BoxLayout` is the default layout manager for a `JFrame`.

ANS: *False.* `BorderLayout` *is the default layout manager for* `JFrame`.

d) Method `setEditable` is a `JTextComponent` method.

ANS: *True*

e) `JPanel` objects are containers to which other GUI components can be attached.

ANS: *True*

f) Class `JFrame` directly extends class `Container`.

ANS: *False.* `JFrame` *inherits directly from* `Frame`.

g) `JApplets` can contain menus.

ANS: *True*

14.7 Write a program that displays a circle of random size and calculates and displays the area, radius, diameter and circumference. Use the following equations: $diameter = 2 \infty radius$, $area = \pi \infty radius^2$, $circumference = 2 \infty \pi \infty radius$. Use the constant `Math.PI` for pi (π). All drawing should be done on a subclass of `JPanel`, and the results of the calculations should be displayed in a read-only `JTextArea`.

ANS:

```java
// Exercise 14.7 Solution: Circle1.java
// Program draws a circle of a random diameter and displays the radius,
// diameter, area and circumference.
import java.awt.*;
import java.awt.event.*;
import javax.swing.*;

public class Circle1 extends JFrame
{
   private JTextArea display;

   public Circle1()
   {
      super( "Circle1" );

      // the panel on which all drawing is done
      CircleCanvas theCanvas = new CircleCanvas();

      // the area for writing information about the circle
      display = new JTextArea( 5, 30 );
      display.setEditable( false );

      display.setText( "The Radius is: " + theCanvas.getRadius() +
         "\nThe Diameter is: " + theCanvas.getDiameter() +
         "\nThe Area is: " + theCanvas.getArea() +
         "\nThe Circumference is: " + theCanvas.getCircumference() );

      Container container = getContentPane();
      container.add( theCanvas, BorderLayout.CENTER );
      container.add( display, BorderLayout.SOUTH );

      setSize( 200, 300 );
      setVisible( true );
   }

   public static void main( String args[] )
   {
      Circle1 application = new Circle1();
```

Fig. S14.1 Solution to Exercise 14.7. (Part 1 of 3.)

```
      application.setDefaultCloseOperation( JFrame.EXIT_ON_CLOSE );
   }

}  // end class Circle1

// class to display circle and calculate circle's dimensions
class CircleCanvas extends JPanel {
   private int radius;

   // generate random radius and set panel size
   public CircleCanvas()
   {
      radius = ( int )( 1 + Math.random() * 100 );
      setSize( 200, 200 );
   }

   // draw circle
   public void paintComponent( Graphics g )
   {
      g.drawOval( 0, 0, 2 * radius, 2 * radius );
   }

   // get diameter of circle
   public int getDiameter()
   {
      return ( 2 * radius );
   }

   // get circumference of circle
   public int getCircumference()
   {
      return ( int )( 2 * Math.PI * radius );
   }

   // get area of circle
   public int getArea()
   {
      return ( int )( Math.PI * radius * radius );
   }

   // get radius of circle
   public int getRadius()
   {
      return radius;
   }

}  // end class CircleCanvas
```

Fig. S14.1 Solution to Exercise 14.7. (Part 2 of 3.)

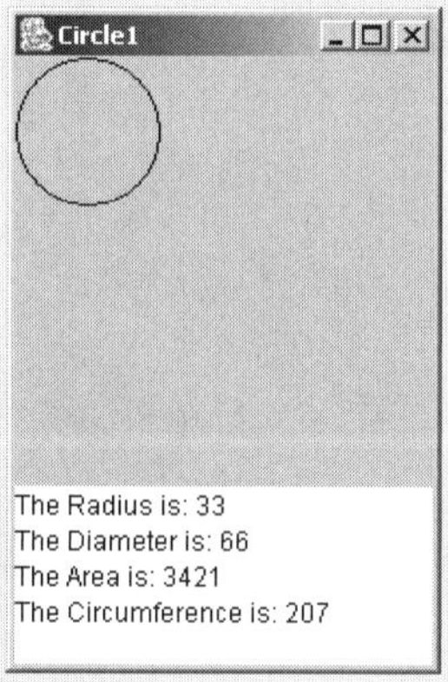

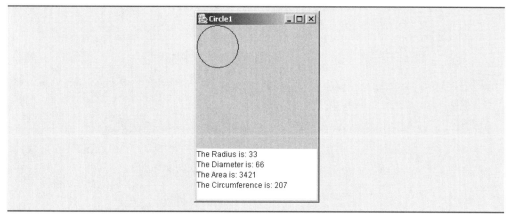

Fig. S14.1 Solution to Exercise 14.7. (Part 3 of 3.)

14.10 Write a program that uses the `paintComponent` method to draw the current value of a `JSlider` on a subclass of `JPanel`. In addition, provide a `JTextField` where a specific value can be entered. The `JTextField` should display the current value of the `JSlider` at all times. A `JLabel` should be used to identify the `JTextField`. The `JSlider` methods `setValue` and `getValue` should be used. [Note: The `setValue` method is a `public` method that does not return a value and takes one integer argument—the `JSlider` value, which determines the position of the thumb.]

ANS:

```java
// Exercise 14.10 Solution: DrawValue.java
// Program draws the value of the scrollbar on a canvas.
import java.awt.*;
import java.awt.event.*;
import javax.swing.*;
import javax.swing.event.*;

public class DrawValue extends JFrame {
   private DrawCanvas canvas;
   private JTextField display;
   private JLabel label;
   private JSlider slider;
   private JPanel panel;

   public DrawValue()
   {
      super( "DrawValue" );

      // create a panel and set its layout
      panel = new JPanel();
      panel.setLayout( new GridLayout( 1, 3 ) );

      label = new JLabel( "Value:" );

```

Fig. S14.2 Solution to Exercise 14.10. (Part 1 of 4.)

```java
      canvas = new DrawCanvas();

      // set up slider
      slider = new JSlider( SwingConstants.HORIZONTAL, 0, 100, 50 );

      // register JSlider event listener
      slider.addChangeListener(

         new ChangeListener() { // anonymous inner class

            // handle change in slider value
            public void stateChanged( ChangeEvent e )
            {
               canvas.setNumber( slider.getValue() );
               display.setText( String.valueOf( slider.getValue() ) );
            }

         }  // end anonymous inner class

      ); // end call to addChangeListener

      display = new JTextField( "50", 5 );
      display.addActionListener(

         new ActionListener() { // anonymous inner class

            // handle action performed event
            public void actionPerformed( ActionEvent e )
            {
               int value = Integer.parseInt( display.getText() );

               if ( value < slider.getMinimum() ||
                  value > slider.getMaximum() )

                  return;

               canvas.setNumber( value );
               slider.setValue( value );
            }

         }  // end anonymous inner class

      ); // end call to addActionListener

      // add components to panel
      panel.add( label );
      panel.add( display );
      panel.add( slider );

      // add panel to GUI
```

Fig. S14.2 Solution to Exercise 14.10. (Part 2 of 4.)

```
      Container container = getContentPane();
      container.add( canvas, BorderLayout.CENTER );
      container.add( panel, BorderLayout.NORTH );

      setSize( 300, 300 );
      setVisible( true );

   } // end DrawValue constructor

   public static void main( String args[] )
   {
      DrawValue application = new DrawValue();
      application.setDefaultCloseOperation( JFrame.EXIT_ON_CLOSE );
   }

} // end class DrawValue

// class to display slider value
class DrawCanvas extends JPanel {
   private int number;

   // set up panel
   public DrawCanvas()
   {
      number = 50;
      setBackground( Color.black );
      setSize( 200, 200 );
   }

   // set number
   public void setNumber( int theNumber )
   {
      number = theNumber;
      repaint();
   }

   // draw number on panel
   public void paintComponent( Graphics g )
   {
      super.paintComponent( g );
      g.setFont( new Font( "Serif", Font.BOLD, 99 ) );
      g.setColor( Color.red );
      g.drawString( String.valueOf( number ),
         getSize().width / 2 - 40, getSize().height / 2 );
   }

} // end class DrawCanvas
```

Fig. S14.2 Solution to Exercise 14.10. (Part 3 of 4.)

Fig. S14.2 Solution to Exercise 14.10. (Part 4 of 4.)

14.11 Modify the program of Fig. 14.13 by adding a minimum of two new tabs.

ANS:

```
// Exercise 14.11 Solution: JTabbedPaneDemo.java
// Demonstrating JTabbedPane.
import java.awt.*;
import javax.swing.*;

public class JTabbedPaneDemo extends JFrame  {

   // set up GUI
   public JTabbedPaneDemo()
   {
      super( "JTabbedPane Demo " );

      // create JTabbedPane
      JTabbedPane tabbedPane = new JTabbedPane();

      // set up panel1 and add it to JTabbedPane
      JLabel label1 = new JLabel( "panel one", SwingConstants.CENTER );
      JPanel panel1 = new JPanel();
      panel1.add( label1 );
      tabbedPane.addTab( "Tab One", null, panel1, "First Panel" );

      // set up panel2 and add it to JTabbedPane
      JLabel label2 = new JLabel( "panel two", SwingConstants.CENTER );
      JPanel panel2 = new JPanel();
      panel2.setBackground( Color.yellow );
      panel2.add( label2 );
      tabbedPane.addTab( "Tab Two", null, panel2, "Second Panel" );

      // set up panel3 and add it to JTabbedPane
```

Fig. S14.3 Solution to Exercise 14.11. (Part 1 of 3.)

```java
      JLabel label3 = new JLabel( "panel three" );
      JPanel panel3 = new JPanel();
      panel3.setLayout( new BorderLayout() );
      panel3.add( new JButton( "North" ), BorderLayout.NORTH );
      panel3.add( new JButton( "West" ), BorderLayout.WEST );
      panel3.add( new JButton( "East" ), BorderLayout.EAST );
      panel3.add( new JButton( "South" ), BorderLayout.SOUTH );
      panel3.add( label3, BorderLayout.CENTER );
      tabbedPane.addTab( "Tab Three", null, panel3, "Third Panel" );

      // set up panel4 and add it to JTabbedPane
      JLabel label4 = new JLabel( "panel four" );
      JPanel panel4 = new JPanel();
      panel4.setBackground( Color.black );
      JLabel number = new JLabel( "50" );
      number.setFont( new Font( "Serif", Font.BOLD, 99 ) );
      number.setForeground( Color.red );
      panel4.add( number );
      tabbedPane.addTab( "Tab Four", null, panel4, "Fourth Panel" );

      // set up panel5 and add it to JTabbedPane
      JLabel label5 = new JLabel( "panel five" );
      JPanel panel5 = new JPanel();
      JSlider slider =
         new JSlider( SwingConstants.HORIZONTAL, 0, 100, 50 );
      panel5.add( slider );
      tabbedPane.addTab( "Tab Five", null, panel5, "Fifth Panel" );

      // add JTabbedPane to container
      getContentPane().add( tabbedPane );

      setSize( 250, 200 );
      setVisible( true );

   } // end constructor

   public static void main( String args[] )
   {
      JTabbedPaneDemo tabbedPaneDemo = new JTabbedPaneDemo();
      tabbedPaneDemo.setDefaultCloseOperation( JFrame.EXIT_ON_CLOSE );
   }

} // end class JTabbedPaneDemo
```

Fig. S14.3 Solution to Exercise 14.11. (Part 2 of 3.)

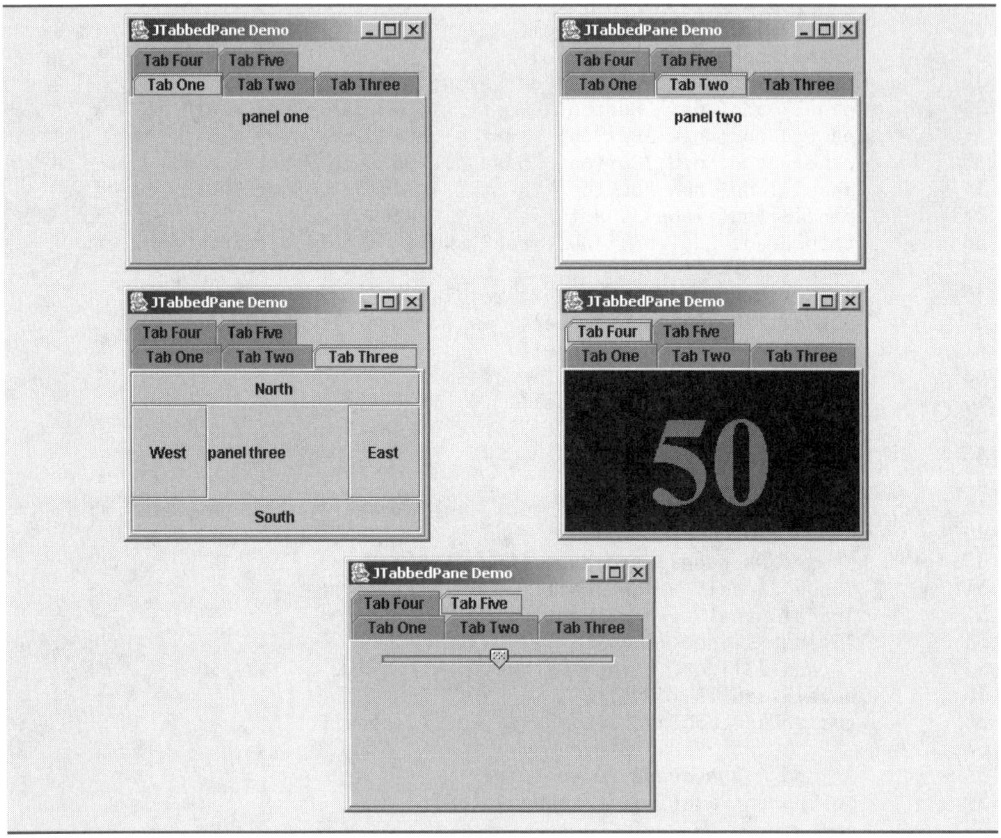

Fig. S14.3 Solution to Exercise 14.11. (Part 3 of 3.)

14.12 Declare a subclass of `JPanel` called `MyColorChooser` that provides three `JSlider` objects and three `JTextField` objects. Each `JSlider` represents the values from 0–255 for the red, green and blue parts of a color. Use the red, green and blue values as the arguments to the `Color` constructor to create a new `Color` object. Display the current value of each `JSlider` in the corresponding `JTextField`. When the user changes the value of the `JSlider`, the `JTextField` should be changed accordingly. Declare class `MyColorChooser` so it can be reused in other applications or applets. Use your new GUI component as part of an applet that displays the current `Color` value by drawing a filled rectangle.

ANS: `MyColorChooser.java`.

```
// Exercise 14.12 Solution: MyColorChooser.java
// JPanel subclass
import java.awt.*;
import java.awt.event.*;
import javax.swing.*;
import javax.swing.event.*;

```

Fig. S14.4 Solution to Exercise 14.12: MyColorChooser.java. (Part 1 of 3.)

```
public class MyColorChooser extends JPanel {
   private JSlider redSlider, blueSlider, greenSlider;
   private JTextField redDisplay, blueDisplay, greenDisplay;
   private JLabel redLabel, blueLabel, greenLabel;
   private Color color;

   // set up GUI
   public MyColorChooser()
   {
      // create sliders and labels
      redLabel = new JLabel( "Red:" );
      redSlider = new JSlider( SwingConstants.HORIZONTAL, 0, 255, 1 );
      redDisplay = new JTextField( "0", 4 );
      redDisplay.setEditable( false );

      greenLabel = new JLabel( "Green:" );
      greenSlider = new JSlider( SwingConstants.HORIZONTAL, 0, 255, 1 );
      greenDisplay = new JTextField( "0", 4 );
      greenDisplay.setEditable( false );

      blueLabel = new JLabel( "Blue:" );
      blueSlider = new JSlider( SwingConstants.HORIZONTAL, 0, 255, 1 );
      blueDisplay = new JTextField( "0", 4 );
      blueDisplay.setEditable( false );

      setLayout( new GridLayout( 3, 3 ) );

      // add sliders and labels to layout
      add( redLabel );
      add( redSlider );
      add( redDisplay );
      add( greenLabel );
      add( greenSlider );
      add( greenDisplay );
      add( blueLabel );
      add( blueSlider );
      add( blueDisplay );

      // add listeners to Sliders
      redSlider.addChangeListener( new ChangeHandler() );
      greenSlider.addChangeListener( new ChangeHandler() );
      blueSlider.addChangeListener( new ChangeHandler() );

      color = Color.black;
   }

   // get color
   public Color getColor()
   {
      return color;
```

Fig. S14.4 Solution to Exercise 14.12: MyColorChooser.java. (Part 2 of 3.)

```
   }

   // get red slider
   public JSlider getRedSlider()
   {
      return redSlider;
   }

   // get green slider
   public JSlider getGreenSlider()
   {
      return greenSlider;
   }

   // get blue slider
   public JSlider getBlueSlider()
   {
      return blueSlider;
   }

   // inner class to handle slider events
   private class ChangeHandler implements ChangeListener {

      // handle change in slider value
      public void stateChanged( ChangeEvent e )
      {
         int red = redSlider.getValue();
         int green = greenSlider.getValue();
         int blue = blueSlider.getValue();

         color = new Color( red, green, blue );

         redDisplay.setText( String.valueOf( red ) );
         greenDisplay.setText( String.valueOf( green ) );
         blueDisplay.setText( String.valueOf( blue ) );
      }

   } // end private inner class ChangeHandler

} // end class MyColorChooser
```

Fig. S14.4 Solution to Exercise 14.12: MyColorChooser.java. (Part 3 of 3.)

ANS: `Palette.java`.

```
// Exercise 14.12 Solution: Palette.java
// Program allows the user to create a custom color.
import java.awt.*;
import java.awt.event.*;
import javax.swing.*;
```

Fig. S14.5 Solution to Exercise 14.12: Palette.java. (Part 1 of 3.)

```
import javax.swing.event.*;

public class Palette extends JApplet implements ChangeListener {
   private MyColorChooser colorChooser;
   private JPanel drawPanel;

   // set up GUI
   public void init()
   {
      // create a new color chooser
      colorChooser = new MyColorChooser();

      // create sliders
      JSlider red = colorChooser.getRedSlider();
      red.addChangeListener( this );

      JSlider green = colorChooser.getGreenSlider();
      green.addChangeListener( this );

      JSlider blue = colorChooser.getBlueSlider();
      blue.addChangeListener( this );

      drawPanel = new JPanel();

      // add components to GUI
      Container container = getContentPane();
      container.add( colorChooser, BorderLayout.SOUTH );
      container.add( drawPanel, BorderLayout.CENTER );

      this.repaint();
   }

   public void stateChanged( ChangeEvent event )
   {
      draw();
   }

   // draw directly on JPanel
   private void draw()
   {
      Graphics g = drawPanel.getGraphics();
      g.setColor( colorChooser.getColor() );
      g.fillRect( 50, 50, 150, 150 );
   }

   // draw directly on JPanel
   public void paint( Graphics gg )
   {
      super.paint( gg );
      draw();
```

Fig. S14.5 Solution to Exercise 14.12: Palette.java. (Part 2 of 3.)

```
    }

} // end class Palette
```

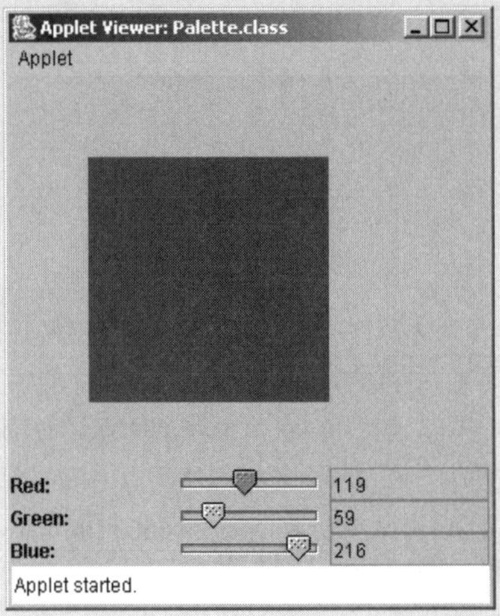

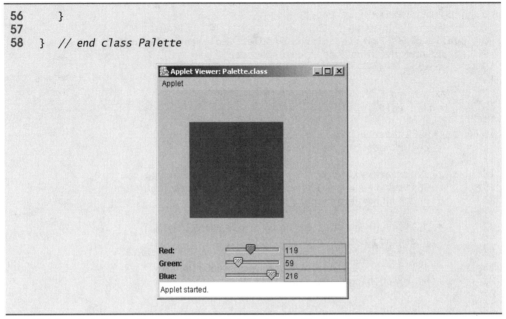

Fig. S14.5 Solution to Exercise 14.12: Palette.java. (Part 3 of 3.)

15

Exception Handling

Solutions to Selected Exercises

15.16 Until this chapter, we have found that dealing with errors detected by constructors is a bit awkward. Explain why exception handling is an effective means for dealing with constructor failure.

ANS: *A thrown exception passes to the outside world the information about the failed constructor and the responsibility to deal with the failure. Exceptions thrown in constructors cause objects built as part of the object being constructed to be marked for eventual garbage collection.*

15.18 Use inheritance to create an exception superclass and various exception subclasses. Write a program to demonstrate that the `catch` specifying the superclass catches subclass exceptions.

ANS:

```
// Exercise 15.18 Solution: Demo.java
// Program demonstrates that the exception
// superclass will catch the subclass exceptions

// exception subclasses
class ExceptionA extends Exception {}

class ExceptionB extends ExceptionA {}

class ExceptionC extends ExceptionB {}

public class Demo {

   public static void main( String args[] )
   {
      // throw ExceptionC
      try {
         throw new ExceptionC();
      }

      // catch ExceptionA and all subclasses
```

Fig. S15.1 Solution to Exercise 15.18. (Part 1 of 2.)

```
      catch( ExceptionA exception1 ) {
         System.err.println( "First Exception subclass caught. \n" );
      }

      // throw ExceptionB
      try {
         throw new ExceptionB();
      }

      // catch ExceptionA and all subclasses
      catch( ExceptionA exception2 ) {
         System.err.println( "Second Exception subclass caught. \n" );
      }

   } // end method main

} // end class Demo
```

```
First Exception subclass caught.

Second Exception subclass caught.
```

Fig. S15.1 Solution to Exercise 15.18. (Part 2 of 2.)

15.20 Write a program that shows that the order of `catch` clauses is important. If you try to catch a superclass exception type before a subclass type, the compiler should generate errors. Explain why these errors occur.

ANS:

```
// Exercise 15.20 part II Solution: CompileError.java
// Program generates a compiler error.
import java.io.*;

public class CompileError {

   public static void main( String args[] )
   {
      try {
         throw new IOException();
      }

      // superclass exception
      catch ( Exception exception ) {
         exception.printStackTrace();
      }

      // subclass exception
      catch ( IOException ioException ) {
```

Fig. S15.2 Solution to Exercise 15.20. (Part 1 of 2.)

```
            System.err.println( "IOException" );
         }
      }

   } // end class CompileError
```

```
CompileError.java:19: exception java.io.IOException has already been caught
      catch ( IOException ioException ) {
      ^
1 error
```

Fig. S15.2 Solution to Exercise 15.20. (Part 2 of 2.)

15.22 Write a program that illustrates rethrowing an exception.

ANS:

```
// Exercise 15.22 Solution: Demo4.java
// Program demonstrates rethrowing an exception

public class Demo4 {

   public static void main( String args[] )
   {
      // call someMethod
      try {
         someMethod();
      }

      // catch Exceptions thrown from someMethod
      catch( Exception exception ) {
          System.err.println( exception.getMessage() + "\n" );
          exception.printStackTrace();
      }
   }

   // call someMethod2; rethrow Exceptions back to main
   public static void someMethod() throws Exception
   {
      // call someMethod2
      try {
         someMethod2();
      }

      // catch Exceptions thrown from someMethod2
      catch( Exception exception2 ) {
         throw exception2;   // rethrow the Exception
      }
   }

   // throw Exception back to someMethod
```

Fig. S15.3 Solution to Exercise 15.22. (Part 1 of 2.)

```
    public static void someMethod2() throws Exception
    {
       throw new Exception( "Exception thrown in someMethod2" );
    }

} // end class Demo4
```

```
Exception thrown in someMethod2

java.lang.Exception: Exception thrown in someMethod2
        at Demo4.someMethod2(Demo4.java:37)
        at Demo4.someMethod(Demo4.java:25)
        at Demo4.main(Demo4.java:10)
```

Fig. S15.3 Solution to Exercise 15.22. (Part 2 of 2.)

16

Multithreading

Solutions to Selected Exercises

16.3 State whether each of the following is *true* or *false*. If *false*, explain why.

a) Method `sleep` does not consume processor time while a thread sleeps.

ANS: *True.*

b) Declaring a method `synchronized` guarantees that deadlock cannot occur.

ANS: *False. Deadlocks can occur if the lock on an object is never released.*

c) `Thread` methods `suspend`, `resume` and `stop` are deprecated.

ANS: *True.*

16.4 Define each of the following terms.

a) thread

ANS: *An individual execution context of a program.*

b) multithreading

ANS: *The ability of more than one thread to execute concurrently.*

c) *Ready* state

ANS: *A state in which the thread is capable of running (if the processor becomes available).*

d) *Blocked* state

ANS: *A state in which the thread cannot use the processor. For example, the blocked state occurs when the thread issues an I/O request.*

e) preemptive scheduling

ANS: *A thread of higher priority enters a running state and is assigned the processor. The thread "preempted" from the processor is placed back in the ready state according to its priority.*

f) `Runnable` interface

ANS: *An interface that provides a* `run` *method. By implementing the* `Runnable` *interface, any class can be executed as a separate thread.*

g) monitor

ANS: *A monitor "watches" shared data between threads. A monitor is responsible for locking an object (i.e., allowing only one thread at a time to execute* `synchronized` *methods on the object).*

h) `notify` method

ANS: *Notifies a waiting thread that an object's lock has been released and that the waiting thread can now attempt to obtain the lock for itself.*

i) producer/consumer relationship

ANS: *A relationship in which a producer and a consumer share common data. The producer typically wants to "produce" (add information) and the consumer wants to "eat" (remove information).*

16.6 What is timeslicing? Give a fundamental difference in how scheduling is performed on Java systems that support timeslicing vs. scheduling on Java systems that do not support timeslicing. Why would a thread ever want to call `yield`?

ANS: *Timeslicing specifies that each thread can use the processor for a limited amount of time. When a thread's timeslice expires, a thread of equal priority gets a chance to execute. Systems that do not support timeslicing will not preempt a thread with the same priority. The waiting thread cannot execute until the thread in the processor has completed its task or removes itself from the processor.*

16.9 Write a Java program to demonstrate that as a high-priority thread executes, it will delay the execution of all lower priority threads.

ANS:

```java
// Exercise 16.9 Solution: Demo.java
// Program priority of threads.
import java.awt.*;
import java.awt.event.*;
import javax.swing.*;

public class Demo extends JFrame {
   private HighThread high;
   private LowThread low;
   private JTextArea output;

   // Demo constructor
   public Demo()
   {
      super( "Demo" );

      // create GUI
      output = new JTextArea( 10, 20 );
      JScrollPane scrollPane = new JScrollPane( output );
      Container container = getContentPane();
      container.add( scrollPane );
      setSize( 250, 200 );
      setVisibility( true );

      // initialize threads
      low = new LowThread( output );
      high = new HighThread( output );

```

Fig. S16.1 Solution to Exercise 16.9. (Part 1 of 3.)

```
      // start threads
      low.start();
      high.start();
   }

   public static void main( String args[] )
   {
      Demo application = new Demo();
      application.setDefaultCloseOperation( JFrame.EXIT_ON_CLOSE );
   }

}  // end class Demo

// subclass of Thread
class HighThread extends Thread {
   private JTextArea display;

   // HighThread constructor
   public HighThread( JTextArea textArea )
   {
      display = textArea;
      setPriority( Thread.MAX_PRIORITY );
   }

   // action to perform on execution
   public void run()
   {
      for ( int x = 0; x < 100; x++ )
         SwingUtilities.invokeLater(

            new Runnable() { // anonymous inner class

               public void run()
               {
                  display.append( "High Priority Thread\n" );
               }

            } // end anonymous inner class

         ); // end call to invokeLater

   } // end method run

}  // end class HighThread

// subclass of Thread
class LowThread extends Thread {
   private JTextArea display;

   // LowThread constructor
```

Fig. S16.1 Solution to Exercise 16.9. (Part 2 of 3.)

```
   public LowThread( JTextArea textArea )
   {
      display = textArea;
      setPriority( Thread.MIN_PRIORITY );
   }

   // action to perform on execution
   public void run()
   {
      for ( int y = 0; y < 100; y++ )
         SwingUtilities.invokeLater(

            new Runnable() { // anonymous inner class

               public void run()
               {
                  display.append( "Low Priority Thread\n" );
               }

            } // end anonymous inner class

         ); // end call to invokeLater

   } // end method run

} // end class LowThread
```

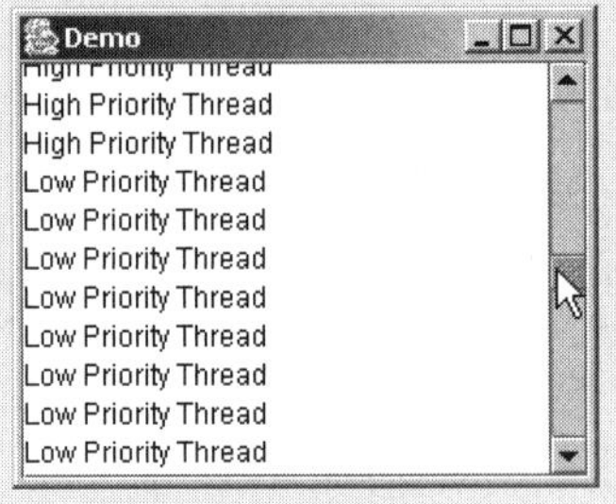

Fig. S16.1 Solution to Exercise 16.9. (Part 3 of 3.)

16.11 Write a Java program that demonstrates a high priority thread using `sleep` to give lower priority threads a chance to run.

ANS:

```
// Exercise 16.11 Solution: Demo3.java
// Program demonstrates high priority threads
import java.awt.*;
import java.awt.event.*;
import javax.swing.*;

```

Fig. S16.2 Solution to Exercise 16.11. (Part 1 of 4.)

```
public class Demo3 extends JFrame {
   private HighThread high;
   private LowThread low;
   private JTextArea output;

   public Demo3()
   {
      super( "Demo3" );

      // set up GUI
      output = new JTextArea( 10, 20 );
      getContentPane().add( output );
      setSize( 250, 200 );
      setVisible( true );

      // initialize threads
      high = new HighThread( output );
      low = new LowThread( output );

      // start threads
      high.start();
      low.start();
   }

   public static void main( String args[] )
   {
      Demo3 application = new Demo3();
      application.setDefaultCloseOperation( JFrame.EXIT_ON_CLOSE );
   }

} // end class Demo3

// subclass of Thread
class HighThread extends Thread {
   private JTextArea display;

   public HighThread( JTextArea textArea )
   {
      display = textArea;
      setPriority( Thread.MAX_PRIORITY );
   }

   // action to perform on execution
   public void run()
   {
      for ( int x = 0; x < 5; x++ ) {
         try {
            sleep( 100 );
         }

```

Fig. S16.2 Solution to Exercise 16.11. (Part 2 of 4.)

```
            // process exception from sleep
            catch ( Exception exception ) {
               JOptionPane.showMessageDialog( null, exception.toString(),
                  "Exception", JOptionPane.ERROR_MESSAGE );
            }

            SwingUtilities.invokeLater(

               new Runnable() { // anonymous inner class

                  public void run()
                  {
                     display.append( "High Priority Thread\n" );
                  }

               } // end anonymous inner class

            ); // end call to invokeLater

         } // end for

      } // end method run

   }  // end class HighThread

   // subclass of Thread
   class LowThread extends Thread {
      private JTextArea display;

      public LowThread( JTextArea textArea )
      {
         display = textArea;
         setPriority( Thread.MIN_PRIORITY );
      }

      // action to perform on execution
      public void run()
      {
         for ( int y = 0; y < 5; y++ )
            SwingUtilities.invokeLater(

               new Runnable() { // anonymous inner class

                  public void run()
                  {
                     display.append( "Low Priority Thread\n" );
                  }

               } // end anonymous inner class

```

Fig. S16.2 Solution to Exercise 16.11. (Part 3 of 4.)

```
      ); // end call to invokeLater

   } // end method run

} // end class LowThread
```

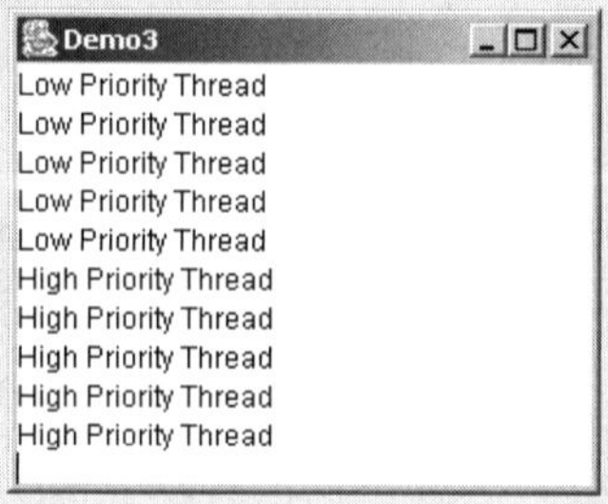

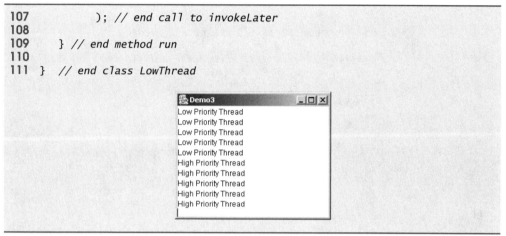

Fig. S16.2 Solution to Exercise 16.11. (Part 4 of 4.)

16.15 Write a program that bounces a blue ball inside an applet. The ball should begin moving with a `mousePressed` event. When the ball hits the edge of the applet, the ball should bounce off the edge and continue in the opposite direction.

ANS:

```
// Exercise 16.15 Solution: Ball.java
// Program bounces a ball around the applet
import java.awt.*;
import java.awt.event.*;
import javax.swing.*;

public class Ball extends JApplet implements Runnable
{
   private Thread blueBall;
   private boolean xUp, yUp, bouncing;
   private int x, y, xDx, yDy;
   private final int MAX_X = 200, MAX_Y = 200;

   public void init()
   {
      // initialize values
      xUp = false;
      yUp = false;
      xDx = 1;
      yDy = 1;
      bouncing = false;

      // let Ball Applet be its own MouseListener
      addMouseListener(

         new MouseListener() {
```

Fig. S16.3 Solution to Exercise 16.15. (Part 1 of 4.)

```java
            public void mousePressed( MouseEvent event )
            {
               createBall( event ); // delegate call to ball starter
            }

            public void mouseExited( MouseEvent event ) {}

            public void mouseClicked( MouseEvent event ) {}

            public void mouseReleased( MouseEvent event ) {}

            public void mouseEntered( MouseEvent event ) {}
         }
      );

      setSize( MAX_X, MAX_Y ); // set size of Applet
   }

   // creates a ball and sets it in motion if no ball exists
   private void createBall( MouseEvent event )
   {
      if ( blueBall == null ) {
         x = event.getX();
         y = event.getY();
         blueBall = new Thread( this );

         bouncing = true; // start ball's bouncing
         blueBall.start();
      }
   }

   // called if applet is closed.  by setting blueBall to null,
   // threads will be ended.
   public void stop()
   {
      blueBall = null;
   }

   // draws ball at current position
   public void paint( Graphics g )
   {
      super.paint( g );

      if ( bouncing ) {
         g.setColor( Color.blue );
         g.fillOval( x, y, 10, 10 );
      }
   }

```

Fig. S16.3 Solution to Exercise 16.15. (Part 2 of 4.)

```
   // action to perform on execution, bounces ball
   // perpetually until applet is closed.
   public void run()
   {
      while ( true ) {

         // sleep for a random interval
         try {
            blueBall.sleep( 20 );
         }

         // process InterruptedException during sleep
         catch ( InterruptedException exception ) {
            System.err.println( exception.toString() );
         }

         // determine new x position
         if ( xUp == true )
            x += xDx;
         else
            x -= xDx;

         // determine new y position
         if ( yUp == true )
            y += yDy;
         else
            y -= yDy;

         // randomize variables for creating next move
         if ( y <= 0 ) {
            yUp = true;
            yDy = ( int ) ( Math.random() * 5 + 2 );
         }

         else if ( y >= MAX_Y - 10 ) {
            yDy = ( int ) ( Math.random() * 5 + 2 );
            yUp = false;
         }

         if ( x <= 0 ) {
            xUp = true;
            xDx = ( int ) ( Math.random() * 5 + 2 );
         }

         else if ( x >= MAX_X - 10 ) {
            xUp = false;
            xDx = ( int ) ( Math.random() * 5 + 2 );
         }

         repaint();
```

Fig. S16.3 Solution to Exercise 16.15. (Part 3 of 4.)

```

      }  // end while

   }  // end method run

}  // end class Ball
```

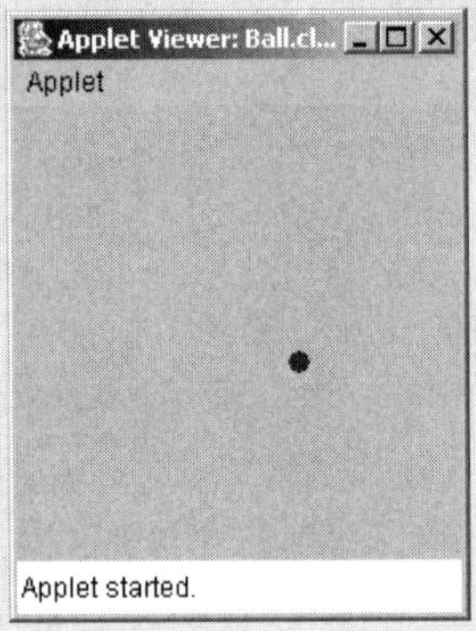

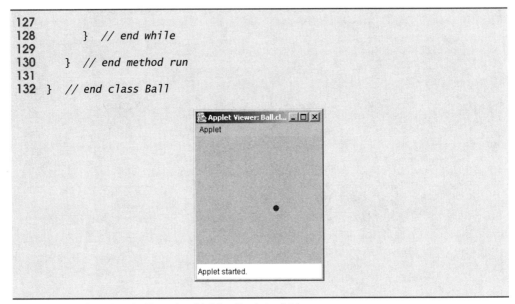

Fig. S16.3 Solution to Exercise 16.15. (Part 4 of 4.)

17

Files and Streams

Solutions to Selected Exercises

17.5 Fill in the blanks in each of the following statements:

a) Computers store large amounts of data on secondary storage devices as __________.

ANS: *files*

b) A(n) __________ is composed of several fields.

ANS: *record*

c) To facilitate the retrieval of specific records from a file, one field in each record is chosen as a(n) __________.

ANS: *key*

d) The majority of information stored in computer systems is stored in __________ files.

ANS: *sequential*

e) The standard stream objects are __________, __________ and __________.

ANS: `System.in`, `System.out`, `System.err`

17.6 Determine which of the given statements are *true* and which are *false*. If *false*, explain why.

a) The impressive functions performed by computers essentially involve the manipulation of zeros and ones.

ANS: *True.*

b) People specify programs and data items as characters; computers then manipulate and process these characters as groups of zeros and ones.

ANS: *True.*

c) A person's five-digit zip code is an example of a numeric field.

ANS: *True.*

d) A person's street address is generally considered to be an alphabetic field.

ANS: *False. This would be a field consisting of letters, digits and spaces (an alphanumeric field) represented with a* `String`.

e) Data items represented in computers form a data hierarchy in which data items become larger and more complex as we progress from fields to characters to bits and so on.

ANS: *False. Data becomes more complex as we progress from bits to characters to fields, etc.*

f) A record key identifies a record as belonging to a particular field.

ANS: *False. A record key identifies a record as belonging to a particular person or entity.*

g) Companies store all their information in a single file in order to facilitate computer processing of the information. When a program creates a file, the file is automatically retained by the computer for future reference.

ANS: *False. Companies typically store information in multiple files.*

17.11 *(Telephone-Number Word Generator)* Standard telephone keypads contain the digits zero through nine. The numbers two through nine each have three letters associated with them. (See Fig. 17.3.) Many people find it difficult to memorize phone numbers, so they use the correspondence between digits and letters to develop seven-letter words that correspond to their phone numbers. For example, a person whose telephone number is 686-2377 might use the correspondence indicated in Fig. 17.3 to develop the seven-letter word "NUMBERS." Each seven-letter word corresponds to exactly one seven-digit telephone number. The restaurant wishing to increase its takeout business could surely do so with the number 825-3688 (i.e., "TAKEOUT").

Each seven-letter phone number corresponds to many separate seven-letter words. Unfortunately, most of these words represent unrecognizable juxtapositions of letters. It is possible, however, that the owner of a barbershop would be pleased to know that the shop's telephone number, 424-7288, corresponds to "HAIRCUT." The owner of a liquor store would, no doubt, be delighted to find that the store's number, 233-7226,

Account number	Dollar amount
300	83.89
700	80.78
700	1.53

Fig. S17.1 Additional transaction records,

Record #	Tool name	Quantity	Cost
3	Electric sander	18	35.99
19	Hammer	128	10.00
26	Jigsaw	16	14.25

Fig. S17.2 Data for Exercise 17.10. (Part 1 of 2.)

Record #	Tool name	Quantity	Cost
39	Lawn mower	10	79.50
56	Power saw	8	89.99
76	Screwdriver	236	4.99
81	Sledgehammer	32	19.75
88	Wrench	65	6.48

Fig. S17.2 Data for Exercise 17.10. (Part 2 of 2.)

Digit	Letters
2	A B C
3	D E F
4	G H I
5	J K L
6	M N O
7	P R S
8	T U V
9	W X Y

Fig. S17.3 Telephone key pad digits and letters.

corresponds to "BEERCAN." A veterinarian with the phone number 738-2273 would be pleased to know that the number corresponds to the letters "PETCARE." An automotive dealership would be pleased to know that the dealership number, 639-2277, corresponds to "NEWCARS."

Write a program that, given a seven-digit number, uses a `PrintStream` object to write to a file every possible seven-letter word combination corresponding to that number. There are 2187 (3^7) such combinations. Avoid phone numbers with the digits 0 and 1.

ANS:

```
// Exercise 17.11 Solution: Phone.java
// Note: phone number must be input in the form #######.
// Only the digits 2 thru 9 are recognized.
import java.io.*;
import java.awt.*;
import java.awt.event.*;
import javax.swing.*;

public class Phone extends JFrame
{
   private int phoneNumber[];
   private JTextField input;
```

Fig. S17.4 Solution for Exercise 17.11. (Part 1 of 4.)

```
   private JLabel prompt;

   public Phone()
   {
      super( "Phone" );
      input = new JTextField( 15 );
      input.addActionListener(

         new ActionListener() { // anonymous inner class

            public void actionPerformed( ActionEvent event )
            {
               calculate(); // calculate character sequences
            }

         } // end anonymous inner class

      ); // end call to addActionListener

      prompt = new JLabel(
         "Enter phone number (digits greater than 1 only):" );

      Container container = getContentPane();
      container.setLayout( new FlowLayout() );
      container.add( prompt );
      container.add( input );

      setSize( 300, 100 );
      setVisible( true );
   }

   // output letter combinations to file
   private void calculate()
   {
      String letters[][] = { { "" },
         { "" },              { "A", "B", "C" }, { "D", "E", "F" },
         { "G", "H", "I" }, { "J", "K", "L" }, { "M", "N", "O" },
         { "P", "R", "S" }, { "T", "U", "V" }, { "W", "X", "Y" } };

      long phoneNumber = Long.parseLong( input.getText() );
      int digits[] = new int[ 7 ];
      for ( int i = 0; i < 7; i++ ) {
         digits[i] = ( int )(phoneNumber % 10);
         phoneNumber /= 10;
      }

      PrintStream output = null;

      try {
         output = new PrintStream( new FileOutputStream( "phone.dat" ) );
```

Fig. S17.4 Solution for Exercise 17.11. (Part 2 of 4.)

```
      }

      catch( IOException exception ) {
         JOptionPane.showMessageDialog( null, exception.toString(),
            "Exception", JOptionPane.ERROR_MESSAGE );

         System.exit( 1 );
      }

      input.setText( "Please wait..." );

      int loop[] = new int[ 7 ];

      // output all possible combinations
      for ( loop[ 0 ] = 0; loop[ 0 ] <= 2; loop[ 0 ]++ )
         for ( loop[ 1 ] = 0; loop[ 1 ] <= 2; loop[ 1 ]++ )
            for ( loop[ 2 ] = 0; loop[ 2 ] <= 2; loop[ 2 ]++ )
               for ( loop[ 3 ] = 0; loop[ 3 ] <= 2; loop[ 3 ]++ )
                  for ( loop[ 4 ] = 0; loop[ 4 ] <= 2; loop[ 4 ]++ )
                     for ( loop[ 5 ] = 0; loop[ 5 ] <= 2; loop[ 5 ]++ )
                        for ( loop[ 6 ] = 0; loop[ 6 ] <= 2; loop[6]++ ) {
                           for ( int i = 6; i >= 0; i-- )
                              output.print(
                                 letters[ digits[ i ] ][ loop[ i ] ] );

                           output.println();
                        }

      input.setText( "Done" );

      output.close(); // close output stream

   } // end method actionPerformed

   public static void main( String args[] )
   {
      Phone application = new Phone();
      application.setDefaultCloseOperation( JFrame.EXIT_ON_CLOSE );
   }

} // end class Phone
```

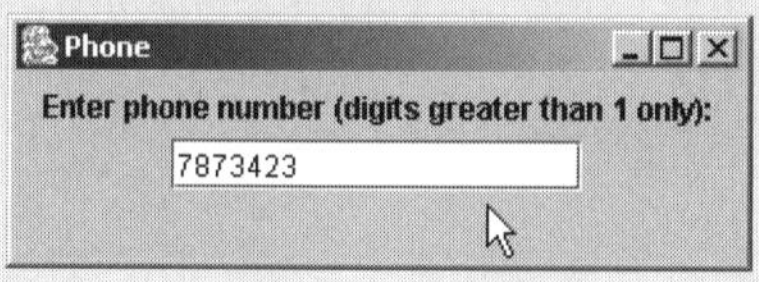

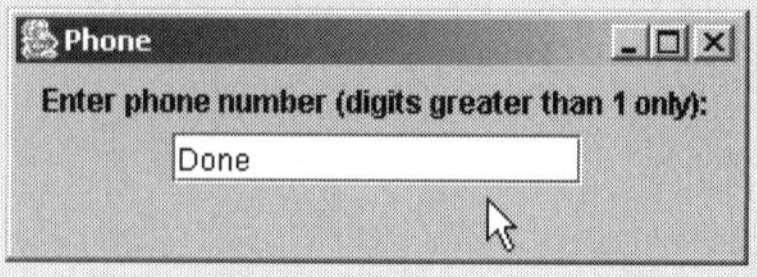

Fig. S17.4 Solution for Exercise 17.11. (Part 3 of 4.)

```
PTPDGAD
RTPDGAD
STPDGAD
PUPDGAD
RUPDGAD
SUPDGAD
PVPDGAD
...
```

Fig. S17.4 Solution for Exercise 17.11. (Part 4 of 4.)

18

Networking

Solutions to Selected Exercises

18.3 Distinguish between connection-oriented and connectionless network services.

ANS: *Connection-oriented services maintain a connection while data is being transferred. Connectionless services do not maintain a connection. Connection-oriented services are generally slower but more reliable.*

18.4 How does a client determine the host name of the client computer?

ANS: `InetAddress.getLocalHost().getHostName()`.

18.5 Under what circumstances would a `SocketException` be thrown?

ANS: *If a* `DatagramSocket` *cannot be constructed properly, a* `SocketException` *is thrown.*

18.6 How can a client get a line of text from a server?

ANS: *Through the* `Socket` *using a stream object (e.g., such as* `ObjectInputStream`*).*

18.7 Describe how a client connects to a server.

ANS: *A client can read a file through a* `URL` *connection by creating a* `URL` *object and issuing an* `openStream` *method call on the* `URL` *object. The* `openStream` *call returns an* `InputStream` *object that can be used to read bytes from the file. Also, a* `DataInputStream` *object can be chained to the* `InputStream` *returned from* `openStream` *to allow other data types to be read from the file on the server.*

18.8 Describe how a server sends data to a client.

ANS: *A client connects to the server by creating a socket using the* `Socket` *class constructor. The name of the server and the port to connect to are passed to the* `Socket` *constructor. Information can be exchanged between the client and server using the socket's* `InputStream` *and* `OutputStream`.

18.14 Use a socket connection to allow a client to specify a file name and have the server send the contents of the file or indicate that the file does not exist.

ANS:

```java
// Exercise 18.14 Solution: Server.java
// Program receives file name from client and sends
// contents of file back to the client if file exists.
import java.net.*;
import java.io.*;

public class Server {
   private ServerSocket server;
   private Socket connection;
   private BufferedReader input;
   private BufferedWriter output;

   // constructor
   public Server()
   {
      // create ServerSocket
      try {
         server = new ServerSocket( 5000, 10 );
      }

      // process problems communicating with server
      catch( IOException exception ) {
         exception.printStackTrace();
         System.exit( 0 );
      }
   }

   // run server
   public void runServer()
   {
      // wait for connection, get streams, read file
      try {

         // allow server to accept connection
         connection = server.accept();

         // set up output stream
         output = new BufferedWriter( new OutputStreamWriter(
            connection.getOutputStream() ) );

         // flush output buffer to send header information
         output.flush();

         // set up input stream
         input = new BufferedReader( new InputStreamReader(
            connection.getInputStream() ) );

         // receive file name from client
```

Fig. S18.1 Solution to Exercise 18.14: Server.java. (Part 1 of 3.)

```
         File file = new File( input.readLine() );

         String result;

         // send file to client
         if ( file.exists() ) {
            BufferedReader fileInput = new BufferedReader(
               new InputStreamReader( new FileInputStream( file ) ) );

            // write first 13 characters
            output.write( "The file is:\n", 0, 13 );
            output.flush();

            // read first line of file
            result = fileInput.readLine();

            while ( result != null ) {
               output.write( result + '\n', 0, result.length() + 1 );
               output.flush();
               result = fileInput.readLine();
            }
         }

         // file does not exist
         else {
            result = file.getName() + " does not exist\n";
            output.write( result, 0, result.length() );
            output.flush();
         }

         // close streams and socket
         output.close();
         input.close();
         connection.close();
      }

      // process problems communicating with server
      catch( IOException ioException ) {
         System.err.println( "IOException has occurred!" );
         ioException.printStackTrace();

         System.exit( 0 );
      }

   } // end method runServer

   public static void main( String args[] )
   {
      Server application = new Server();
      application.runServer();
```

Fig. S18.1 Solution to Exercise 18.14: Server.java. (Part 2 of 3.)

```
    }

} // end class Server
```

Fig. S18.1 Solution to Exercise 18.14: Server.java. (Part 3 of 3.)

```
// Exercise 18.14 Solution: Client.java
// Program receives a file name from user, sends file name
// to server and displays file contents if file exists.
import java.awt.*;
import java.net.*;
import java.io.*;
import java.awt.event.*;
import javax.swing.*;

public class Client extends JFrame implements ActionListener {
   private JTextField fileField;
   private JTextArea contents;
   private BufferedReader bufferInput;
   private BufferedWriter bufferOutput;
   private Socket connection;
   private JPanel panel;
   private JLabel label;
   private JScrollPane scroller;

   // set up GUI, connect to server, get streams
   public Client()
   {
      // set up GUI
      label = new JLabel( "Enter file name to retrieve:" );

      panel = new JPanel();
      panel.setLayout( new GridLayout( 1, 2, 0, 0 ) );
      panel.add( label );

      fileField = new JTextField();
      fileField.addActionListener( this );
      panel.add( fileField );

      contents = new JTextArea();
      scroller = new JScrollPane( contents );

      Container container = getContentPane();
      container.setLayout( new BorderLayout() );
      container.add( panel, BorderLayout.NORTH );
      container.add( scroller, BorderLayout.CENTER );

      // connect to server, get streams
```

Fig. S18.2 Solution to Exercise 18.14: Client.java. (Part 1 of 3.)

```
      try {

         // create Socket to make connection to server
         connection = new Socket( InetAddress.getLocalHost(), 5000 );

         // set up output stream
         bufferOutput = new BufferedWriter( new OutputStreamWriter(
            connection.getOutputStream() ) );

         // flush output buffer to send header information
         bufferOutput.flush();

         // set up input stream
         bufferInput = new BufferedReader( new InputStreamReader(
            connection.getInputStream() ) );
      }

      // process problems communicating with server
      catch( IOException ioException ) {
         ioException.printStackTrace();
      }

      setSize( 500, 500 );
      setVisible( true );
   }

   // process file name entered by user
   public void actionPerformed( ActionEvent event )
   {
      // display contents of file
      try {
         String fileName = event.getActionCommand() + "\n";
         bufferOutput.write( fileName, 0, fileName.length() );
         bufferOutput.flush();
         String output = bufferInput.readLine();

         contents.setText( output );

         // if file exists, dislay file contents
         if ( output.equals( "The file is:" ) ) {
            output = bufferInput.readLine();

            while ( output != null ) {
               contents.append( output + "\n" );
               output = bufferInput.readLine();
            }
         }

         fileField.setEditable( false );
```

Fig. S18.2 Solution to Exercise 18.14: Client.java. (Part 2 of 3.)

```
            fileField.setBackground( Color.lightGray );
            fileField.removeActionListener( this );

            // close streams and socket
            bufferOutput.close();
            bufferInput.close();
            connection.close();
         }

         // end of file
         catch ( EOFException eofException ) {
            System.out.println( "End of file" );
         }

         // process problems communicating with server
         catch ( IOException ioException ) {
            ioException.printStackTrace();
         }
      }

      public static void main( String args[] )
      {
         Client application = new Client();
         application.setDefaultCloseOperation( JFrame.EXIT_ON_CLOSE );
      }

   } // end class Client
```

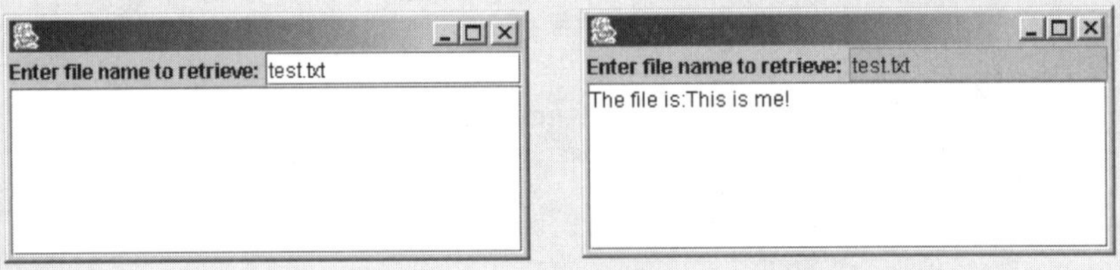

Fig. S18.2 Solution to Exercise 18.14: Client.java. (Part 3 of 3.)

18.17 Multithreaded servers are quite popular today, especially because of the increasing use of multiprocessing servers. Modify the simple server application presented in Section 18.6 to be a multi-threaded server. Then use several client applications and have each of them connect to the server simultaneously. Use a `Vector` to store the client threads. `Vector` provides several methods of use in this exercise. Method `size` determines the number of elements in a `Vector`. Method `get` returns the element (as an `Object` reference) in the location specified by its argument. Method `add` places its argument at the end of the `Vector`. Method `remove` deletes its argument from the `Vector`. Method `lastElement` returns an `Object` reference to the last object you inserted in the `Vector`.

ANS:

```
// Exercise 18.17 Solution: Server2.java
// Program sets up a Server that receives connections from clients, sends
// strings to the clients and receives string from the clients.
import java.io.*;
import java.net.*;
import java.awt.*;
import java.awt.event.*;
import java.util.*;
import javax.swing.*;

public class Server2 extends JFrame {
   private JTextField enterField;
   private JTextArea display;
   private JScrollPane scroller;
   private Vector clients;
   private int numberOfClients;

   // set up GUI
   public Server2()
   {
      super( "Server" );

      numberOfClients = 0;

      // create enterField and register listener
      enterField = new JTextField();
      enterField.setEnabled( false );
      enterField.addActionListener(

         new ActionListener() {  // anonymous inner class

            // send message to clients
            public void actionPerformed( ActionEvent event )
            {
               for ( int i = 0; i < clients.size(); i++ )
                  ( ( ClientThread ) clients.elementAt( i ) ).sendData(
                     event.getActionCommand() );

               enterField.setText( "" );
            }
         }
      );

      display = new JTextArea();
      display.setEnabled( false );
      scroller = new JScrollPane( display );

      Container container = getContentPane();
```

Fig. S18.3 Solution to Exercise 18.17: Server2.java. (Part 1 of 5.)

```
      container.add( enterField, BorderLayout.NORTH );
      container.add( scroller, BorderLayout.CENTER );

      setSize( 300, 150 );
      setVisible( true );

   } // end constructor Server2

   // set up and run server
   public void runServer()
   {
      // set up server and process connections
      try {

         // create ServerSocket
         ServerSocket server = new ServerSocket( 5558, 100 );

         clients = new Vector();

         // accept connections and add ClientThreads to Vector
         while ( true ) {
            display.append( "Waiting for connection\n" );
            numberOfClients++;
            clients.add( new ClientThread( server.accept(),
               display, numberOfClients ) );
            ( ( ClientThread ) clients.lastElement() ).start();

            enterField.setEnabled( true );
         }
      }

      // process problems with I/O
      catch ( IOException ioException ) {
         ioException.printStackTrace();
      }

   } // end method runServer

   public static void main( String args[] )
   {
      Server2 application = new Server2();
      application.setDefaultCloseOperation( JFrame.EXIT_ON_CLOSE );
      application.runServer();
   }

   // private inner class ClientThread manages each Client as a thread
   private class ClientThread extends Thread {
      private int clientNumber;
      private Socket connection;
      private ObjectOutputStream output;
```

Fig. S18.3 Solution to Exercise 18.17: Server2.java. (Part 2 of 5.)

```java
        private ObjectInputStream input;
        private JTextArea display;

        // set up a Client thread
        public ClientThread( Socket socket, JTextArea display, int number )
        {
           this.display = display;
           clientNumber = number;
           connection = socket;

           // obtain streams from Socket
           try {
              output = new ObjectOutputStream(
                 connection.getOutputStream() );
              output.flush();

              input = new ObjectInputStream( connection.getInputStream() );

              sendData( "Connection successful" );

              this.display.append( "\nConnection " +
                 clientNumber + " received from: " +
                 connection.getInetAddress().getHostName() + "\n" );
           }

           // process problems with IO
           catch ( IOException ioException ) {
              ioException.printStackTrace();
           }

        } // end constructor ClientThread

        // send message to client
        public void sendData( String message )
        {
           // send object to client
           try {
              output.writeObject( "SERVER>>> " + message );
              output.flush();
              display.append( "\nSERVER>>>" + message );
           }

           // process problems sending object
           catch ( IOException ioException ) {
              display.append( "\nError writing object" );
           }
        }

        // control thread's execution
        public void run()
```

Fig. S18.3 Solution to Exercise 18.17: Server2.java. (Part 3 of 5.)

```
      {
         String message = null;

         // process connection
         try {

            // read message from client
            do {

               try {
                  message = ( String ) input.readObject();
                  display.append( "\n" + message );
                  display.setCaretPosition( display.getText().length() );
               }

               // process problems reading from client
               catch ( ClassNotFoundException classNotFoundException ) {
                  display.append( "\nUnknown object type received" );
               }

            } while ( !message.equals( "CLIENT>>> TERMINATE" ) );

            display.append( "\nClient terminated connection" );
            display = null;
         }

         // process problems with I/O
         catch ( IOException ioException ) {
            System.out.println( "Client terminated connection" );
         }

         // close streams and socket
         finally {

            try {
               output.close();
               input.close();
               connection.close();
            }

            // process problems with I/O
            catch ( IOException ioException ) {
               ioException.printStackTrace();
            }

            clients.remove( this );
         }

      } // end method run

   } // end class ClientThread
```

Fig. S18.3 Solution to Exercise 18.17: Server2.java. (Part 4 of 5.)

```
}  // end class Server2
```

Fig. S18.3 Solution to Exercise 18.17: Server2.java. (Part 5 of 5.)

```
// Exercise 18.17 Solution: Client2.java
// Program sets up a Client that will read information
// sent from a Server and display the information.
import java.io.*;
import java.net.*;
import java.awt.*;
import java.awt.event.*;
import java.util.*;
import javax.swing.*;

public class Client2 extends JFrame {
   private JTextField enterField;
   private JTextArea displayArea;
   private JScrollPane scroller;
   ObjectOutputStream output;
   ObjectInputStream input;
   String message = "";

   // set up GUI
   public Client2()
   {
      super( "Client" );

      addWindowListener(  // set closing operation

         new WindowAdapter() {

            public void windowClosing( WindowEvent e ) {

               sendData( "TERMINATE" );
               System.exit( 0 );
            }
         }
      );

      // create enterField and register listener
      enterField = new JTextField();
      enterField.setEnabled( false );
      enterField.addActionListener(

         new ActionListener() {  // anonymous inner class

            // send message to server
            public void actionPerformed( ActionEvent event )
```

Fig. S18.4 Solution to Exercise 18.17: Client2.java. (Part 1 of 4.)

```
               {
                  sendData( event.getActionCommand() );
                  enterField.setText( "" );
               }

            } // end anonymous inner class

         ); // end call to addActionListener

         displayArea = new JTextArea();
         displayArea.setEnabled( false );
         scroller = new JScrollPane( displayArea );

         Container container = getContentPane();
         container.add( enterField, BorderLayout.NORTH );
         container.add( scroller, BorderLayout.CENTER );

         setSize( 300, 150 );
         setVisible( true );

      } // end constructor Client2

      // connect to server, get streams, process connection
      public void runClient()
      {
         Socket client;

         // connect to server, get streams, process connection
         try {
            displayArea.setText( "Attempting connection\n" );

            // create Socket to make connection to server
           client = new Socket( InetAddress.getByName( "127.0.0.1" ), 5558 );

            // display connection information
            displayArea.append( "Connected to: " +
               client.getInetAddress().getHostName() );

            // set up output stream for objects
            output = new ObjectOutputStream( client.getOutputStream() );

            // flush output buffer to send header information
            output.flush();

            // set up input stream for objects
            input = new ObjectInputStream( client.getInputStream() );

            displayArea.append( "\nGot I/O streams\n" );

            // enable enterField so client user can send messages
```

Fig. S18.4 Solution to Exercise 18.17: Client2.java. (Part 2 of 4.)

```
         enterField.setEnabled( true );

         // process messages sent from server
         do {

            // read message and display it
            try {
               message = ( String ) input.readObject();
               displayArea.append( "\n" + message );
               displayArea.setCaretPosition(
                  displayArea.getText().length() );
            }

            // catch problems reading from server
            catch ( ClassNotFoundException classNotFoundException ) {
               displayArea.append( "\nUnknown object type received" );
            }

         } while ( !message.equals( "SERVER>>> TERMINATE" ) );

         displayArea.append( "\nClosing connection.\n" );

         // close streams and socket
         output.close();
         input.close();
         client.close();

         displayArea.append( "Connection closed." );

      }  // end try

      // server closed connection
      catch ( EOFException eofException ) {
         System.err.println( "Server terminated connection" );
      }

      // process problems communicating with server
      catch ( IOException ioException ) {
         ioException.printStackTrace();
      }

   } // end method runClient

   // send message to server
   private void sendData( String string )
   {
      // send object to client
      try {
         message = string;
         output.writeObject( "CLIENT>>> " + string );
```

Fig. S18.4 Solution to Exercise 18.17: Client2.java. (Part 3 of 4.)

```
            output.flush();
            displayArea.append( "\nCLIENT>>> " + string );
         }

         // process problems sending object
         catch ( IOException ioException ) {
            displayArea.append( "\nError writing object" );
            ioException.printStackTrace();
         }
      }

   public static void main( String args[] )
   {
      final Client2 application = new Client2();
      application.runClient();
   }

} // end class Client2
```

Fig. S18.4 Solution to Exercise 18.17: Client2.java. (Part 4 of 4.)

19

Multimedia: Images, Animation, Audio and Video

Solutions to Selected Exercises

19.4 Describe the Java methods for playing and manipulating audio clips.

ANS: *Class* `Applet` *method* `play` *and the* `AudioClip` *interface method* `play` *both load the sound and play it once.* `AudioClip` *method* `loop` *continuously loops the audio clip in the background.* `AudioClip` *method* `stop` *terminates an audio clip that is currently playing.*

19.6 *(Randomly Erasing an Image)* Suppose an image is displayed in a rectangular screen area. One way to erase the image is simply to set every pixel to the same color immediately, but this is a dull visual effect. Write a Java program that displays an image and then erases it by using random-number generation to select individual pixels to erase. After most of the image is erased, erase all of the remaining pixels at once. You can draw individual pixels as a line that starts and ends at the same coordinates. You might try several variants of this problem. For example, you might display lines randomly or display shapes randomly to erase regions of the screen.

ANS:

```
// Exercise 19.6 Solution: Eraser.java
// Program slowly erases an image.
import java.awt.*;
import java.awt.event.*;
import javax.swing.*;

public class Eraser extends JApplet implements ActionListener {
   private ImageIcon image;
   private int imageWidth, imageHeight, count, numberOfTimes;
   private boolean showImage;
   private Timer timer;

   // initialize variables, start timer
   public void init()
   {
      showImage = true;
      count = 0;
```

Fig. S19.1 Solution to Exercise 19.6. (Part 1 of 3.)

```

      image = new ImageIcon( "icons2.gif" );
      timer = new Timer( 1, this );
      timer.start();

      imageWidth = image.getIconWidth();
      imageHeight = image.getIconHeight();
      numberOfTimes = imageWidth * imageHeight;
   }

   // draw on JApplet
   public void paint( Graphics g )
   {
      // draw image only once
      if ( showImage == true ) {
         image.paintIcon( this, g, 0, 0 );
         showImage = false;
      }

      g.setColor( getBackground() );

      // loop to increase speed
      for ( int reps = 0; reps < 30; reps++ ) {

         // generate random coordinates within image
         int x = ( int ) ( Math.random() * imageWidth );
         int y = ( int ) ( Math.random() * imageHeight );

         // erase random pixels
         g.drawLine( x, y, x, y );
      }

      // erase remaining pixels when most of image has been erased
      if ( count > numberOfTimes * .95 ) {
         g.fillRect( 0, 0, imageWidth, imageHeight );
      }

      count += 30;

   } // end method paint

   // respond to Timer's events
   public void actionPerformed( ActionEvent event )
   {
      repaint();
   }

} // end class Eraser
```

Fig. S19.1 Solution to Exercise 19.6. (Part 2 of 3.)

Fig. S19.1 Solution to Exercise 19.6. (Part 3 of 3.)

19.8 *(Image Flasher)* Create a Java program that repeatedly flashes an image on the screen. Do this by alternating the image with a plain background-color image.

ANS:

```
// Exercise 19.8 Solution: Flash2.java
// Program flashes an image.
import java.awt.*;
import java.awt.event.*;
import javax.swing.*;

public class Flash2 extends JPanel implements ActionListener {
   private ImageIcon image;
   private int imageWidth, imageHeight;
   private boolean flash;
   private Timer timer;

   // initialize variables, set background color, start timer
   public void init()
   {
      flash = true;

      setBackground( Color.blue );

      image = new ImageIcon( "icons2.gif" );
      imageWidth = image.getIconWidth();
      imageHeight = image.getIconHeight();

      // create and start Timer
      timer = new Timer( 500, this );
      timer.start();
   }

   // draw on JApplet
   public void paint( Graphics g )
   {
      g.setColor( getBackground() );

      // draw image
      if ( flash == true )
         image.paintIcon( this, g, 20, 20 );
```

Fig. S19.2 Solution to Exercise 19.8. (Part 1 of 2.)

```java

      // draw rectangle over image
      else
         g.fillRect( 20, 20, imageWidth, imageHeight );
   }

   // respond to Timer's events
   public void actionPerformed( ActionEvent event )
   {
      flash = !flash;
      repaint();
   }

   public static void main( String args[] )
   {
      Flash2 flash2 = new Flash2();
      JFrame window = new JFrame( "Flashing Images" );
      window.getContentPane().add( flash2 );
      window.setDefaultCloseOperation( JFrame.EXIT_ON_CLOSE );
      window.pack();
      window.setSize( 380, 120 );
      window.setVisible( true );
   }

} // end class Flash2
```

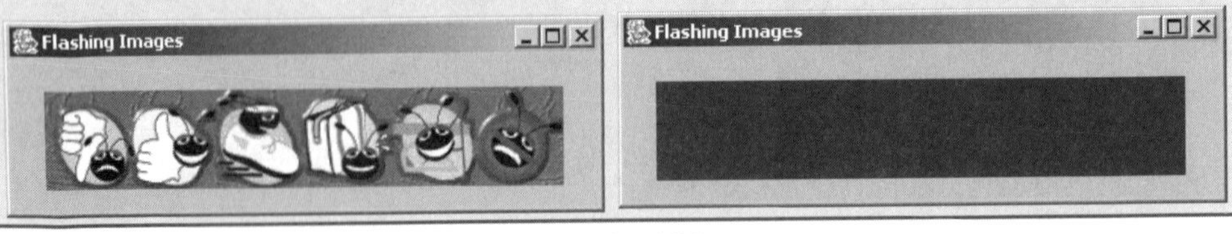

Fig. S19.2 Solution to Exercise 19.8. (Part 2 of 2.)

19.10 *(Calling Attention to an Image)* If you want to emphasize an image, you might place a row of simulated light bulbs around your image. You can let the light bulbs flash in unison, or you can let them fire on and off in sequence one after the other.

ANS:

```java
// Exercise 19.10 Solution: Flash3.java
// Program highlights an image.
import java.awt.*;
import java.awt.event.*;
import javax.swing.*;

public class Flash3 extends JApplet {
   private MyCanvas theCanvas;

```

Fig. S19.3 Solution to Exercise 19.10. (Part 1 of 4.)

```
   // set up GUI to contain a MyCanvas
   public void init()
   {
      // create an image icon
      ImageIcon image1 = new ImageIcon( "icons2.gif" );

      int width = image1.getIconWidth();
      int height = image1.getIconHeight();

      int wide = 12;
      int high = 12;
      Image image2 = createImage( wide, high );
      Image image3 = createImage( wide, high );

      // create canvas and add to GUI
      theCanvas = new MyCanvas( image1.getImage(),
         image2, image3, width, height, wide, high );
      getContentPane().add( theCanvas, BorderLayout.CENTER );
   }

} // end class Flash3

// MyCanvas displays a flashing border
class MyCanvas extends JPanel implements ActionListener {
   private Image image1, image2, image3;
   private Graphics graph2, graph3;
   private Image[] lights;
   private int numLights, rows, columns,
      count, wide, high, width, height;
   private Timer timer;

   // constructor
   public MyCanvas( Image i1, Image i2, Image i3,
      int w, int h, int w2, int h2 )
   {
      int width = w;
      int height = h;
      wide = w2;
      high = h2;
      image1 = i1;
      image2 = i2;
      image3 = i3;

      // create and start a timer
      timer = new Timer( 300, this );
      timer.start();

      // create a yellow light
      graph2 = image2.getGraphics();
      graph2.setColor( Color.black );
```

Fig. S19.3 Solution to Exercise 19.10. (Part 2 of 4.)

```
      graph2.fillRect( 0, 0, wide, high );
      graph2.setColor( Color.yellow );
      graph2.fillOval( 0, 0, 10, 10 );

      // create a white light
      graph3 = image3.getGraphics();
      graph3.setColor( Color.black );
      graph3.fillRect( 0, 0, wide, high );
      graph3.setColor( Color.white );
      graph3.fillOval( 0, 0, 10, 10 );

      // initialize values and create array
      rows = width / wide + 2;
      columns = height / high;
      numLights = 2 * rows + 2 * columns;
      lights = new Image[ numLights ];

      // used to make the lights blink
      int count = 0;

      setSize( wide * rows, high * ( columns + 2 ) );

      repaint();
   }

   // override to produce blinking lights effect
   public void paintComponent( Graphics g )
   {
      super.paintComponent( g );

      // determine whether light is "on" or "off"
      for ( int on = 0; on < numLights; on += 2 ) {

         if ( count == 0 ) {
            lights[ on ] = image2;
            lights[ on + 1 ] = image3;
         }

         else {
            lights[ on ] = image3;
            lights[ on + 1 ] = image2;
         }
      }

      // actually set position of light and draw
      for ( int on = 0; on < numLights; on++ ) {

         // reposition all lights
         // top side, left to right
         if ( on < rows )
```

Fig. S19.3 Solution to Exercise 19.10. (Part 3 of 4.)

```
            g.drawImage( lights[ on ], on * wide, 0, this );

         // right side, top to bottom
         else if ( on >= rows && on < ( rows + columns ) )
            g.drawImage( lights[ on ], (rows - 1) * wide,
               ( on - rows + 1 ) * high, this );

         // bottom side, right to left
         else if ( on >= ( rows + columns ) &&
            on < ( rows * 2 + columns ) ) {

            int xValue = rows - ( on - (rows + columns) ) - 1;
            g.drawImage( lights[ on ],  xValue * wide,
               ( columns + 1 ) * high, this );
         }

         // left side, bottom to top
         else {
            int yValue =
               columns - ( on - ( 2 * rows ) - columns );
            g.drawImage( lights[ on ], 0, yValue * high, this );
         }

      } // end for loop

      g.drawImage( image1, wide, high, wide * (rows - 2 ),
         high * columns, this );

      // Change ++count to y to get the blinking effect
      count = ++count % 2;

   }  // end method paintComponent

   // action to perform when timer indicates
   public void actionPerformed( ActionEvent event )
   {
      repaint();
   }

}  // end class MyCanvas
```

Fig. S19.3 Solution to Exercise 19.10. (Part 4 of 4.)

19.11 *(Image Zooming)* Create a program that enables you to zoom in on or away from an image.

ANS:

```java
// Exercise 19.11 Solution: Zoom.java
// Program zooms an image.
import java.awt.*;
import java.awt.event.*;
import javax.swing.*;

public class Zoom extends JApplet
{
   private ImageIcon image;
   private JButton zoomIn, zoomOut;
   private JPanel drawingPanel, buttonPanel;
   private int imageWidth, imageHeight;

   // set up GUI, initialize variables
   public void init()
   {
      image = new ImageIcon( "icons2.gif" );

      buttonPanel = new JPanel();
      zoomIn = new JButton( "Zoom In" );
      zoomIn.addActionListener(

         new ActionListener() {

            public void actionPerformed( ActionEvent event )
            {
               // zoom in
               imageWidth *= 2;
               imageHeight *= 2;

               // refresh image
               repaint();
            }
         }
      );
      buttonPanel.add( zoomIn );

      zoomOut = new JButton( "Zoom Out" );
      zoomOut.addActionListener(

         new ActionListener() {

            public void actionPerformed( ActionEvent event )
            {
               // zoom out
               imageWidth /= 2;
               imageHeight /= 2;
```

Fig. S19.4 Solution to Exercise 19.11. (Part 1 of 2.)

```java

               // refresh image
               repaint();
            }
         }
      );
      buttonPanel.add( zoomOut );

      imageWidth = image.getIconWidth();
      imageHeight = image.getIconHeight();

      drawingPanel = new JPanel();
      drawingPanel.setSize( 800, 200 );

      // add components to content pane
      Container container = getContentPane();
      container.add( drawingPanel, BorderLayout.CENTER );
      container.add( buttonPanel, BorderLayout.SOUTH );

   } // end method init

   // draw image with appropriate dimensions
   public void paint( Graphics g )
   {
      super.paint( g );

      g.drawImage( image.getImage(), 0, 0, imageWidth,
         imageHeight, drawingPanel );

      buttonPanel.repaint();
   }

} // end class Zoom
```

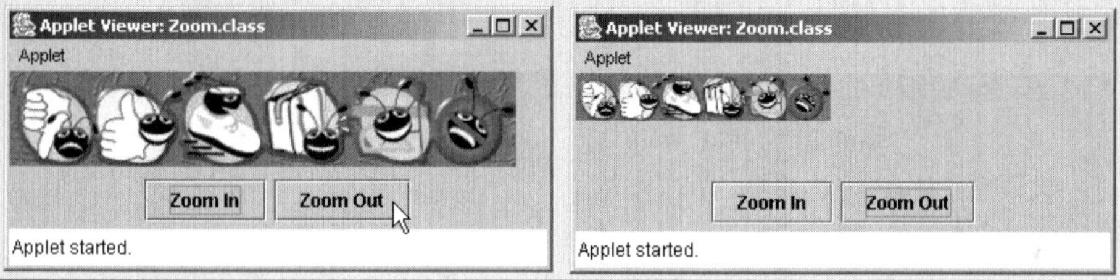

Fig. S19.4 Solution to Exercise 19.11. (Part 2 of 2.)

20

Data Structures

Solutions to Selected Exercises

20.6 Write a program that concatenates two linked-list objects of characters. Class `ListConcatenate` should include a method `concatenate` that takes references to both list objects as arguments and concatenates the second list to the first list.

ANS:

```
// Exercise 20.6 Solution: ListConcatenate.java
// Program concatenates two lists
import com.deitel.jhtp5.ch20.*;

public class ListConcatenate {

   public static void main( String args[] )
   {
      // create two linked lists
      List list1 = new List();
      List list2 = new List();

      // create objects to store in list1
      Character a1 = new Character( '5' );
      Character b1 = new Character( '@' );
      Character c1 = new Character( 'V' );
      Character d1 = new Character( '+' );

      // use List insert methods
      System.out.println( "List 1:" );
      list1.insertAtFront( a1 );
      list1.print();
      list1.insertAtFront( b1 );
      list1.print();
      list1.insertAtBack( c1 );
      list1.print();
      list1.insertAtBack( d1 );
```

Fig. S20.1 Solution to Exercise 20.6. (Part 1 of 3.)

```
        list1.print();

        // create objects to store in list2
        Character a2 = new Character( 'P' );
        Character b2 = new Character( 'c' );
        Character c2 = new Character( 'M' );
        Character d2 = new Character( '&' );

        // use List insert methods
        System.out.println( "List 2:" );
        list2.insertAtFront( a2 );
        list2.print();
        list2.insertAtFront( b2 );
        list2.print();
        list2.insertAtBack( c2 );
        list2.print();
        list2.insertAtBack( d2 );
        list2.print();

        // concatenate lists using method concatenate
        concatenate( list1, list2 );
        System.out.println( "Concatenated list is:" );
        list1.print();
    }

    // concatenates two lists and stores the results in the first list
    public static void concatenate( List one, List two )
    {
        while ( !two.isEmpty() )
            one.insertAtBack( two.removeFromFront() );
    }

} // end class ListConcatenate
```

Fig. S20.1 Solution to Exercise 20.6. (Part 2 of 3.)

```
List 1:
The list is: 5

The list is: @ 5

The list is: @ 5 V

The list is: @ 5 V +

List 2:
The list is: P

The list is: c P

The list is: c P M

The list is: c P M &

Concatenated list is:
The list is: @ 5 V + c P M &
```

Fig. S20.1 Solution to Exercise 20.6. (Part 3 of 3.)

20.8 Write a program that inserts 25 random integers from 0 to 100 in order into a linked list object. The program should calculate the sum of the elements and the floating-point average of the elements.

ANS:

```java
// Exercise 20.8 Solution: ListTest.java
// Program inserts and sorts random numbers in a list,
// prints the sum, and displays the average.
import com.deitel.jhtp5.ch20.*;

class List2 extends List {

   // constructor takes name
   public List2( String name )
   {
      super( name );
   }

   // default constructor
   public List2()
   {
      super();
   }

   // insert number into the sorted list
   public void insert( Integer number )
```

Fig. S20.2 Solution to Exercise 20.8. (Part 1 of 3.)

```java
    {
        // number is the first element in list
        if ( isEmpty() ) {
            ListNode newNode = new ListNode( number );
            firstNode = lastNode = newNode;
        }

        // list already contains elements
        else {

            // if number is less than first value
            if ( ( ( Integer ) firstNode.getObject() ).intValue() >
                                                number.intValue() )

                insertAtFront( number );

            // if number is greater than last value
            else if ( ( ( Integer ) lastNode.getObject() ).intValue() <
                                                number.intValue() )

                insertAtBack( number );

            // search through list for correct placement
            else {
                ListNode current = firstNode.getNext();
                ListNode previous = firstNode;
                ListNode newNode = new ListNode( number );

                while ( current != lastNode && ( ( Integer )
                    current.getObject() ).intValue() < number.intValue() ) {

                    previous = current;
                    current = current.getNext();
                }

                // insert node into list by changing references
                previous.setNext( newNode );
                newNode.setNext( current );
            }
        }

    } // end method insert

    // calculates and returns sum of every value in list
    public int add()
    {
        int sum = 0;
        ListNode current = firstNode;

        // cycle through list adding values to total
```

Fig. S20.2 Solution to Exercise 20.8. (Part 2 of 3.)

```
      while ( current != null ) {
         sum += ( ( Integer ) current.getObject() ).intValue();
         current = current.getNext();
      }

      return sum;
   }

}  // end class List2

// class tests List2 by inserting random numbers
public class ListTest {

   public static void main( String args[] )
   {
      List2 list = new List2();
      Integer newNumber = null;

      // create Integers to store in list
      for ( int k = 1; k <= 25; k++ ) {
         newNumber = new Integer( ( int ) ( Math.random() * 101 ) );
         list.insert( newNumber );
      }

      list.print();

      int sum = list.add();
      System.out.println( "Sum is: " + sum + "\nAverage: " +
         ( ( float ) sum / 25.0f ) );
   }

}  // end class ListTest
```

```
The list is: 2 6 8 8 9 11 24 24 26 34 34 40 45 49 52 55 69 71 73 75 82 85 87 92 93

Sum is: 1154
Average: 46.16
```

Fig. S20.2 Solution to Exercise 20.8. (Part 3 of 3.)

20.10 Write a program that inputs a line of text and uses a stack object to print the words of the line in reverse order.

ANS:

```
// Exercise 20.10 Solution: StackTest.java
// Program prints the words of a line in reverse
import java.awt.*;
import java.util.*;
```

Fig. S20.3 Solution to Exercise 20.10. (Part 1 of 3.)

```
import java.awt.event.*;
import javax.swing.*;

import com.deitel.jhtp5.ch20.*;

public class StackTest extends JFrame {

   private JTextField inputField, outputField;
   private JLabel prompt;
   private JPanel panel;

   public StackTest()
   {
      super( "Reversing a string" );

      // create stack
      final StackComposition stack = new StackComposition();

      // create GUI components
      prompt = new JLabel( "Enter String:" );
      inputField = new JTextField( 20 );

      inputField.addActionListener(

         new ActionListener() { // anonymous inner class

            public void actionPerformed( ActionEvent event )
            {
               // take each word from tokenizer and push on stack
               String text = inputField.getText();
               StringTokenizer tokenizer = new StringTokenizer( text );
               StringBuffer buffer = new StringBuffer( text.length() );

               while ( tokenizer.hasMoreTokens() )
                  stack.push( tokenizer.nextToken() );

               // build reverse string by popping words from stack.
               while ( !stack.isEmpty() ) {
                  Object removedObject = stack.pop();
                  buffer.append( removedObject.toString() + " " );
               }

               outputField.setText( buffer.toString() );
            }

         } // end anonymous inner class
      );

      outputField = new JTextField( 20 );
      outputField.setEditable( false );
```

Fig. S20.3 Solution to Exercise 20.10. (Part 2 of 3.)

```java

      // set up layout and add components
      Container container = getContentPane();
      container.setLayout( new FlowLayout() );
      JPanel panel = new JPanel();
      panel.add( prompt );
      panel.add( inputField );
      container.add( panel );
      container.add( outputField );

      setSize( 400, 100 );
      setVisible( true );
   }

   public static void main( String args[] )
   {
      StackTest application = new StackTest();
      application.setDefaultCloseOperation( JFrame.EXIT_ON_CLOSE );
   }

} // end class StackTest
```

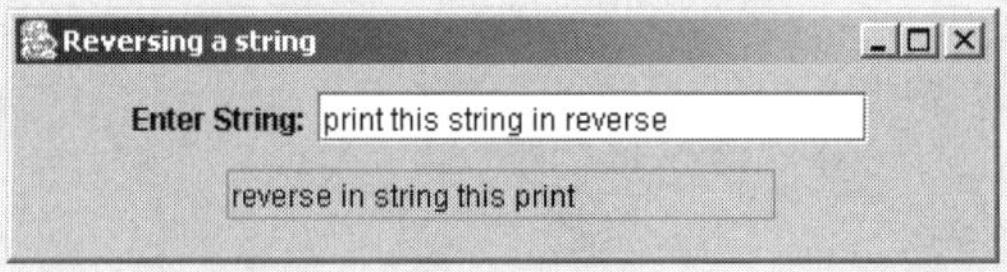

Fig. S20.3 Solution to Exercise 20.10. (Part 3 of 3.)

20.11 Write a program that uses a stack to determine whether a string is a palindrome (i.e., the string is spelled identically backward and forward). The program should ignore spaces and punctuation.

ANS:

```java
// Exercise 20.11 Solution: StackTest2.java
// Program tests for a palindrome.
import java.awt.*;
import java.util.*;
import java.awt.event.*;
import javax.swing.*;
import com.deitel.jhtp5.ch20.*;

public class StackTest2 extends JFrame {
   private JLabel output;

   public StackTest2()
   {
      // create stack
      final StackComposition stack = new StackComposition();

```

Fig. S20.4 Solution to Exercise 20.11. (Part 1 of 3.)

```
      // create GUI components
      final JLabel prompt = new JLabel( "Enter String:" );
      final JTextField input = new JTextField( 20 );
      input.addActionListener(

         new ActionListener() { // anonymous inner class

            public void actionPerformed( ActionEvent event )
            {
               String text = input.getText();
               char letter;

               // cycle through input one char at a time to
               // create stack of all relevant characters
               for ( int i = 0; i < text.length(); i++ ) {
                  letter = text.charAt( i );

                  if ( Character.isLetterOrDigit( letter ) )
                     stack.push( new Character( letter ) );
               }

               Object removedObject = null;
               boolean flag = false;

               // test for palindrome
               try {

                  for ( int count = 0; count < text.length()
                     && !stack.isEmpty(); count++ ) {

                     letter = text.charAt( count );

                     // ignore spaces and punctuation
                     if ( !Character.isLetterOrDigit( letter ) )
                        continue;

                     removedObject = stack.pop();

                     // not palindrome
                     if ( letter != ( ( Character )
                           removedObject ).charValue() ) {
                        flag = true;
                        break;
                     }
                  }

                  // palindrome
                  if ( flag == false )
                     output.setText( "Palindrome" );

```

Fig. S20.4 Solution to Exercise 20.11. (Part 2 of 3.)

```
                  // not palindrome
                  else
                     output.setText( "Not a Palindrome" );
               }

               // catch operations performed on empty list
               catch ( EmptyListException exception ) {
                  System.err.println( "\n" + exception.toString() );
               }

            } // end method actionPerformed

         } // end anonymous inner class
      );

      output = new JLabel( " " );

      // add components to GUI
      Container container = getContentPane();
      container.setLayout( new BorderLayout() );
      container.add( prompt, BorderLayout.NORTH );
      container.add( input, BorderLayout.CENTER );
      container.add( output, BorderLayout.SOUTH );

      setSize( 400, 80 );
      setVisible( true );
   }

   public static void main( String args[] )
   {
      StackTest2 application = new StackTest2();
      application.setDefaultCloseOperation( JFrame.EXIT_ON_CLOSE );
   }

} // end class StackTest2
```

Fig. S20.4 Solution to Exercise 20.11. (Part 3 of 3.)

20.16 Modify Fig. 20.17 and Fig. 20.18 to allow the binary tree to contain duplicates.

```
package com.deitel.jhtp5.ch20;

// class TreeNode definition
public class TreeNode {

```

```
   // public access members
   public TreeNode leftNode;
   public int data;
   public TreeNode rightNode;

   // initialize data and make this a leaf node
   public TreeNode( int nodeData )
   {
      data = nodeData;
      leftNode = rightNode = null;  // node has no children
   }

   // locate insertion point and insert new node
   public synchronized void insert( int insertValue )
   {
      // insert in left subtree
      if ( insertValue < data ) {

         // insert new TreeNode
         if ( leftNode == null )
            leftNode = new TreeNode( insertValue );

         else // continue traversing left subtree
            leftNode.insert( insertValue );
      }

      // insert in right subtree
      else {

         // insert new TreeNode
         if ( rightNode == null )
            rightNode = new TreeNode( insertValue );

         else // continue traversing right subtree
            rightNode.insert( insertValue );
      }

   } // end method insert

   // get right child
   public synchronized TreeNode getRight()
   {
      return rightNode;
   }

   // get left child
   public synchronized TreeNode getLeft()
   {
      return leftNode;
   }

```

```
   // return the data
   public synchronized Object getData()
   {
      return new Integer( data );
   }

}  // end class TreeNode
```

ANS:

```
// Exercise 20.16 Solution: TreeTest.java
// This program tests the Tree class. The solution to 20.16 is mostly
// found in the code of TreeNode, in package com.deitel.jhtp5.ch20
import java.util.*;
import com.deitel.jhtp5.ch20.*;

public class TreeTest {

   public static void main( String args[] )
   {
      Tree tree = new Tree();
      int intVal;

      System.out.println( "Inserting the following values: " );

      // randomly generate numbers and insert in the tree
      for ( int i = 1; i <= 10; i++ ) {
         intVal = ( int ) ( Math.random() * 100 );
         System.out.print( intVal + " " );
         tree.insertNode( intVal );
      }

      // print each of the traversals
      System.out.println ( "\n\nPreorder traversal" );
      tree.preorderTraversal();

      System.out.println ( "\n\nInorder traversal" );
      tree.inorderTraversal();

      System.out.println ( "\n\nPostorder traversal" );
      tree.postorderTraversal();
      System.out.println();
   }

}  // end class Tree
```

Fig. S20.6 Solution to Exercise 20.16. (Part 1 of 2.)

```
Inserting the following values:
42 11 97 76 83 85 83 19 44 64

Preorder traversal
42 11 19 97 76 44 64 83 85 83

Inorder traversal
11 19 42 44 64 76 83 83 85 97

Postorder traversal
19 11 64 44 83 85 83 76 97 42
```

Fig. S20.6 Solution to Exercise 20.16. (Part 2 of 2.)

20.17 Write a program based on the program of Fig. 20.5 and Fig. 20.6 that inputs a line of text, tokenizes the sentence into separate words (you might want to use the `StreamTokenizer` class from the `java.io` package), inserts the words in a binary search tree and prints the inorder, preorder and post-order traversals of the tree.

ANS:

```java
// Exercise 20.17 Solution: TreeNode2.java
// Class TreeNode2 definition.

public class TreeNode2 {

   // public access members
   public TreeNode2 leftNode;
   public String data;
   public TreeNode2 rightNode;

   // initialize data and make this a leaf node
   public TreeNode2( String value )
   {
      data = value;
      leftNode = rightNode = null;  // node has no children
   }

   // get right child
   public synchronized TreeNode2 getRight()
   {
      return rightNode;
   }

   // get left child
   public synchronized TreeNode2 getLeft()
   {
      return leftNode;
   }
```

Fig. S20.7 Solution to Exercise 20.17: TreeNode2.java. (Part 1 of 2.)

```
   // return the data
   public synchronized Object getData()
   {
      return data;
   }

   // insert node
   public void insert( String string )
   {
      // insert in left subtree
      if ( string.compareTo( data ) < 0 ) {

         // insert new TreeNode2
         if ( leftNode == null )
            leftNode = new TreeNode2( string );

         else // continue traversing left subtree
            leftNode.insert( string );
      }

      // insert in right subtree
      else {

         // insert new TreeNode2
         if ( rightNode == null )
            rightNode = new TreeNode2( string );

         else // continue traversing right subtree
            rightNode.insert( string );
      }
   }

}  // end class TreeNode2
```

Fig. S20.7 Solution to Exercise 20.17: TreeNode2.java. (Part 2 of 2.)

ANS:

```
// Exercise 20.17 Solution: Tree2.java
// Class Tree2 definition.
import com.deitel.jhtp5.ch20.*;

public class Tree2 {
   private TreeNode2 root;

   public Tree2()
   {
      root = null;
   }
```

Fig. S20.8 Solution to Exercise 20.17: Tree2.java. (Part 1 of 3.)

```java

   // begin preorder traversal
   public synchronized void preorderTraversal()
   {
      preorderHelper( root );
   }

   // recursive method to perform preorder traversal
   private void preorderHelper( TreeNode2 node )
   {
      if ( node == null )
         return;

      System.out.print( node.data + " " ); // output node data
      preorderHelper( node.leftNode );     // traverse left subtree
      preorderHelper( node.rightNode );    // traverse right subtree
   }

   // begin inorder traversal
   public synchronized void inorderTraversal()
   {
      inorderHelper( root );
   }

   // recursive method to perform inorder traversal
   private void inorderHelper( TreeNode2 node )
   {
      if ( node == null )
         return;

      inorderHelper( node.leftNode );      // traverse left subtree
      System.out.print( node.data + " " ); // output node data
      inorderHelper( node.rightNode );     // traverse right subtree
   }

   // begin postorder traversal
   public synchronized void postorderTraversal()
   {
      postorderHelper( root );
   }

   // recursive method to perform postorder traversal
   private void postorderHelper( TreeNode2 node )
   {
      if ( node == null )
         return;

      postorderHelper( node.leftNode );    // traverse left subtree
      postorderHelper( node.rightNode );   // traverse right subtree
      System.out.print( node.data + " " ); // output node data
```

Fig. S20.8 Solution to Exercise 20.17: Tree2.java. (Part 2 of 3.)

```
   }

   public void insertNode( String string )
   {
      // tree is empty
      if ( root == null )
         root = new TreeNode2( string );

      else // call TreeNode2 method insert on root
         root.insert( string );
   }

}  // end class Tree2
```

Fig. S20.8 Solution to Exercise 20.17: Tree2.java. (Part 3 of 3.)

ANS:

```
// Exercise 20.17 Solution: Tree2Test.java
// Program tests the Tree2 class.
import java.awt.*;
import java.util.*;
import java.awt.event.*;
import javax.swing.*;

public class Tree2Test extends JFrame {
   private JLabel prompt;
   private JTextField inputField;

   public Tree2Test()
   {
      super( "Tokenizer" );
      prompt = new JLabel( "Enter String:" );
      inputField = new JTextField( 25 );
      inputField.addActionListener(

         new ActionListener() {

            public void actionPerformed( ActionEvent event )
            {
               Tree2 tree = new Tree2();

               StringTokenizer tokens =
                  new StringTokenizer( inputField.getText() );

               while ( tokens.hasMoreTokens() )
                  tree.insertNode( tokens.nextToken() );

               System.out.println( "\n\nPreorder traversal" );
               tree.preorderTraversal();
```

Fig. S20.9 Solution to Exercise 20.17: Tree2Test.java. (Part 1 of 2.)

```
                    System.out.println( "\n\nInorder traversal" );
                    tree.inorderTraversal();

                    System.out.println( "\n\nPostorder traversal" );
                    tree.postorderTraversal();
                }
            }
        );

        Container container = getContentPane();
        container.add( prompt, BorderLayout.NORTH );
        container.add( inputField, BorderLayout.SOUTH );

        setSize( 400, 100 );
        setVisible( true );
    }

    public static void main( String args[] )
    {
        Tree2Test application = new Tree2Test();
        application.setDefaultCloseOperation( JFrame.EXIT_ON_CLOSE );
    }

} // end class Tree2Test
```

```
Preorder traversal
I have been a inserted into tree

Inorder traversal
I a been have inserted into tree

Postorder traversal
a been tree into inserted have I
```

Fig. S20.9 Solution to Exercise 20.17: Tree2Test.java. (Part 2 of 2.)

20.19 Write a method `depth` that receives a binary tree and determines how many levels it has.

ANS:

```
// Fig. 20.17: Tree.java
// Definition of class TreeNode and class Tree.
```

Fig. S20.10 Solution to Exercise 20.19. (Part 1 of 4.)

```java

class TreeNode {

   // package access members
   TreeNode leftNode;
   int data;
   TreeNode rightNode;

   // initialize data and make this a leaf node
   public TreeNode( int nodeData )
   {
      data = nodeData;
      leftNode = rightNode = null;  // node has no children
   }

   // locate insertion point and insert new node; ignore duplicate values
   public synchronized void insert( int insertValue )
   {
      // insert in left subtree
      if ( insertValue < data ) {

         // insert new TreeNode
         if ( leftNode == null )
            leftNode = new TreeNode( insertValue );

         else // continue traversing left subtree
            leftNode.insert( insertValue );
      }

      // insert in right subtree
      else if ( insertValue > data ) {

         // insert new TreeNode
         if ( rightNode == null )
            rightNode = new TreeNode( insertValue );

         else // continue traversing right subtree
            rightNode.insert( insertValue );
      }

   } // end method insert

   public TreeNode getLeft()
   {
      return leftNode;
   }

   public TreeNode getRight()
   {
      return rightNode;
```

Fig. S20.10 Solution to Exercise 20.19. (Part 2 of 4.)

```java
   }

} // end class TreeNode

// class Tree definition
public class Tree {
   private TreeNode root;

   public TreeNode getRoot()
   {
      return root;
   }

   // construct an empty Tree of integers
   public Tree()
   {
      root = null;
   }

   // insert a new node in the binary search tree
   public synchronized void insertNode( int insertValue )
   {
      if ( root == null )
         root = new TreeNode( insertValue ); // create the root node here

      else
         root.insert( insertValue ); // call the insert method
   }

   // begin preorder traversal
   public synchronized void preorderTraversal()
   {
      preorderHelper( root );
   }

   // recursive method to perform preorder traversal
   private void preorderHelper( TreeNode node )
   {
      if ( node == null )
         return;

      System.out.print( node.data + " " ); // output node data
      preorderHelper( node.leftNode );     // traverse left subtree
      preorderHelper( node.rightNode );    // traverse right subtree
   }

   // begin inorder traversal
   public synchronized void inorderTraversal()
   {
      inorderHelper( root );
```

Fig. S20.10 Solution to Exercise 20.19. (Part 3 of 4.)

```
    }

    // recursive method to perform inorder traversal
    private void inorderHelper( TreeNode node )
    {
       if ( node == null )
          return;

       inorderHelper( node.leftNode );       // traverse left subtree
       System.out.print( node.data + " " ); // output node data
       inorderHelper( node.rightNode );      // traverse right subtree
    }

    // begin postorder traversal
    public synchronized void postorderTraversal()
    {
       postorderHelper( root );
    }

    // recursive method to perform postorder traversal
    private void postorderHelper( TreeNode node )
    {
       if ( node == null )
          return;

       postorderHelper( node.leftNode );     // traverse left subtree
       postorderHelper( node.rightNode );    // traverse right subtree
       System.out.print( node.data + " " ); // output node data
    }

 } // end class Tree
```

```
Inserting the following values:
66 79 32 81 39 90 71 16 80 66

Preorder traversal
66 32 16 39 79 71 81 80 90

Inorder traversal
16 32 39 66 71 79 80 81 90

Postorder traversal
16 39 32 71 80 90 81 79 66

Tree has a depth of: 3
```

Fig. S20.10 Solution to Exercise 20.19. (Part 4 of 4.)

20.20 (*Recursively Print a List Backwards*) Write a method `printListBackwards` that recursively outputs the items in a linked list object in reverse order. Write a test program that creates a sorted list of integers and prints the list in reverse order.

ANS:

```
// Exercise 20.20 Solution: List3.java
// Class List3 definition.
import com.deitel.jhtp5.ch20.*;

public class List3 extends List {

   public List3( String string )
   {
      super( string );
   }

   public List3()
   {
      this( "list" );
   }

   // insert Integer
   public void insert( Integer number )
   {
      // empty list
      if ( isEmpty() ) {
         ListNode newNode = new ListNode( number );
         firstNode = lastNode = newNode;
      }

      // insert into list
      else {

         // insert at front
         if ( ( ( Integer ) firstNode.getObject() ).intValue() >
                                          number.intValue() )

            insertAtFront( number );

         // insert at back
         else if ( ( ( Integer ) lastNode.getObject() ).intValue() <
                                              number.intValue() )

            insertAtBack( number );

         // insert in middle of list
         else {
            ListNode current = firstNode.getNext();
            ListNode previous = firstNode;
            ListNode newNode = new ListNode( number );

            // locate proper place to insert
            while ( current != lastNode && ( ( Integer )
```

Fig. S20.11 Solution to Exercise 20.20: List3.java. (Part 1 of 2.)

```
                  current.getObject() ).intValue() < number.intValue() ) {

                  previous = current;
                  current = current.getNext();
               }

               previous.setNext( newNode );
               newNode.setNext( current );
            }
         }

      } // end method insert

      // print list backwards
      public void printListBackwards()
      {
         System.out.print( "\nReverse ordered list: " );
         reverse( firstNode );
         System.out.println();
      }

      private void reverse( ListNode currentNode )
      {
         if ( currentNode == null )
            return;

         else
            reverse( currentNode.getNext() );

         System.out.print( ( ( Integer )
            currentNode.getObject() ).intValue() + " " );
      }

   } // end class List3
```

Fig. S20.11 Solution to Exercise 20.20: List3.java. (Part 2 of 2.)

ANS:

```
// Exercise 20.20 Solution: List2Test.java
// Program recursively prints a list of random numbers backwards.

public class List2Test {

   public static void main( String args[] )
   {
      List3 list = new List3();
      Integer number = null;

      // create objects to store in the List
```

Fig. S20.12 Solution to Exercise 20.20: List2Test.java. (Part 1 of 2.)

```
      for ( int i = 1; i <= 25; i++ ) {
         number = new Integer( ( int ) ( Math.random() * 101 ) );
         list.insert( number );
      }

      list.print();
      list.printListBackwards();
   }

} // end class List2Test
```

```
The list is: 0 6 11 16 19 32 35 36 36 41 44 48 48 49 52 58 59 65 65 72 73 79 79
84 95


Reverse ordered list: 95 84 79 79 73 72 65 65 59 58 52 49 48 48 44 41 36 36 35
32 19 16 11 6 0
```

Fig. S20.12 Solution to Exercise 20.20: List2Test.java. (Part 2 of 2.)

20.23 (*Binary Tree Search*) Write method `binaryTreeSearch`, which attempts to locate a specified value in a binary search tree object. The method should take as an argument a search key to be located. If the node containing the search key is found, the method should return a reference to that node; otherwise, the method should return a null reference.

ANS:

```
// Exercise 20.23 Solution: Tree4.java
// Class Tree4 definition.
import com.deitel.jhtp5.ch20.*;

public class Tree4 extends Tree {

   // begin binary tree search
   public TreeNode binaryTreeSearch( Integer key )
   {
      return search( root, key );
   }

   // recursive method to perform binary tree search
   private TreeNode search( TreeNode currentNode, Integer key )
   {
      // key not found
      if ( currentNode == null )
         return null;

      // key found
      if ( key.intValue() ==
         ( ( Integer ) currentNode.getData() ).intValue() )
```

Fig. S20.13 Solution to Exercise 20.23: Tree4.java. (Part 1 of 2.)

```
        return currentNode;

      // traverse down left child subtree
      else if ( key.intValue() <
         ( ( Integer ) currentNode.getData() ).intValue() )

         return search(  currentNode.getLeft(), key );

      //  traverse down right child subtree
      else
         return search(  currentNode.getRight(), key );
   }

}  // end class Tree4
```

Fig. S20.13 Solution to Exercise 20.23: Tree4.java. (Part 2 of 2.)

ANS:

```
// Exercise 20.23 Solution: Tree3Test.java
// Program performs a binary tree search.
import java.util.*;
import com.deitel.jhtp5.ch20.TreeNode;

public class Tree3Test {

   public static void main( String args[] )
   {
      Tree4 tree = new Tree4();
      int number;

      System.out.println( "Inserting the following values: " );

      // create Objects to store in tree
      for ( int i = 1; i <= 10; i++ ) {
         number = ( int ) ( Math.random() * 100 );
         System.out.print( number + " " );
         tree.insertNode( number );
      }

      // create Object to search for in tree
      int searchNumber = ( int ) ( Math.random() * 100 );

      // search
      TreeNode myNode =
         tree.binaryTreeSearch( new Integer( searchNumber ) );

      // Object not in tree
      if ( myNode == null )
```

Fig. S20.14 Solution to Exercise 20.23: Tree3Test.java. (Part 1 of 2.)

```
         System.out.println(
            "\n" + searchNumber + " is not in the tree." );

      // Object found in tree
      else
         System.out.println(
            "\n" + searchNumber + " found in the tree." );
   }

} // end Tree3Test
```

```
Inserting the following values:
59 37 43 73 39 6 89 36 94 65
88 is not in the tree.
```

Fig. S20.14 Solution to Exercise 20.23: Tree3Test.java. (Part 2 of 2.)

20.25 (*Printing Trees*) Write a recursive method `outputTree` to display a binary tree object on the screen. The method should output the tree row-by-row, with the top of the tree at the left of the screen and the bottom of the tree toward the right of the screen. Each row is output vertically. For example, the binary tree illustrated in Fig. 20.20 is output as shown in Fig. 20.21.

Note that the rightmost leaf node appears at the top of the output in the rightmost column and the root node appears at the left of the output. Each column of output starts five spaces to the right of the preceding column. Method `outputTree` should receive an argument `totalSpaces` representing the number of spaces preceding the value to be output. (This variable should start at zero so the root node is output at the left of the screen.) The method uses a modified inorder traversal to output the tree—it starts at the rightmost node in the tree and works back to the left. The algorithm is as follows:

While the reference to the current node is not null, perform the following:
    Recursively call `outputTree` with the right subtree of the current node and `totalSpaces` + 5.
    Use a `for` statement to count from 1 to `totalSpaces` and output spaces.
    Output the value in the current node.
    Set the reference to the current node to refer to the left subtree of the current node.
    Increment `totalSpaces` by 5.

ANS:

```
// Exercise 20.25 Solution: Tree2.java
// Class Tree which can print itself.
import com.deitel.jhtp5.ch20.*;

public class Tree2 {
   private TreeNode root;

   public Tree2()
   {
      root = null;
```

Fig. S20.15 Solution to Exercise 20.25: Tree2.java. (Part 1 of 3.)

```
   }

   // insert a new node in the binary search tree
   public synchronized void insertNode( Integer value )
   {
      if ( root == null )
         root = new TreeNode( value.intValue() );

      else
         root.insert( value.intValue() );
   }

   // begin preorder traversal
   public synchronized void preorderTraversal()
   {
      preorderHelper( root );
   }

   // recursive method to perform preorder traversal
   private void preorderHelper( TreeNode node )
   {
      if ( node == null )
         return;

      System.out.print( node.data + " " );
      preorderHelper( node.leftNode );
      preorderHelper( node.rightNode );
   }

   // begin inorder traversal
   public synchronized void inorderTraversal()
   {
      inorderHelper( root );
   }

   // recursive method to perform inorder traversal
   private void inorderHelper( TreeNode node )
   {
      if ( node == null )
         return;

      inorderHelper( node.leftNode );
      System.out.print( node.data + " " );
      inorderHelper( node.rightNode );
   }

   // begin postorder traversal
   public synchronized void postorderTraversal()
   {
      postorderHelper( root );
```

Fig. S20.15 Solution to Exercise 20.25: Tree2.java. (Part 2 of 3.)

```
    }

    // recursive method to perform postorder traversal
    private void postorderHelper( TreeNode node )
    {
       if ( node == null )
          return;

       postorderHelper( node.leftNode );
       postorderHelper( node.rightNode );
       System.out.print( node.data + " " );
    }

    // begin printing tree
    public void outputTree()
    {
       outputTreeHelper( root, 0 );
    }

    // recursive method to print tree
    private void outputTreeHelper( TreeNode currentNode, int spaces )
    {
       // recursively print right branch, then left
       if ( currentNode != null ) {
          outputTreeHelper( currentNode.getRight(), spaces + 5 );

          for ( int k = 1; k <= spaces; k++ )
             System.out.print( " " );

          System.out.println( currentNode.getData().toString() );
          outputTreeHelper( currentNode.getLeft(), spaces + 5 );
       }
    }

 } // end class Tree2
```

Fig. S20.15 Solution to Exercise 20.25: Tree2.java. (Part 3 of 3.)

ANS:

```
// Exercise 20.25 Solution: Tree2Test.java
// This program tests the Tree2 class.
import java.util.*;

public class Tree2Test {

   public static void main( String args[] )
   {
      Tree2 tree = new Tree2();
      int intVal;
```

Fig. S20.16 Solution to Exercise 20.25: Tree2Test.java. (Part 1 of 2.)

```

      System.out.println( "Inserting the following values: " );

      // create Objects to store in tree
      for ( int i = 1; i <= 10; i++ ) {
         intVal = ( int ) ( Math.random() * 100 );
         System.out.print( intVal + " " );
         tree.insertNode( new Integer( intVal ) );
      }

      // run three different traversal types
      System.out.println ( "\n\nPreorder traversal" );
      tree.preorderTraversal();

      System.out.println ( "\n\nInorder traversal" );
      tree.inorderTraversal();

      System.out.println ( "\n\nPostorder traversal" );
      tree.postorderTraversal();

      // print a depiction of the tree
      System.out.println( "\n\n" );
      tree.outputTree();
   }

}  // end class Tree2Test
```

```
Inserting the following values:
45 22 83 15 49 53 23 30 83 36

Preorder traversal
45 22 15 23 30 36 83 49 53

Inorder traversal
15 22 23 30 36 45 49 53 83

Postorder traversal
15 36 30 23 22 53 49 83 45


     83
               53
          49
45
                    36
               30
          23
     22
          15
```

Fig. S20.16 Solution to Exercise 20.25: Tree2Test.java. (Part 2 of 2.)

21

Java Utilities Package and Bit Manipulation

Solutions to Selected Exercises

21.4 Define each of the following terms in the context of hashing:

a) key

ANS: *Value used to determine the hash table cell where the data is stored.*

b) collision

ANS: *A situation where two keys hash into the same cell.*

c) hashing transformation

ANS: *A high-speed scheme for converting an application key into a table cell.*

d) load factor

ANS: *The ratio of the number of occupied cells in the hash table to the size of the hash table.*

e) space/time trade-off

ANS: *When the load factor is increased, the result is better memory utilization. However, the program runs slower due to increased hashing collisions.*

f) `Hashtable` class

ANS: *Java utilities package class that enables programmers to use hashing.*

g) capacity of a `Hashtable`

ANS: *The number of cells in a hash table.*

21.5 Explain briefly the operation of each of the following methods of class `Vector`:

a) `add`

ANS: *Adds one element to the end of the vector.*

b) `insertElementAt`

ANS: *Inserts one element at the specified position.*

c) `set`

ANS: *Sets the element at the specified position.*

d) `remove`

ANS: *Removes the first occurence of an element from the vector.*

e) `removeAllElements`

ANS: *Removes all vector elements.*

f) `removeElementAt`

ANS: *Removes the element at the specified position.*

g) `firstElement`

ANS: *Returns a reference to the first element in the vector.*

h) `lastElement`

ANS: *Returns a reference to the last element in the vector.*

i) `isEmpty`

ANS: *Determines whether or not a vector is empty.*

j) `contains`

ANS: *Determines if a vector contains a specified search key.*

k) `indexOf`

ANS: *Returns the position of the first occurence of a specified object.*

l) `size`

ANS: *The current number of elements in the vector.*

m) `capacity`

ANS: *The number of elements available for storage (used and unused).*

21.9 Explain briefly the operation of each of the following methods of class `Hashtable`:

a) `put`

ANS: *Adds a key/value pair into the table.*

b) `get`

ANS: *Locate the value associated with the specified key.*

c) `isEmpty`

ANS: *Returns a* `boolean` *value indicating whether or not the hash table is empty.*

d) `containsKey`

ANS: *Determine whether specified key is in the hash table.*

e) `contains`

ANS: *Determine whether specified* `Object` *is in the hash table.*

f) `keys`

ANS: *Return an* `Enumeration` *of the keys in the hash table.*

21.13 Why might you want to use objects of class `BitSet`? Explain the operation of each of the following methods of class `BitSet`:

a) `set`

ANS: *Sets the specified bit to on.*

b) `clear`

ANS: *Sets the specified bits to off.*

c) `get`

ANS: *Determines whether or not the specified bit is on.*

d) `and`

ANS: *Performs a bitwise logical AND.*

e) `or`

ANS: *Performs a bitwise logical OR.*

f) `xor`

ANS: *Performs a bitwise logical XOR.*

g) `size`

ANS: *Returns the size of the bit set.*

h) `equals`

ANS: *Compares two bit sets for equality.*

i) `toString`

ANS: *Converts a bit set to a* `String`.

21.14 Write a program that right shifts an integer variable four bits to the right with sign extension, then shifts the same integer variable four bits to the right with zero extension. The program should print the integer in bits before and after each shift operation. Run your program once with a positive integer and once with a negative integer.

ANS:

```java
// Exercise 21.14 Solution: BitShift.java
// Using the bitwise shift operators
import java.awt.*;
import java.awt.event.*;
import javax.swing.*;
import javax.swing.event.*;

public class BitShift extends JFrame
{
   private JLabel prompt, originalBitLabel, signBitLabel, zeroBitLabel;
   private JTextField inputValue, originalBitField,
      signBitField, zeroBitField;
   private JButton rightSign, rightZero;
   private int number;

   public BitShift()
   {
      super( "BitShifting" );
      prompt = new JLabel( "Enter integer to shift " );
      inputValue = new JTextField( 8 );
```

Fig.S 21.1 Solution to Exercise 21.14. (Part 1 of 4.)

```
        originalBitLabel = new JLabel( "Bit representation: " );
        originalBitField = new JTextField( 22 );
        originalBitField.setEditable( false );

        // components related to the right shift w/ sign extension
        rightSign = new JButton( ">>" );
        rightSign.addActionListener(

           new ActionListener() { // anonymous inner class

              public void actionPerformed( ActionEvent event )
              {
                 // shift bits
                 number = Integer.parseInt( inputValue.getText() );
                 originalBitField.setText( getBits( number ) );

                 int number2 = number >> 4;
                 signBitField.setText( getBits( number2 ) );

                 rightSign.setEnabled( false );
                 rightZero.setEnabled( true );
              }

           } // end anonymous inner class

        ); // end call to addActionListener

        signBitLabel = new JLabel(
           "After right shift with sign extension: " );
        signBitField = new JTextField( 22 );
        signBitField.setEditable( false );

        // components related to the right shift w/ zero extension
        rightZero = new JButton( ">>>" );
        rightZero.addActionListener(

           new ActionListener() { // anonymous inner class

              public void actionPerformed( ActionEvent event )
              {
                 // shift bits
                 int number2 = number >>> 4;
                 zeroBitField.setText( getBits( number2 ) );
                 rightZero.setEnabled( false );
              }

           } // end anonymous inner class

        ); // end call to addActionListener

```

Fig.S 21.1 Solution to Exercise 21.14. (Part 2 of 4.)

```
      rightZero.setEnabled( false );
      zeroBitLabel = new JLabel(
            "After right shift with zero extension: " );
      zeroBitField = new JTextField( 22 );
      zeroBitField.setEditable( false );

      // add components to container
      Container container = getContentPane();
      container.setLayout( new FlowLayout() );
      container.add( prompt );
      container.add( inputValue );
      container.add( originalBitLabel );
      container.add( originalBitField );
      container.add( rightSign );
      container.add( signBitLabel );
      container.add( signBitField );
      container.add( rightZero );
      container.add( zeroBitLabel );
      container.add( zeroBitField );

      setSize(260, 350);
      setVisible( true );
   }

   // return String containing the bit representation of the int
   public String getBits( int value )
   {
      int displayMask = 1 << 31;
      StringBuffer buffer = new StringBuffer( 35 );

      for ( int c = 1; c <= 32; c++ ) {

         // use AND operator and mask to get
         // binary representation of value
         buffer.append( ( value & displayMask ) == 0 ? '0' : '1' );
         value <<= 1;

         // spacing
         if ( c % 8 == 0 )
            buffer.append( ' ' );
      }

      return buffer.toString();
   }

   public static void main( String args[] )
   {
      BitShift application = new BitShift();
      application.setDefaultCloseOperation( JFrame.EXIT_ON_CLOSE );
   }
```

Fig.S 21.1 Solution to Exercise 21.14. (Part 3 of 4.)

```java

} // end class BitShift
```

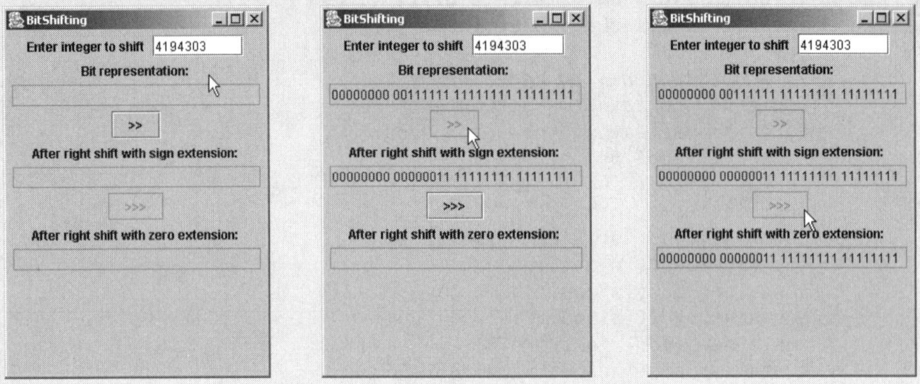

Fig.S 21.1 Solution to Exercise 21.14. (Part 4 of 4.)

21.15 Show how shifting an integer left by one can be used to perform multiplication by two and how shifting an integer right by one can be used to perform division by two. Be careful to consider issues related to the sign of an integer.

ANS:

```java
// Exercise 21.15 Solution: BitShift2.java
// Using the bitwise shift operators
import java.awt.*;
import java.awt.event.*;
import javax.swing.*;
import javax.swing.event.*;

public class BitShift2 extends JFrame {
   private JLabel prompt, status;
   private JTextField value, bits;
   private JButton multiply, divide;

   public BitShift2()
   {
      prompt = new JLabel( "Enter integer to shift " );
      status = new JLabel( "" );

      value = new JTextField( 8 );
      bits = new JTextField( 22 );
      bits.setEditable( false );

      multiply = new JButton( "<< (Multiply by 2)" );
      divide = new JButton( ">> (Divide by 2)" );
```

Fig. S21.2 Solution to Exercise 21.15. (Part 1 of 3.)

```
      multiply.addActionListener(

         new ActionListener() { // anonymous inner class

            public void actionPerformed( ActionEvent event )
            {
               // bit shift
               int number = Integer.parseInt( value.getText() );
               number <<= 1;

               // display results
               value.setText( Integer.toString( number ) );
               bits.setText( getBits( number ) );

            }

         } // end anonymous inner class

      ); // end call to addActionListener

      divide.addActionListener(

         new ActionListener() { // anonymous inner class

            public void actionPerformed( ActionEvent event )
            {
               // bit shift
               int number = Integer.parseInt( value.getText() );
               number >>= 1;

               // display results
               value.setText( Integer.toString( number ) );
               bits.setText( getBits( number ) );
            }

         } // end anonymous inner class

      ); // end call to addActionListener

      Container container = getContentPane();
      container.setLayout( new FlowLayout() );
      container.add( prompt );
      container.add( value );
      container.add( multiply );
      container.add( divide );
      container.add( bits );
      container.add( status );

      setSize( 260, 300 );
      setVisible( true );
```

Fig. S21.2 Solution to Exercise 21.15. (Part 2 of 3.)

```java
   }

   // return String containing the bit representation of the int
   public String getBits( int value )
   {
      int displayMask = 1 << 31;
      StringBuffer buffer = new StringBuffer( 35 );

      for ( int count = 1; count <= 32; count++ ) {
         buffer.append( ( value & displayMask ) == 0 ? '0' : '1' );
         value <<= 1;

         if ( count % 8 == 0 )
            buffer.append( ' ' );
      }

      return buffer.toString();
   }

   public static void main( String args[] )
   {
      BitShift2 application = new BitShift2();
      application.setDefaultCloseOperation( JFrame.EXIT_ON_CLOSE );
   }

}  // end class BitShift2
```

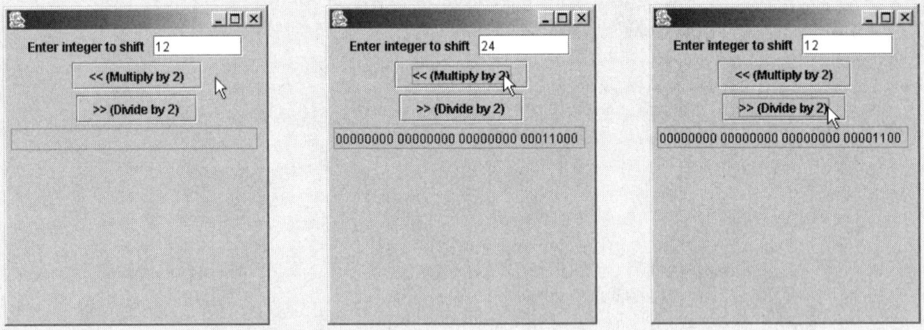

Fig. S21.2 Solution to Exercise 21.15. (Part 3 of 3.)

21.18 Modify your solution to Exercise 20.12 to use class Stack.

ANS:

```java
// Exercise 21.18 Solution: InfixToPostfixConverter.java
// Program converts infix arithmetic expression to a postfix
// expression. Assume a valid expression is entered.
```

Fig. S21.3 Solution to Exercise 21.18. (Part 1 of 4.)

```java
import java.awt.*;
import java.awt.event.*;
import java.util.*;
import javax.swing.*;

public class InfixToPostfixConverter extends JFrame
{
   private JLabel prompt, postfixLabel;
   private JTextField infixField, postfixField;

   public InfixToPostfixConverter()
   {
      prompt = new JLabel( "Enter infix arithmetic expression: " );
      infixField = new JTextField( 20 );
      infixField.addActionListener(

         new ActionListener() { // anonymous inner class

            public void actionPerformed( ActionEvent event )
            {
               // call convertToPostfix
               StringBuffer input = new StringBuffer(
                  infixField.getText() );
               postfixField.setEnabled( true );
               postfixField.setText( convertToPostfix(
                  input ).toString() );
               postfixField.setEditable( false );
            }

         } // end anonymous inner class

      ); // end call to addActionListener

      postfixLabel = new JLabel( "Expression in postfix notation: " );
      postfixField = new JTextField( 20 );
      postfixField.setEnabled( false );

      Container container = getContentPane();
      container.setLayout( new FlowLayout() );
      container.add( prompt );
      container.add( infixField );
      container.add( postfixLabel );
      container.add( postfixField );

      setSize( 260, 150 );
      setVisible( true );
   }

   public StringBuffer convertToPostfix( StringBuffer infix )
   {
```

Fig. S21.3 Solution to Exercise 21.18. (Part 2 of 4.)

```
      StringBuffer postfix = new StringBuffer();
      Stack stack = new Stack();
      stack.push( new Character( '(' ) );
      infix.append( ")" );

      int index = 0;

      // convert expression
      while( !stack.isEmpty() ) {
         char temp = infix.charAt( index );

         // digits
         if ( Character.isDigit( temp ) )
            postfix.append( temp );

         // left parenthesis
         else if ( temp == '(' )
            stack.push( new Character( temp ) );

         // operators
         else if ( isOperator( temp ) ) {
            char top = ( ( Character ) stack.peek() ).charValue();

            while ( isOperator( top ) && !precedence( top, temp ) ) {

               postfix.append( ( ( Character) stack.pop() ).charValue() );
               top = ( ( Character ) stack.peek() ).charValue();
            }

            stack.push( new Character( temp ) );
         }

         // right parenthesis
         else {

            while ( ( ( Character ) stack.peek() ).charValue() != '(' )
               postfix.append( ( (Character) stack.pop() ).charValue() );

            stack.pop();
         }

         index++;
      }

      return postfix;

   } // end method convertToPostfix

   // determine if c is an operator
   public boolean isOperator( char c )
```

Fig. S21.3 Solution to Exercise 21.18. (Part 3 of 4.)

```java
    {
       if ( c == '+' || c == '-' || c == '*' ||
          c == '/' || c == '^' || c == '%' )
          return true;

       return false;
    }

    // return true if operator1 has lower precedence than operator2
    public boolean precedence( char operator1, char operator2 )
    {
       if ( ( operator1 == '+' || operator1 == '-' ) &&
            operator2 != '+' && operator2 != '-' )
          return true;

       else if ( operator1 != '^' && operator2 == '^' )
          return true;

       return false;
    }

    public static void main( String args[] )
    {
       InfixToPostfixConverter application = new InfixToPostfixConverter();
       application.setDefaultCloseOperation( JFrame.EXIT_ON_CLOSE );
    }

 } // end class InfixToPostfixConverter
```

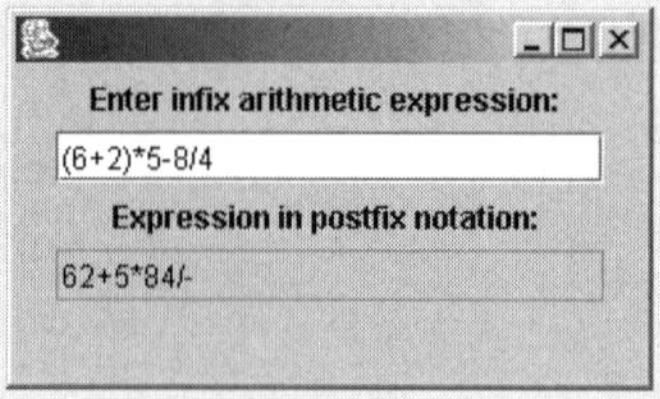

Fig. S21.3 Solution to Exercise 21.18. (Part 4 of 4.)

22

Collections

Solutions to Selected Exercises

22.3 Define each of the following terms:

a) `Collection`

ANS: *Interface* `Collection` *is the root interface in the collections hierarchy from which interfaces* `Set` *and* `List` *are derived.*

b) `Collections`

ANS: *Class* `Collections` *provides* `static` *methods that manipulate collections polymorphically. These methods implement algorithms for searching, sorting, etc.*

c) `Comparator`

ANS: *An object that specifies how a collections objects are ordered.*

d) `List`

ANS: *An interface that descibes the implemention for linked lists.*

22.5 Explain briefly the operation of each of the following `Iterator`-related methods:

a) `iterator`

ANS: *Returns an iterator for a collection.*

b) `hasNext`

ANS: *Determines if a collection has a next element.*

c) `next`

ANS: *Returns the next element in a collection.*

22.6 Determine whether each statement is *true* or *false*. If *false*, explain why.

a) Elements in a `Collection` must be sorted in ascending order before a `binarySearch` may be performed.

ANS: *True.*

b) Method `first` gets the first element in a `TreeSet`.

ANS: *False. The elements need only be sorted.*

c) A `List` created with `Arrays` method `asList` is resizable.

ANS: *False. The* `List` *is fixed length.*

d) Class `Arrays` provides static method `sort` for sorting array elements.

ANS: *True.*

22.7 Rewrite method `printList` of Fig. 22.4 to use a `ListIterator`.

ANS:

```
// Exercise 22.7 Solution: ListTest.java
// Program modifies and prints Lists.
import java.util.*;

public class ListTest {
   private String colors[] = { "black", "yellow", "green",
      "blue", "violet", "silver" };
   private String colors2[] = { "gold", "white", "brown",
      "blue", "gray", "silver" };

   // set up and manipulate LinkedList objects
   public ListTest()
   {
      LinkedList link = new LinkedList();
      LinkedList link2 = new LinkedList();

      // add elements to each list
      for ( int count = 0; count < colors.length; count++ ) {
         link.add( colors[ count ] );
         link2.add( colors2[ count ] );
      }

      link.addAll( link2 );            // concatenate lists
      link2 = null;                    // release resources

      printList( link );

      uppercaseStrings( link );

      printList( link );

      System.out.print( "\nDeleting elements 4 to 6..." );
      removeItems( link, 4, 7 );

      printList( link );
   }

   // output List contents
   public void printList( List list )
   {
      ListIterator iterator = list.listIterator();

```

Fig. S22.1 Solution to Exercise 22.7. (Part 1 of 2.)

```
      System.out.println( "\nlist: " );

      while ( iterator.hasNext() )
         System.out.print( ( String )iterator.next() + " " );

      System.out.println();
   }

   // locate String objects and convert to uppercase
   public void uppercaseStrings( List list )
   {
      ListIterator iterator = list.listIterator();

      while ( iterator.hasNext() ) {
         Object object = iterator.next();   // get item

         if ( object instanceof String )    // check for String
            iterator.set( ( ( String ) object ).toUpperCase() );
      }
   }

   // obtain sublist and use clear method to delete sublist items
   public void removeItems( List list, int start, int end )
   {
      list.subList( start, end ).clear();   // remove items
   }

   public static void main( String args[] )
   {
      new ListTest();
   }

} // end class ListTest
```

```
list:
black yellow green blue violet silver gold white brown blue gray silver

list:
BLACK YELLOW GREEN BLUE VIOLET SILVER GOLD WHITE BROWN BLUE GRAY SILVER

Deleting elements 4 to 6...
list:
BLACK YELLOW GREEN BLUE WHITE BROWN BLUE GRAY SILVER
```

Fig. S22.1 Solution to Exercise 22.7. (Part 2 of 2.)

22.8 Rewrite lines 14–21 in Fig. 22.4 to be more concise by using the `asList` method and the `LinkedList` constructor that takes a `Collection` argument.

ANS:

```
// Exercise 22.8 Solution: ListTest2.java
// Program modifies and prints Lists.
import java.util.*;

public class ListTest2 {
   private String colors[] = { "black", "yellow", "green",
      "blue", "violet", "silver" };
   private String colors2[] = { "gold", "white", "brown",
      "blue", "gray", "silver" };

   // set up and manipulate LinkedList objects
   public ListTest2()
   {
      LinkedList link = new LinkedList( Arrays.asList( colors ) );
      LinkedList link2 = new LinkedList( Arrays.asList( colors2 ) );

      link.addAll( link2 );          // concatenate lists
      link2 = null;                  // release resources

      printList( link );

      uppercaseStrings( link );

      printList( link );

      System.out.print( "\nDeleting elements 4 to 6..." );
      removeItems( link, 4, 7 );

      printList( link );
   }

   // output List contents
   public void printList( List list )
   {
      ListIterator iterator = list.listIterator();

      System.out.println( "\nlist: " );

      while ( iterator.hasNext() )
         System.out.print( iterator.next() + " " );

      System.out.println();
   }

   // locate String objects and convert to uppercase
   public void uppercaseStrings( List list )
   {
      ListIterator iterator = list.listIterator();
```

Fig. S22.2 Solution to Exercise 22.8. (Part 1 of 2.)

```

      while ( iterator.hasNext() ) {
         Object object = iterator.next();   // get item

         if ( object instanceof String )    // check for String
            iterator.set( ( ( String ) object ).toUpperCase() );
      }
   }

   // obtain sublist and use clear method to delete sublist items
   public void removeItems( List list, int start, int end )
   {
      list.subList( start, end ).clear();   // remove items
   }

   public static void main( String args[] )
   {
      new ListTest2();
   }

} // end class ListTest2
```

```
list:
black yellow green blue violet silver gold white brown blue gray silver

list:
BLACK YELLOW GREEN BLUE VIOLET SILVER GOLD WHITE BROWN BLUE GRAY SILVER

Deleting elements 4 to 6...
list:
BLACK YELLOW GREEN BLUE WHITE BROWN BLUE GRAY SILVER
```

Fig. S22.2 Solution to Exercise 22.8. (Part 2 of 2.)

22.12 Rewrite your solution to Exercise 20.8 to use a `LinkedList` collection.

ANS:

```
// Exercise 22.12 Solution: ListTest3.java
// Program inserts and sorts random numbers in a list,
// prints the sum, and displays the average.
import java.util.*;

public class ListTest3 {

   public static void main( String args[] )
   {
      LinkedList list = new LinkedList();
      Integer newNumber = null;
```

Fig. S22.3 Solution to Exercise 22.12. (Part 1 of 2.)

```

        // Create objects to store in the List
        for ( int k = 0; k < 25; k++ ) {
           newNumber = new Integer( ( int ) ( Math.random() * 101 ) );
           list.add( newNumber );
        }

        Collections.sort( list );
        System.out.println( list.toString() );

        int count = 0;

        ListIterator iterator = list.listIterator();

        while ( iterator.hasNext() )
           count += ( ( Integer ) iterator.next() ).intValue();

        System.out.println( "Sum is: " + count + "\nAverage is: " +
              ( ( double ) count / list.size() ) );
     }

  } // end class ListTest3
```

```
[3, 6, 7, 18, 27, 30, 32, 36, 41, 44, 50, 50, 52, 52, 55, 56, 63, 67, 71, 74,
85, 88, 95, 99, 100]
Sum is: 1301
Average is: 52.04
```

Fig. S22.3 Solution to Exercise 22.12. (Part 2 of 2.)

22.16 Write a program that uses a `StringTokenizer` to tokenize a line of text input by the user and places each token in a tree. Print the elements of the sorted tree.

ANS:

```
// Exercise 22.16 Solution: TreeTest.java
// Program tokenizes text input by user and places each
// token in a tree. Sorted tree elements are then printed.
import java.awt.*;
import java.util.*;
import java.awt.event.*;
import javax.swing.*;

public class TreeTest extends JFrame {
   private JLabel prompt;
   private JTextField input;
   private JTextArea display;
   private JPanel panel;

```

Fig. S22.4 Solution to Exercise 22.16. (Part 1 of 3.)

```
   public TreeTest()
   {
      super( "Tokenizer" );

      prompt = new JLabel( "Enter String:" );
      input = new JTextField( 25 );

      input.addActionListener(

         new ActionListener() { // anonymous inner class

            // tokenize input text and add each token to tree
            public void actionPerformed( ActionEvent event )
            {
               TreeSet tree = new TreeSet();
               StringTokenizer tokenizer =
                  new StringTokenizer( input.getText() );

               while ( tokenizer.hasMoreTokens() )
                  tree.add( tokenizer.nextToken() );

               // print tree in text area
               display.setText( tree.toString() );
            }

         } // end anonymous inner class

      ); // end call to addActionListener

      panel = new JPanel();
      panel.add( prompt, BorderLayout.NORTH );
      panel.add( input, BorderLayout.SOUTH );

      display = new JTextArea();

      Container container = getContentPane();
      container.add( panel, BorderLayout.NORTH );
      container.add( new JScrollPane( display ), BorderLayout.CENTER );

      setSize( 400, 100 );
      setVisible( true );
   }

   public static void main( String args[] )
   {
      TreeTest application = new TreeTest();
      application.setDefaultCloseOperation( JFrame.EXIT_ON_CLOSE );
   }

} // end class TreeTest
```

Fig. S22.4 Solution to Exercise 22.16. (Part 2 of 3.)

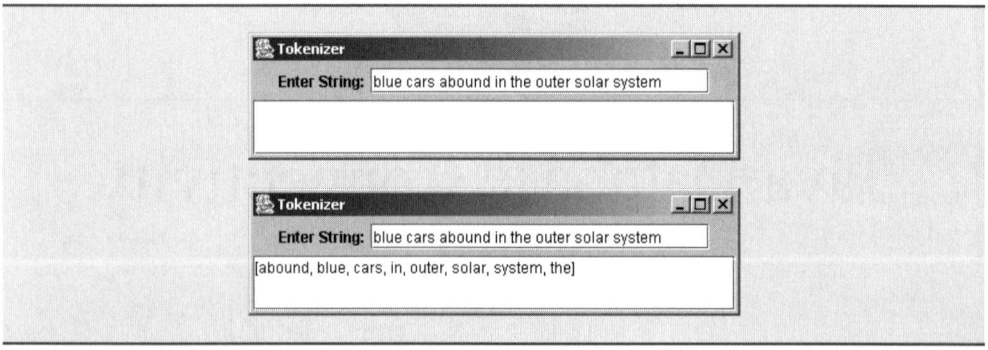
Tokenizer
Enter String:
blue cars abound in the outer solar system
Tokenizer
Enter String:
blue cars abound in the outer solar system
[abound, blue, cars, in, outer, solar, system, the]

Fig. S22.4 Solution to Exercise 22.16. (Part 3 of 3.)

23

Java Database Connectivity (JDBC)

Solutions to Selected Exercises

23.2 Using the techniques shown in this chapter, define a complete query application for the `books` database. Provide a series of predefined queries, with an appropriate name for each query, displayed in a `JComboBox`. Also allow users to supply their own queries and add them to the `JComboBox`. Provide the following predefined queries:

a) Select all authors from the `authors` table.
b) Select all publishers from the `publishers` table.
c) Select a specific author and list all books for that author. Include the title, year and ISBN. Order the information alphabetically by the author's last name and first name.
d) Select a specific publisher and list all books published by that publisher. Include the title, year and ISBN. Order the information alphabetically by title.
e) Provide any other queries you feel are appropriate.

ANS:

```
// Exercise 23.2 Solution: DisplayQueryResults.java
import java.sql.*;
import javax.swing.*;
import java.awt.*;
import java.awt.event.*;
import java.util.*;

public class DisplayQueryResults extends JFrame {
   private Connection connection;
   private Statement statement;
   private ResultSet resultSet;
   private ResultSetMetaData rsMetaData;
   private JTable table;
   private JComboBox inputQuery;
   private JButton submitQuery;
   private JTextField input;

   public DisplayQueryResults()
```

Fig. S23.1 Solution to Exercise 23.2. (Part 1 of 7.)

```
   {
      super( "Select Query. Click Submit to See Results." );

      // The URL specifying the books database to which this program
      // connects to using JDBC
      String url = "jdbc:db2j:books";

      // Load the driver to allow connection to the database
      try {
         Class.forName( "com.ibm.db2j.jdbc.DB2jDriver" );

         connection = DriverManager.getConnection( url );
      }
      catch ( ClassNotFoundException cnfex ) {
         System.err.println( "Failed to load JDBC driver." );
         cnfex.printStackTrace();
         System.exit( 1 );  // terminate program
      }
      catch ( SQLException sqlex ) {
         System.err.println( "Unable to connect" );
         sqlex.printStackTrace();
         System.exit( 1 );  // terminate program
      }

      String names[] = { "All authors", "All publishers", "All books",
         "A specific author", "A specific publisher" };

      // If connected to database, set up GUI
      inputQuery = new JComboBox( names );

      submitQuery = new JButton( "Submit query" );
      submitQuery.addActionListener(

         new ActionListener() {

            public void actionPerformed( ActionEvent e )
            {
               getTable();
            }
         }
      );

      JPanel topPanel = new JPanel();
      input = new JTextField( 20 );
      input.addActionListener(

         new ActionListener() {

            public void actionPerformed( ActionEvent e )
            {
```

Fig. S23.1 Solution to Exercise 23.2. (Part 2 of 7.)

```
               try {
                  String query = input.getText();
                  statement = connection.createStatement();
                  resultSet = statement.executeQuery( query );
                  displayResultSet( resultSet );
               }
               catch ( SQLException sqlex ) {
                  sqlex.printStackTrace();
               }
            }
         }
      );

      JPanel centerPanel = new JPanel();
      centerPanel.setLayout( new FlowLayout() );
     centerPanel.add( new JLabel( "Enter query, author or publisher:" ) );
      centerPanel.add( input );
      topPanel.setLayout( new BorderLayout() );
      topPanel.add( inputQuery, BorderLayout.NORTH );
      topPanel.add( centerPanel, BorderLayout.CENTER );
      topPanel.add( submitQuery, BorderLayout.SOUTH );

      table = new JTable( 4, 4 );

      Container c = getContentPane();
      c.setLayout( new BorderLayout() );
      c.add( topPanel, BorderLayout.NORTH );
      c.add( table, BorderLayout.CENTER );

      getTable();

      setSize( 500, 500 );
      setVisible( true );

   } // end constructor DisplayQueryResult

   private void getTable()
   {
      try {
         int selection = inputQuery.getSelectedIndex();
         String query = null;

         switch ( selection ) {
            case 0:
               query = "SELECT * FROM Authors";
               break;
            case 1:
               query = "SELECT * FROM Publishers";
               break;
```

Fig. S23.1 Solution to Exercise 23.2. (Part 3 of 7.)

```
            case 2:
               query = "SELECT * FROM TITLES";
               break;
            case 3:
               query = "SELECT Authors.LastName, Authors.FirstName, "+
                  "Titles.Title, Titles.Price, " + "Titles.ISBN FROM " +
                  "Titles INNER JOIN (AuthorISBN INNER JOIN Authors ON" +
                  " AuthorISBN.AuthorID = Authors.AuthorID) ON " +
                  "Titles.ISBN = AuthorISBN.ISBN WHERE Authors.LastName" +
                  " = '" + input.getText() + "' ORDER BY " +
                  "Authors.LastName, Authors.FirstName ASC";
                  break;
            case 4:
               query = "SELECT Publishers.PublisherName, Titles.Title, " +
                  "Titles.Price, Titles.ISBN FROM Titles INNER JOIN " +
                  "Publishers ON Publishers.PublisherID = " +
                  "Titles.PublisherID WHERE Publishers.PublisherName = '"
                  + input.getText() + "' ORDER BY Titles.Title ASC";
                  break;
         }

         statement = connection.createStatement();
         resultSet = statement.executeQuery( query );
         displayResultSet( resultSet );

      } // end try

      catch ( SQLException sqlex ) {
         sqlex.printStackTrace();
      }

   } // end method getTable

   private void displayResultSet( ResultSet rs ) throws SQLException
   {
      // position to first record
      boolean moreRecords = rs.next();

      // If there are no records, display a message
      if ( !moreRecords ) {
         JOptionPane.showMessageDialog( this,
            "ResultSet contained no records" );
         setTitle( "No records to display" );
         return;
      }

      Vector columnHeads = new Vector();
      Vector rows = new Vector();

      try {
```

Fig. S23.1 Solution to Exercise 23.2. (Part 4 of 7.)

```
         // get column heads
         ResultSetMetaData rsmd = rs.getMetaData();

         for ( int i = 1; i <= rsmd.getColumnCount(); ++i )
            columnHeads.addElement( rsmd.getColumnName( i ) );

         // get row data
         do {
            rows.addElement( getNextRow( rs, rsmd ) );
         } while ( rs.next() );

         // display table with ResultSet contents
         table = new JTable( rows, columnHeads );
         JScrollPane scroller = new JScrollPane( table );
         Container c = getContentPane();
         c.remove( 1 );
         c.add( scroller, BorderLayout.CENTER );
         c.validate();

      } // end try

      catch ( SQLException sqlex ) {
         sqlex.printStackTrace();
      }

   } // end method displayResultSet

   private Vector getNextRow( ResultSet rs,
      ResultSetMetaData rsmd ) throws SQLException
   {
      Vector currentRow = new Vector();

      for ( int i = 1; i <= rsmd.getColumnCount(); ++i )
         switch( rsmd.getColumnType( i ) ) {
            case Types.VARCHAR:
            case Types.LONGVARCHAR:
                  currentRow.addElement( rs.getString( i ) );
               break;
            case Types.INTEGER:
                  currentRow.addElement( new Long( rs.getLong( i ) ) );
               break;
            case Types.REAL:
                  currentRow.addElement( new Float( rs.getDouble( i ) ) );
               break;
            default:
               System.out.println( "Type was: " +
                  rsmd.getColumnTypeName( i ) );
         }

      return currentRow;
```

Fig. S23.1 Solution to Exercise 23.2. (Part 5 of 7.)

```

   } // end method getNextRow

   public void shutDown()
   {
      try {
         connection.close();
      }
      catch ( SQLException sqlex ) {
         System.err.println( "Unable to disconnect" );
         sqlex.printStackTrace();
      }
   }

   public static void main( String args[] )
   {
      final DisplayQueryResults app = new DisplayQueryResults();
      app.addWindowListener(

         new WindowAdapter() {

            public void windowClosing( WindowEvent e )
            {
               app.shutDown();
               System.exit( 0 );
            }
         }
      );
   }

} // end class DisplayQueryResults
```

Fig. S23.1 Solution to Exercise 23.2. (Part 6 of 7.)

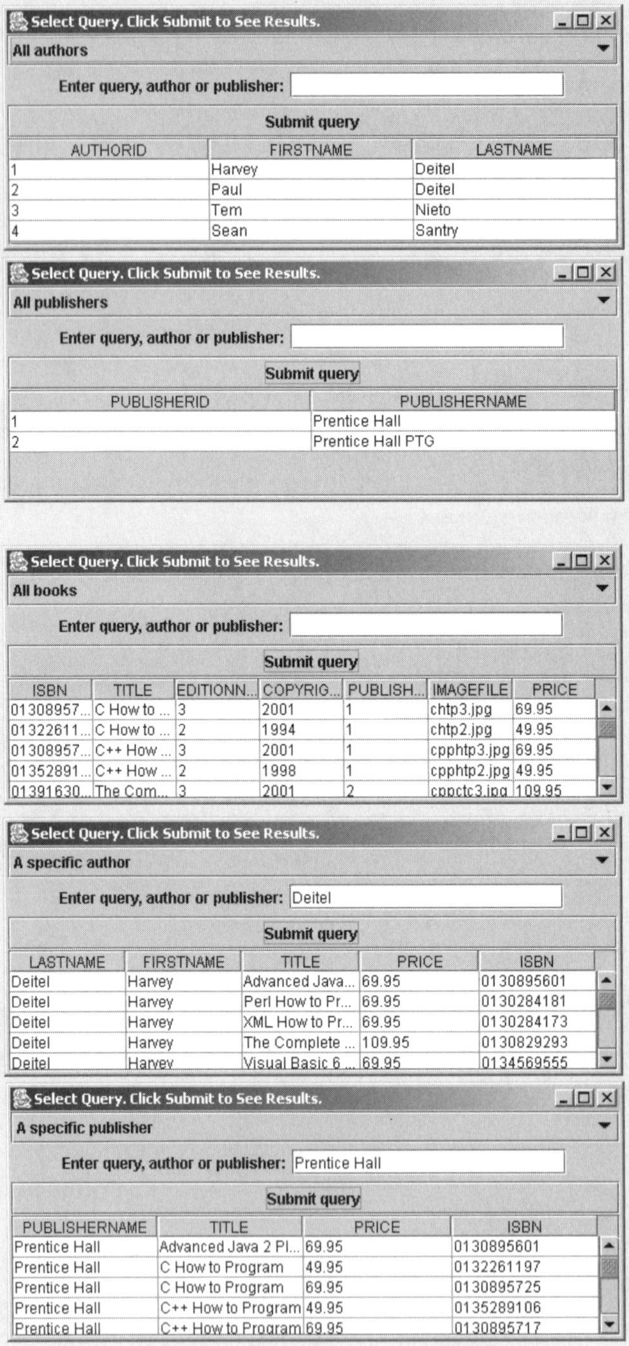
Select Query. Click Submit to See Results.
All authors
Enter query, author or publisher:
Submit query
AUTHORID FIRSTNAME LASTNAME
1 Harvey Deitel
2 Paul Deitel
3 Tem Nieto
4 Sean Santry
Select Query. Click Submit to See Results.
All publishers
Enter query, author or publisher:
Submit query
PUBLISHERID PUBLISHERNAME
1 Prentice Hall
2 Prentice Hall PTG
Select Query. Click Submit to See Results.
All books
Enter query, author or publisher:
Submit query
ISBN TITLE EDITIONN... COPYRIG... PUBLISH... IMAGEFILE PRICE
01308957... C How to ... 3 2001 1 chtp3.jpg 69.95
01322611... C How to ... 2 1994 1 chtp2.jpg 49.95
01308957... C++ How ... 3 2001 1 cpphtp3.jpg 69.95
01352891... C++ How ... 2 1998 1 cpphtp2.jpg 49.95
Select Query. Click Submit to See Results.
A specific author
Enter query, author or publisher: Deitel
Submit query
LASTNAME FIRSTNAME TITLE PRICE ISBN
Deitel Harvey Advanced Java... 69.95 0130895601
Deitel Harvey Perl How to Pr... 69.95 0130284181
Deitel Harvey XML How to Pr... 69.95 0130284173
Deitel Harvey The Complete ... 109.95 0130829293
Select Query. Click Submit to See Results.
A specific publisher
Enter query, author or publisher: Prentice Hall
Submit query
PUBLISHERNAME TITLE PRICE ISBN
Prentice Hall Advanced Java 2 Pl... 69.95 0130895601
Prentice Hall C How to Program 49.95 0132261197
Prentice Hall C How to Program 69.95 0130895725
Prentice Hall C++ How to Program 49.95 0135289106

Fig. S23.1 Solution to Exercise 23.2. (Part 7 of 7.)

23.4 In Section 10.7, we introduced an employee-payroll hierarchy to calculate each employee's payroll. In this exercise, we provide a database of employees that corresponds to the employee-payroll hierarchy. (A SQL script to create the employee database is provided with the examples for this chapter on the CD that accompanies this text and on our Web site `www.deitel.com`.) Write an application that allows:

a) Add employees to the Employee table.
b) For each employee added to the table, add payroll to the corresponding table. For example, for a salaried employee add the payroll information to the salariedEmployees table.

ANS:

```java
// Exercise 23.4 solution: AddEmployees.java
import java.sql.*;
import java.awt.*;
import java.awt.event.*;
import java.util.*;
import javax.swing.*;

public class AddEmployees extends JFrame {
   private Connection connection;
   private Statement statement;
   private ResultSet resultSet;
   private ResultSetMetaData rsMetaData;
   private Container container;
   private JTable table;
   private JTextField input;
   private JButton addSalariedEmployee, addCommissionEmployee,
      addBasePlusCommissionEmployee, addHourlyEmployee;

   public AddEmployees()
   {
      super( "Add Employees" );

      // The URL specifying the books database to which this program
      // connects to using JDBC
      String url = "jdbc:db2j:employees";

      // Load the driver to allow connection to the database
      try {
         Class.forName( "com.ibm.db2j.jdbc.DB2jDriver" );

         connection = DriverManager.getConnection( url );
      }
      catch ( ClassNotFoundException cnfex ) {
         System.err.println( "Failed to load JDBC driver." );
         cnfex.printStackTrace();
         System.exit( 1 );  // terminate program
      }
      catch ( SQLException sqlex ) {
         System.err.println( "Unable to connect" );
         sqlex.printStackTrace();
```

Fig. S23.2 Solution to Exercise 23.4. (Part 1 of 8.)

```
         System.exit( 1 );  // terminate program
      }

      // if connected to database, set up GUI
      JPanel topPanel = new JPanel();
      topPanel.setLayout( new FlowLayout() );
      topPanel.add( new JLabel( "Enter query to insert employees:" ) );

      input = new JTextField( 50 );
      topPanel.add( input );
      input.addActionListener(

         new ActionListener() {

            public void actionPerformed( ActionEvent e )
            {
               addEmployee( input.getText() );
            }
         }
      );

      // create four buttons that allow user to add specific employee
      JPanel centerPanel = new JPanel();
      centerPanel.setLayout( new FlowLayout() );

      addSalariedEmployee = new JButton( "Add Salaried Employee" );
      addSalariedEmployee.addActionListener( new ButtonHandler() );

      addCommissionEmployee = new JButton( "Add Commission Employee" );
      addCommissionEmployee.addActionListener( new ButtonHandler() );

      addBasePlusCommissionEmployee =
         new JButton( "Add Base Plus Commission Employee" );
      addBasePlusCommissionEmployee.addActionListener(
         new ButtonHandler() );

      addHourlyEmployee = new JButton( "Add Hourly Employee" );
      addHourlyEmployee.addActionListener( new ButtonHandler() );

      // add four buttons to centerPanel
      centerPanel.add( addSalariedEmployee );
      centerPanel.add( addCommissionEmployee );
      centerPanel.add( addBasePlusCommissionEmployee );
      centerPanel.add( addHourlyEmployee );

      JPanel inputPanel = new JPanel();
      inputPanel.setLayout( new BorderLayout() );
      inputPanel.add( topPanel, BorderLayout.NORTH );
      inputPanel.add( centerPanel, BorderLayout.CENTER );

```

Fig. S23.2 Solution to Exercise 23.4. (Part 2 of 8.)

```
      table = new JTable( 4, 4 );

      container = getContentPane();
      container.setLayout( new BorderLayout() );
      container.add( inputPanel, BorderLayout.NORTH );
      container.add( table, BorderLayout.CENTER );

      getTable();

      setSize( 800, 300 );
      setVisible( true );

   } // end constructor AddEmployees

   private void getTable()
   {
      try {
         statement = connection.createStatement();
      resultSet = statement.executeQuery( "SELECT * FROM employees" );
         displayResultSet( resultSet );
      }
      catch ( SQLException sqlex ) {
         sqlex.printStackTrace();
      }
   }

   private void addEmployee( String query )
   {
      try {
         statement = connection.createStatement();
         statement.executeUpdate( query );
         getTable();
      }
      catch ( SQLException sqlex ) {
         sqlex.printStackTrace();
      }
   }

   private void displayResultSet( ResultSet rs ) throws SQLException
   {
      // position to first record
      boolean moreRecords = rs.next();

      // if there are no records, display a message
      if ( !moreRecords ) {
         JOptionPane.showMessageDialog( this,
            "ResultSet contained no records" );
         return;
      }

```

Fig. S23.2 Solution to Exercise 23.4. (Part 3 of 8.)

```
      Vector columnHeads = new Vector();
      Vector rows = new Vector();

      try {
         // get column heads
         ResultSetMetaData rsmd = rs.getMetaData();

         for ( int i = 1; i <= rsmd.getColumnCount(); ++i )
            columnHeads.addElement( rsmd.getColumnName( i ) );

         // get row data
         do {
            rows.addElement( getNextRow( rs, rsmd ) );
         } while ( rs.next() );

         // display table with ResultSet contents
         table = new JTable( rows, columnHeads );
         JScrollPane scroller = new JScrollPane( table );
         container.remove( 1 );
         container.add( scroller, BorderLayout.CENTER );
         container.validate();

      } // end try

      catch ( SQLException sqlex ) {
         sqlex.printStackTrace();
      }

   } // end method displayResultSet

   private Vector getNextRow( ResultSet rs,
      ResultSetMetaData rsmd ) throws SQLException
   {
      Vector currentRow = new Vector();

      for ( int i = 1; i <= rsmd.getColumnCount(); ++i )
         switch( rsmd.getColumnType( i ) ) {
            case Types.VARCHAR:
            case Types.LONGVARCHAR:
               currentRow.addElement( rs.getString( i ) );
               break;
            case Types.INTEGER:
               currentRow.addElement( new Long( rs.getLong( i ) ) );
               break;
            case Types.REAL:
               currentRow.addElement( new Float( rs.getDouble( i ) ) );
               break;
            case Types.DATE:
               currentRow.addElement( rs.getDate( i ) );
               break;
```

Fig. S23.2 Solution to Exercise 23.4. (Part 4 of 8.)

```
            default:
               System.out.println( "Type was: " +
                  rsmd.getColumnTypeName( i ) );
         }

      return currentRow;

   } // end method getNextRow

   public void shutDown()
   {
      try {
         connection.close();
      }
      catch ( SQLException sqlex ) {
         System.err.println( "Unable to disconnect" );
         sqlex.printStackTrace();
      }
   }

   public static void main( String[] args )
   {
      final AddEmployees application = new AddEmployees();
      application.addWindowListener(

         new WindowAdapter() {

            public void windowClosing( WindowEvent e )
            {
               application.shutDown();
               System.exit( 0 );
            }
         }
      );
   }

   // inner class ButtonHandler handles button event
   private class ButtonHandler implements ActionListener {

      public void actionPerformed( ActionEvent event )
      {
         String socialSecurityNumber = JOptionPane.showInputDialog(
            "Employee Social Security Number" );
         String insertQuery = "", displayQuery = "";

         // add salaried employee to table salariedEmployee
         if ( event.getSource() == addSalariedEmployee ) {
            double weeklySalary = Double.parseDouble(
               JOptionPane.showInputDialog( "Weekly Salary:" ) );
            insertQuery = "INSERT INTO salariedEmployees VALUES ( '" +
```

Fig. S23.2 Solution to Exercise 23.4. (Part 5 of 8.)

```
            socialSecurityNumber + "', '" + weeklySalary + "', '0' )";
         displayQuery = "SELECT employees.socialSecurityNumber, " +
            "employees.firstName, employees.lastName, " +
            "employees.employeeType, salariedEmployees.weeklySalary" +
            " FROM employees, salariedEmployees WHERE " +
            "employees.socialSecurityNumber = " +
            "salariedEmployees.socialSecurityNumber";
      }

      // add commission employee to table commissionEmployee
      else if ( event.getSource() == addCommissionEmployee ) {
         int grossSales = Integer.parseInt(
            JOptionPane.showInputDialog( "Gross Sales:" ) );
         double commissionRate = Double.parseDouble(
            JOptionPane.showInputDialog( "Commission Rate:" ) );
         insertQuery = "INSERT INTO commissionEmployees VALUES ( '" +
            socialSecurityNumber + "', '" + grossSales + "', '" +
            commissionRate + "', '0' )";
         displayQuery = "SELECT employees.socialSecurityNumber, " +
            "employees.firstName, employees.lastName, " +
            "employees.employeeType, commissionEmployees.grossSales," +
            " commissionEmployees.commissionRate FROM employees, " +
           "commissionEmployees WHERE employees.socialSecurityNumber="
            + "commissionEmployees.socialSecurityNumber";
      }

      // add base plus commission employee to table
      // basePlusCommissionEmployee
      else if ( event.getSource() == addBasePlusCommissionEmployee ) {
         int grossSales = Integer.parseInt(
            JOptionPane.showInputDialog( "Gross Sales:" ) );
         double commissionRate = Double.parseDouble(
            JOptionPane.showInputDialog( "Commission Rate:" ) );
         double baseSalary = Double.parseDouble(
            JOptionPane.showInputDialog( "Base Salary:" ) );
         insertQuery = "INSERT INTO basePlusCommissionEmployees " +
            "VALUES ( '" + socialSecurityNumber + "', '" + grossSales +
            "', '" + commissionRate + "', '" + baseSalary + "', '0' )";
         displayQuery = "SELECT employees.socialSecurityNumber, " +
            "employees.firstName, employees.lastName, employees." +
            "employeeType, basePlusCommissionEmployees.baseSalary, " +
            "basePlusCommissionEmployees.grossSales, basePlus" +
            "CommissionEmployees.commissionRate FROM employees, " +
            "basePlusCommissionEmployees WHERE " +
            "employees.socialSecurityNumber = " +
            "basePlusCommissionEmployees.socialSecurityNumber";
      }

      // add hourly employee to table hourlyEmployee
      else {
```

Fig. S23.2 Solution to Exercise 23.4. (Part 6 of 8.)

```
            int hours = Integer.parseInt(
               JOptionPane.showInputDialog( "Hours:" ) );
            double wage = Double.parseDouble(
               JOptionPane.showInputDialog( "Wage:" ) );
            insertQuery = "INSERT INTO hourlyEmployees VALUES ( '" +
               socialSecurityNumber + "', '" + hours + "', '" + wage +
               "', '0' )";
            displayQuery = "SELECT employees.socialSecurityNumber, " +
               "employees.firstName, employees.lastName, " +
               "employees.employeeType, hourlyEmployees.hours, " +
               "hourlyEmployees.wage FROM employees, hourlyEmployees " +
               "WHERE employees.socialSecurityNumber = " +
               "hourlyEmployees.socialSecurityNumber";
         }

         // execute insert query and display employee info
         try {
            statement = connection.createStatement();
            statement.executeUpdate( insertQuery );

            // display the employee info
            statement = connection.createStatement();
            resultSet = statement.executeQuery( displayQuery );
            displayResultSet( resultSet );
         }
         catch ( SQLException exception ) {
            exception.printStackTrace();
         }

      } // end method actionPerformed

   } // end inner class ButtonHandler

} // end class AddEmployees
```

Fig. S23.2 Solution to Exercise 23.4. (Part 7 of 8.)

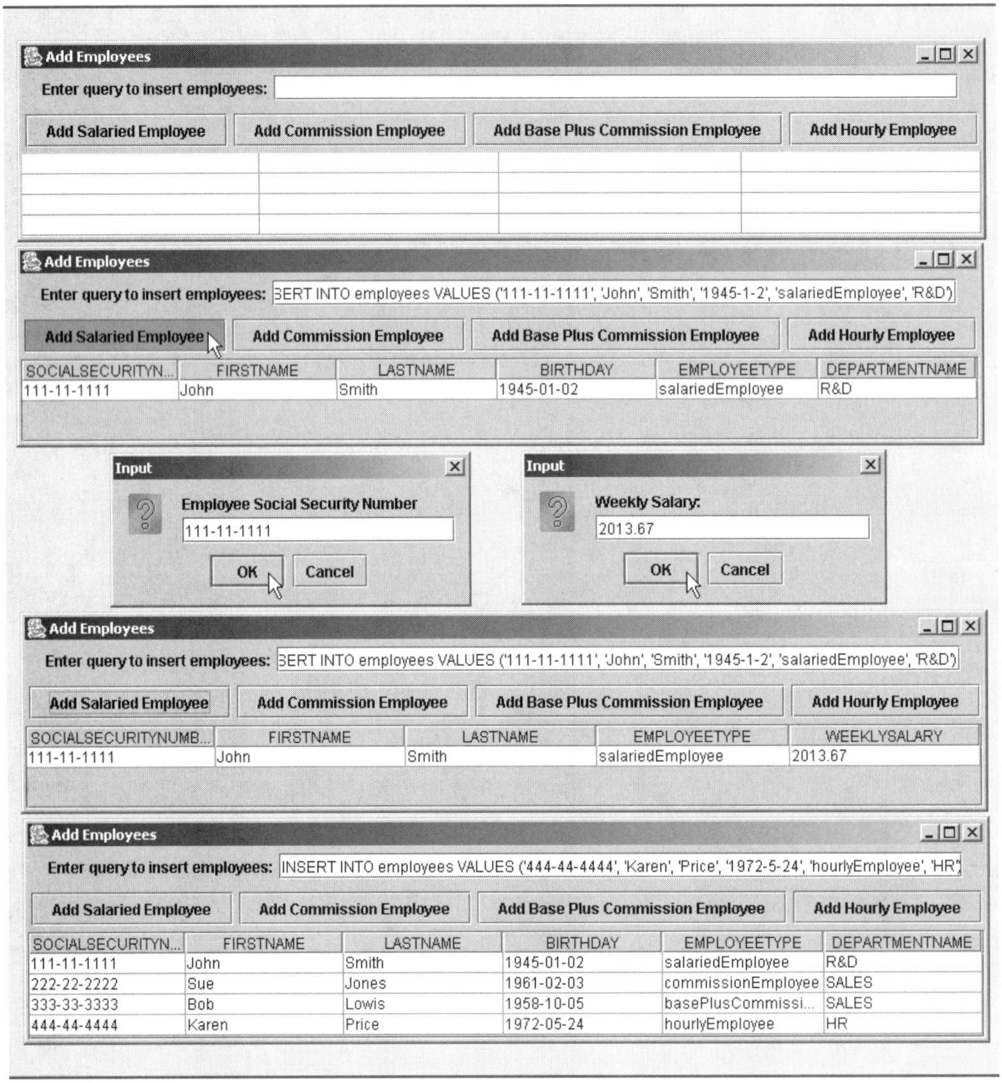

Fig. S23.2 Solution to Exercise 23.4. (Part 8 of 8.)

23.5 Write an application that provides a `JComboBox` and a `JTextArea` to allow the user to perform a query that is either selected from the `JComboBox` or defined in the `JTextArea`. Sample predified querys are:

a) Select all employees working in Department SALES.
b) Select hourly employees working over 30 hours.
c) Select all comission employees in descending order of the comission rate.

ANS:

```
// Exercise 23.5 Solution: DisplayQueryResults.java
import java.sql.*;
import javax.swing.*;
import java.awt.*;
import java.awt.event.*;
import java.util.*;

public class DisplayQueryResults extends JFrame {
   private Connection connection;
   private Statement statement;
   private ResultSet resultSet;
   private ResultSetMetaData rsMetaData;
   private JTable table;
   private JComboBox inputQuery;
   private JButton submitQuery;
   private JTextField input;

   public DisplayQueryResults()
   {
      super( "Select Query. Click Submit to See Results." );

      // The URL specifying the employees database to which this program
      // connects to using JDBC
      String url = "jdbc:db2j:employees";

      // Load the driver to allow connection to the database
      try {
         Class.forName( "com.ibm.db2j.jdbc.DB2jDriver" );

         connection = DriverManager.getConnection( url );
      }
      catch ( ClassNotFoundException cnfex ) {
         System.err.println( "Failed to load JDBC driver." );
         cnfex.printStackTrace();
         System.exit( 1 );  // terminate program
      }
      catch ( SQLException sqlex ) {
         System.err.println( "Unable to connect" );
         sqlex.printStackTrace();
         System.exit( 1 );  // terminate program
      }

      String queries[] = { "Select all employees working in Department " +
         "SALES.", "Select hourly employees working over 30 hours.",
         "Select all comission employees in descending order of the " +
         "comission rate.", "Specify particular query" };

      // If connected to database, set up GUI
```

Fig. S23.3 Solution to Exercise 23.5. (Part 1 of 6.)

```
      inputQuery = new JComboBox( queries );

      submitQuery = new JButton( "Submit query" );
      submitQuery.addActionListener(

         new ActionListener() {

            public void actionPerformed( ActionEvent e )
            {
               getTable();
            }
         }
      );

      JPanel topPanel = new JPanel();
      input = new JTextField( 50 );
      input.addActionListener(

         new ActionListener() {

            public void actionPerformed( ActionEvent e )
            {
               try {
                  String query = input.getText();
                  statement = connection.createStatement();
                  resultSet = statement.executeQuery( query );
                  displayResultSet( resultSet );
               }
               catch ( SQLException sqlex ) {
                  sqlex.printStackTrace();
               }
            }
         }
      );

      JPanel centerPanel = new JPanel();
      centerPanel.setLayout( new FlowLayout() );
      centerPanel.add( new JLabel( "Enter query:" ) );
      centerPanel.add( input );
      topPanel.setLayout( new BorderLayout() );
      topPanel.add( inputQuery, BorderLayout.NORTH );
      topPanel.add( centerPanel, BorderLayout.CENTER );
      topPanel.add( submitQuery, BorderLayout.SOUTH );

      table = new JTable( 4, 4 );

      Container c = getContentPane();
      c.setLayout( new BorderLayout() );
      c.add( topPanel, BorderLayout.NORTH );
      c.add( table, BorderLayout.CENTER );
```

Fig. S23.3 Solution to Exercise 23.5. (Part 2 of 6.)

```

      getTable();

      setSize( 650, 200 );
      setVisible( true );

   } // end constructor DisplayQueryResult

   private void getTable()
   {
      try {
         int selection = inputQuery.getSelectedIndex();
         String query = null;

         switch ( selection ) {
            case 0:
               query = "SELECT * FROM employees WHERE " +
                  "departmentName = 'SALES'";
               break;
            case 1:
               query = "SELECT * FROM hourlyEmployees WHERE hours >= 30";
               break;
            case 2:
               query = "SELECT * FROM commissionEmployees ORDER BY " +
                  "commissionRate DESC";
               break;
            case 3:
               query = input.getText();
                  break;
         }

         statement = connection.createStatement();

         if ( query.substring( 0, 6 ).equals( "SELECT" ) ) {
            resultSet = statement.executeQuery( query );
            displayResultSet( resultSet );
         }

         else statement.executeUpdate( query );

      } // end try

      catch ( SQLException sqlex ) {
         sqlex.printStackTrace();
      }

   } // end method getTable

   private void displayResultSet( ResultSet rs ) throws SQLException
   {
```

Fig. S23.3 Solution to Exercise 23.5. (Part 3 of 6.)

```
      // position to first record
      boolean moreRecords = rs.next();

      // If there are no records, display a message
      if ( !moreRecords ) {
         JOptionPane.showMessageDialog( this,
            "ResultSet contained no records" );
         setTitle( "No records to display" );
         return;
      }

      Vector columnHeads = new Vector();
      Vector rows = new Vector();

      try {
         // get column heads
         ResultSetMetaData rsmd = rs.getMetaData();

         for ( int i = 1; i <= rsmd.getColumnCount(); ++i )
            columnHeads.addElement( rsmd.getColumnName( i ) );

         // get row data
         do {
            rows.addElement( getNextRow( rs, rsmd ) );
         } while ( rs.next() );

         // display table with ResultSet contents
         table = new JTable( rows, columnHeads );
         JScrollPane scroller = new JScrollPane( table );
         Container c = getContentPane();
         c.remove( 1 );
         c.add( scroller, BorderLayout.CENTER );
         c.validate();

      } // end try

      catch ( SQLException sqlex ) {
         sqlex.printStackTrace();
      }

   } // end method displayResultSet

   private Vector getNextRow( ResultSet rs,
      ResultSetMetaData rsmd ) throws SQLException
   {
      Vector currentRow = new Vector();

      for ( int i = 1; i <= rsmd.getColumnCount(); ++i )
         switch( rsmd.getColumnType( i ) ) {
            case Types.VARCHAR:
```

Fig. S23.3 Solution to Exercise 23.5. (Part 4 of 6.)

```
            case Types.LONGVARCHAR:
                  currentRow.addElement( rs.getString( i ) );
               break;
            case Types.INTEGER:
                  currentRow.addElement( new Long( rs.getLong( i ) ) );
               break;
            case Types.REAL:
                  currentRow.addElement( new Float( rs.getDouble( i ) ) );
               break;
            case Types.DATE:
                  currentRow.addElement( rs.getDate( i ) );
              break;
            default:
               System.out.println( "Type was: " +
                  rsmd.getColumnTypeName( i ) );
         }

      return currentRow;

   } // end method getNextRow

   public void shutDown()
   {
      try {
         connection.close();
      }
      catch ( SQLException sqlex ) {
         System.err.println( "Unable to disconnect" );
         sqlex.printStackTrace();
      }
   }

   public static void main( String args[] )
   {
      final DisplayQueryResults app = new DisplayQueryResults();
      app.addWindowListener(

         new WindowAdapter() {

            public void windowClosing( WindowEvent e )
            {
               app.shutDown();
               System.exit( 0 );
            }
         }
      );
   }

} // end class DisplayQueryResults
```

Fig. S23.3 Solution to Exercise 23.5. (Part 5 of 6.)

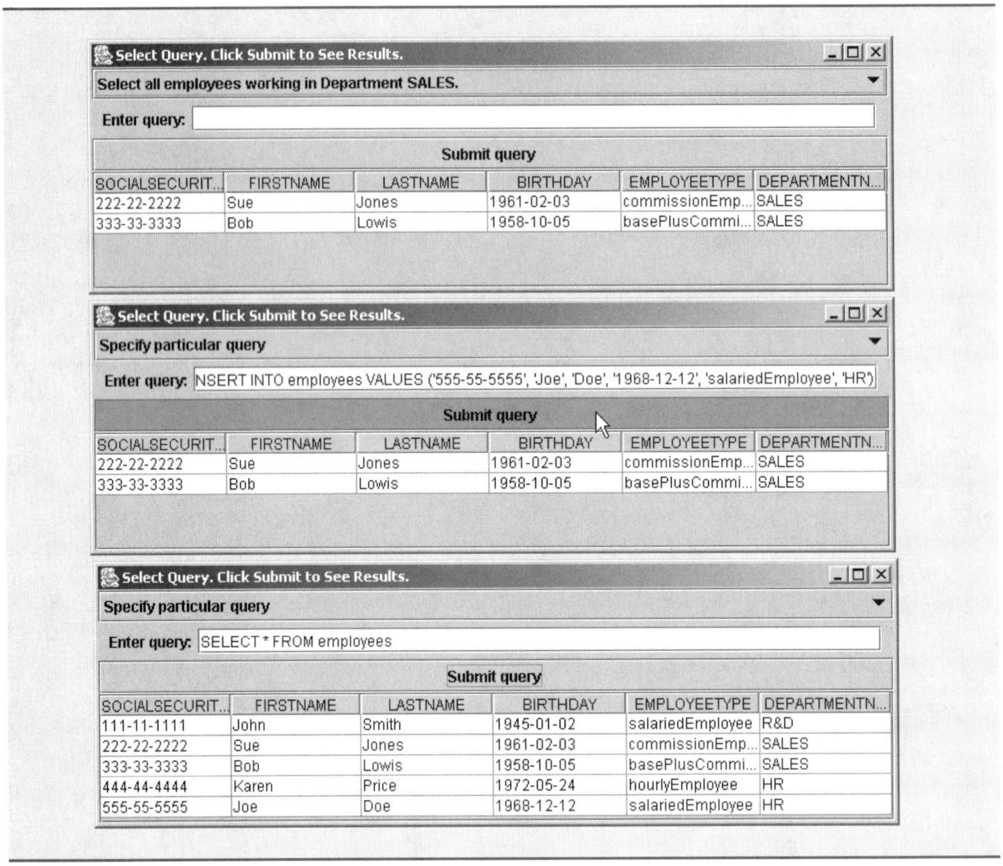
Select Query. Click Submit to See Results.
Select all employees working in Department SALES.
Enter query:
Submit query
SOCIALSECURIT... FIRSTNAME LASTNAME BIRTHDAY EMPLOYEETYPE DEPARTMENTN...
222-22-2222 Sue Jones 1961-02-03 commissionEmp... SALES
333-33-3333 Bob Lowis 1958-10-05 basePlusCommi... SALES
Select Query. Click Submit to See Results.
Specify particular query
Enter query: NSERT INTO employees VALUES ('555-55-5555', 'Joe', 'Doe', '1968-12-12', 'salariedEmployee', 'HR')
Submit query
SOCIALSECURIT... FIRSTNAME LASTNAME BIRTHDAY EMPLOYEETYPE DEPARTMENTN...
222-22-2222 Sue Jones 1961-02-03 commissionEmp... SALES
333-33-3333 Bob Lowis 1958-10-05 basePlusCommi... SALES
Select Query. Click Submit to See Results.
Specify particular query
Enter query: SELECT * FROM employees
Submit query
SOCIALSECURIT... FIRSTNAME LASTNAME BIRTHDAY EMPLOYEETYPE DEPARTMENTN...
111-11-1111 John Smith 1945-01-02 salariedEmployee R&D
222-22-2222 Sue Jones 1961-02-03 commissionEmp... SALES
333-33-3333 Bob Lowis 1958-10-05 basePlusCommi... SALES
444-44-4444 Karen Price 1972-05-24 hourlyEmployee HR
555-55-5555 Joe Doe 1968-12-12 salariedEmployee HR

Fig. S23.3 Solution to Exercise 23.5. (Part 6 of 6.)

24

Servlets

Solution to Selected Exercises

24.3 Create a Web application for dynamic FAQs. The application should obtain the information to create the dynamic FAQ Web page from a database that consists of a `Topics` table and an `FAQ` table. The `Topics` table should have two fields—a unique integer ID for each topic (`topicID`) and a name for each topic (`topicName`). The `FAQ` table should have three fields—the `topicID` (a foreign key), a string representing the question (`question`) and the answer to the question (`answer`). When the servlet is invoked, it should read the data from the database and return a dynamically created Web page containing each question and answer, sorted by topic.

ANS:

```
// Exercise 24.3 solution: FaqListingServlet.java
// Displays all FAQs sorted by topic.
package com.deitel.jhtp5.servlets;

import java.sql.*;
import java.io.*;
import javax.servlet.http.*;
import javax.servlet.*;

public class FaqListingServlet extends HttpServlet {
   private Connection connection;
   private Statement statement;

   // set up database connection and prepare SQL statements
   public void init( ServletConfig config ) throws ServletException
   {
      // attempt database connection and create PreparedStatements
      try {

         System.setProperty( "db2j.system.home",
            config.getInitParameter( "databaseLocation" ) );
```

Fig. S24.1 Solution to Exercise 24.3. (Part 1 of 5.)

```

         Class.forName( config.getInitParameter( "databaseDriver" ) );
         connection = DriverManager.getConnection(
            config.getInitParameter( "databaseName" ) );

         // create Statement to query database
         statement = connection.createStatement();
      }

      // for any exception throw an UnavailableException to
      // indicate that the servlet is not currently available
      catch ( Exception exception ) {
         exception.printStackTrace();
         throw new UnavailableException(exception.getMessage());
      }

   } // end of init method

   // display all FAQs sorted by topic
   public void doGet( HttpServletRequest request,
      HttpServletResponse response )
   {
      String query;

      // set response content type
      response.setContentType( "text/html" );

      // get output stream
      PrintWriter out = null;
      try {
         out = response.getWriter();
      } catch ( Exception exception ) {
         exception.printStackTrace();
         return;
      }

      // start XHTML document
      out.println( "<?xml version = \"1.0\"?>" );

      out.println( "<!DOCTYPE html PUBLIC \"-//W3C//DTD " +
         "XHTML 1.0 Strict//EN\" \"http://www.w3.org" +
         "/TR/xhtml1/DTD/xhtml1-strict.dtd\">" );

      out.println(
         "<html xmlns = \"http://www.w3.org/1999/xhtml\">" );

      // head section of document
      out.println( "<head>" );
      out.println( "<title>FAQ Topics, Questions and Answers" +
                   "</title>" );
```

Fig. S24.1 Solution to Exercise 24.3. (Part 2 of 5.)

```
        out.println( "</head>" );

        // body section of document
        out.println( "<body>" );

        // attempt to retrieve information from database
        ResultSet baseballResults = null;
        ResultSet soccerResults = null;
        ResultSet hockeyResults = null;

        // display information from database
        try {

           // display soccer information
           out.println( "<h2> Soccer </h2> <p>" );

           query = "SELECT TOPICNAME, QUESTION, ANSWER FROM FAQ, TOPICS " +
              "WHERE FAQ.TOPICID = TOPICS.TOPICID AND FAQ.TOPICID = '1'";
           soccerResults = statement.executeQuery( query );

           while ( soccerResults.next() ) {

              // display question
              out.println( "<b>" + soccerResults.getString(
                 "QUESTION" ) + "</b> <br>" );

              // display answer
              out.println( "<i>" + soccerResults.getString(
                 "ANSWER" ) + "</i> <br>" );
           }

           // release ResultSet
           soccerResults.close();

           // display baseball information
           out.println( "<h2> Baseball </h2> <p>" );
           query = "SELECT TOPICNAME, QUESTION, ANSWER FROM FAQ, TOPICS " +
             "WHERE FAQ.TOPICID = TOPICS.TOPICID AND FAQ.TOPICID = '2'";
           baseballResults = statement.executeQuery( query );

           while ( baseballResults.next() ) {

              // display question
              out.println( "<b>" + baseballResults.getString(
                 "QUESTION" ) + "</b> <br>" );

              // display answer
              out.println( "<i>" + baseballResults.getString(
                 "ANSWER" ) + "</i> <br>" );
           }
```

Fig. S24.1 Solution to Exercise 24.3. (Part 3 of 5.)

```

         // release ResultSet
         baseballResults.close();

         // display hockey information
         out.println( "<h2> Hockey </h2> <p>" );
         query = "SELECT TOPICNAME, QUESTION, ANSWER FROM FAQ, TOPICS " +
            "WHERE FAQ.TOPICID = TOPICS.TOPICID AND FAQ.TOPICID = '3'";
         hockeyResults = statement.executeQuery( query );

         while ( hockeyResults.next() ) {

            // display question
            out.println( "<b>" + hockeyResults.getString(
               "QUESTION" ) + "</b> <br>" );

            // display answer
            out.println( "<i>" + hockeyResults.getString(
               "ANSWER" ) + "</i> <br>" );
         }

         // release ResultSet
         hockeyResults.close();
      }

      // catch SQLExceptions
      catch( SQLException exception ) {
         exception.printStackTrace();
         out.println( "<p><h1>... ERROR: could not retrieve" +
                      " information from database</h1>" );
         out.println( "</body></html>" );
         return;
      }

      // finish html document structure
      out.println( "</body>" );
      out.println( "</html>" );

   } // end method doGet

} // end class FaqListingServlet
```

Fig. S24.1 Solution to Exercise 24.3. (Part 4 of 5.)

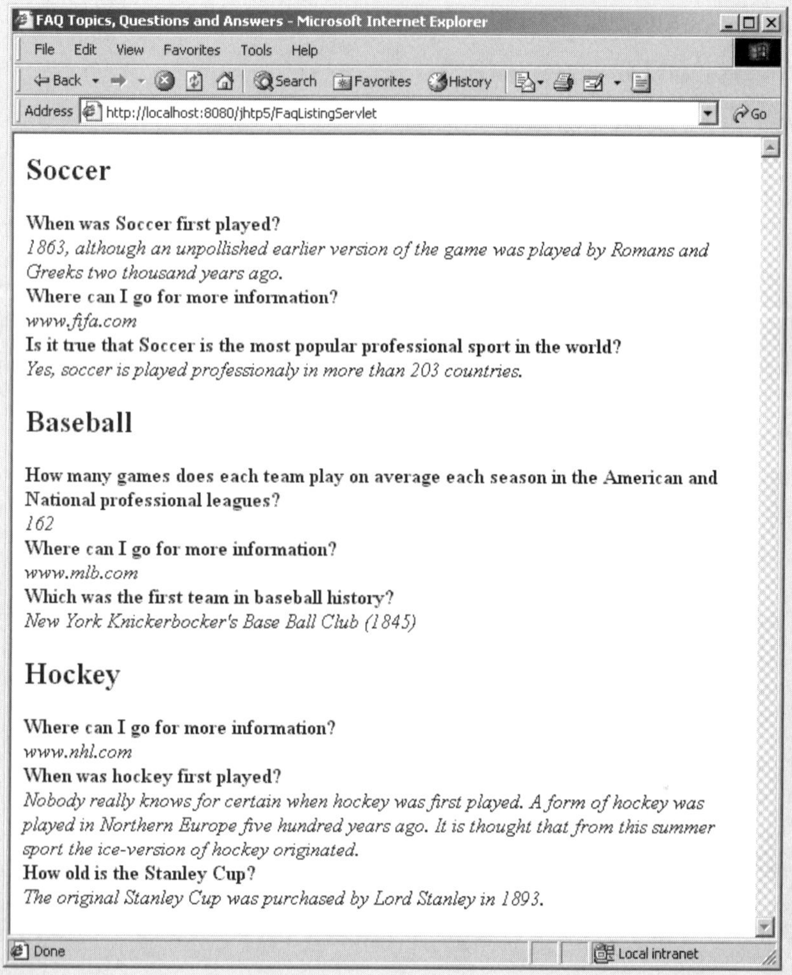

Fig. S24.1 Solution to Exercise 24.3. (Part 5 of 5.)

24.5 Modify the Web application of Fig. 24.20 to allow the user to see the survey results without responding to the survey.

```
<?xml version = "1.0"?>
<!DOCTYPE html PUBLIC "-//W3C//DTD XHTML 1.0 Strict//EN"
   "http://www.w3.org/TR/xhtml1/DTD/xhtml1-strict.dtd">

<!-- Exercise 24.5: Survey2.html -->
```

Fig. S24.2 Exercise 24.5: Survey2.java. (Part 1 of 2.)

```

<html xmlns = "http://www.w3.org/1999/xhtml">
   <head>
      <title>Survey</title>
   </head>

   <body>
      <form method = "post" action = "/jhtp5/animalSurvey2">

         <p>What is your favorite pet?</p>

         <p>
            <input type = "radio" name = "animal"
               value = "1" />Dog<br />
            <input type = "radio" name = "animal"
               value = "2" />Cat<br />
            <input type = "radio" name = "animal"
               value = "3" />Bird<br />
            <input type = "radio" name = "animal"
               value = "4" />Snake<br />
            <input type = "radio" name = "animal"
               value = "5" checked = "checked" />None
         </p>

         <p><input type = "submit" value = "Submit" /></p>

         <p><a href = "/jhtp5/animalSurvey2">See Results</a></p>

      </form>
   </body>
</html>
```

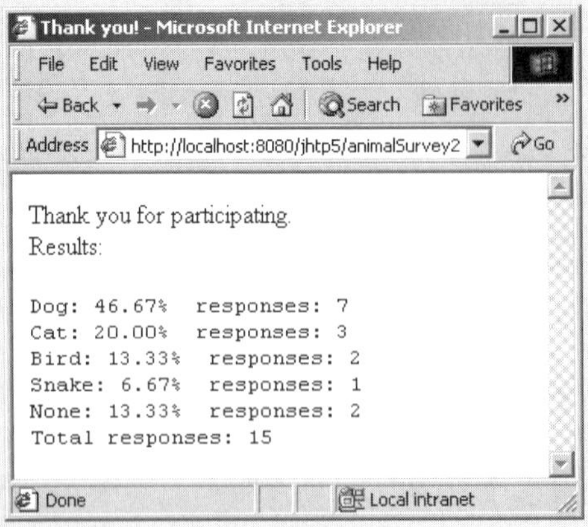

Fig. S24.2 Exercise 24.5: Survey2.java. (Part 2 of 2.)

ANS:

```
// Exercise 24.5 solution: SurveyServlet2.java
// A Web-based survey that uses JDBC from a servlet.
package com.deitel.jhtp5.servlets;

import java.io.*;
import java.text.*;
import java.sql.*;
import javax.servlet.*;
import javax.servlet.http.*;

public class SurveyServlet2 extends HttpServlet {
   private Connection connection;
   private Statement statement;

   // set up database connection and create SQL statement
   public void init( ServletConfig config ) throws ServletException
   {
      // attempt database connection and create Statement
      try {
         System.setProperty( "db2j.system.home",
            config.getInitParameter( "databaseLocation" ) );

         Class.forName( config.getInitParameter( "databaseDriver" ) );
         connection = DriverManager.getConnection(
            config.getInitParameter( "databaseName" ) );

         // create Statement to query database
         statement = connection.createStatement();
      }

      // for any exception throw an UnavailableException to
      // indicate that the servlet is not currently available
      catch ( Exception exception ) {
         exception.printStackTrace();
         throw new UnavailableException( exception.getMessage() );
      }

   }  // end of init method

   // process survey response
   protected void doPost( HttpServletRequest request,
      HttpServletResponse response ) throws ServletException, IOException
   {
      PrintWriter out = response.getWriter();

      // read current survey response
      int value =
         Integer.parseInt( request.getParameter( "animal" ) );
      String query;
```

Fig. S24.3 Solution to Exercise 24.5. (Part 1 of 4.)

```

      // attempt to process a vote and display current results
      try {

         // update total for current survey response
         query = "UPDATE surveyresults SET votes = votes + 1 " +
               "WHERE id = " + value;
         statement.executeUpdate( query );

         displayResults( response );

      } // end try

      // if database exception occurs, return error page
      catch ( SQLException sqlException ) {
         sqlException.printStackTrace();
         out.println( "<title>Error</title>" );
         out.println( "</head>" );
         out.println( "<body><p>Database error occurred. " );
         out.println( "Try again later.</p></body></html>" );
         out.close();
      }

   } // end of doPost method

   // process "get" request from client
   protected void doGet( HttpServletRequest request,
      HttpServletResponse response ) throws ServletException, IOException
   {
      displayResults( response );

   } // end method doGet

   // display results
   public void displayResults( HttpServletResponse response )
         throws ServletException, IOException
   {
      String query;

      // set up response to client
      response.setContentType( "text/html" );
      PrintWriter out = response.getWriter();
      DecimalFormat twoDigits = new DecimalFormat( "0.00" );

      // start XHTML document
      out.println( "<?xml version = \"1.0\"?>" );

      out.println( "<!DOCTYPE html PUBLIC \"-//W3C//DTD " +
         "XHTML 1.0 Strict//EN\" \"http://www.w3.org" +
         "/TR/xhtml1/DTD/xhtml1-strict.dtd\">" );

```

Fig. S24.3 Solution to Exercise 24.5. (Part 2 of 4.)

```
      out.println(
         "<html xmlns = \"http://www.w3.org/1999/xhtml\">" );

      // head section of document
      out.println( "<head>" );

      // attempt to process a vote and display current results
      try {

         // get total of all survey responses
         query = "SELECT sum( votes ) FROM surveyresults";
         ResultSet totalRS = statement.executeQuery( query );
         totalRS.next();
         int total = totalRS.getInt( 1 );

         // get results
         query = "SELECT surveyoption, votes, id FROM surveyresults " +
            "ORDER BY id";
         ResultSet resultsRS = statement.executeQuery( query );
         out.println( "<title>Thank you!</title>" );
         out.println( "</head>" );

         out.println( "<body>" );
         out.println( "<p>Thank you for participating." );
         out.println( "<br />Results:</p><pre>" );

         // process results
         int votes;

         while ( resultsRS.next() ) {
            out.print( resultsRS.getString( 1 ) );
            out.print( ": " );
            votes = resultsRS.getInt( 2 );
            out.print( twoDigits.format(
               ( double ) votes / total * 100 ) );
            out.print( "%  responses: " );
            out.println( votes );
         }

         resultsRS.close();

         out.print( "Total responses: " );
         out.print( total );

         // end XHTML document
         out.println( "</pre></body></html>" );
         out.close();

      } // end try

```

Fig. S24.3 Solution to Exercise 24.5. (Part 3 of 4.)

```
      // if database exception occurs, return error page
      catch ( SQLException sqlException ) {
         sqlException.printStackTrace();
         out.println( "<title>Error</title>" );
         out.println( "</head>" );
         out.println( "<body><p>Database error occurred. " );
         out.println( "Try again later.</p></body></html>" );
         out.close();
      }

   } // end method displayResults

   // close SQL statements and database when servlet terminates
   public void destroy()
   {
      // attempt to close statements and database connection
      try {
         statement.close();
         connection.close();
      }

      // handle database exceptions by returning error to client
      catch( SQLException sqlException ) {
         sqlException.printStackTrace();
      }
   }

} // end class SurveyServlet2
```

Fig. S24.3 Solution to Exercise 24.5. (Part 4 of 4.)

24.7 Write a Web application that consists of a servlet (`DirectoryServlet`) and several Web documents. Document `index.html` should be the first document the user sees. In that document, you should have a series of hyperlinks for other Web pages in your site. When clicked, each hyperlink should invoke the servlet with a `get` request that contains a `page` parameter. The servlet should obtain parameter `page` and redirect the request to the appropriate document.

ANS:

```
<?xml version = "1.0"?>
<!DOCTYPE html PUBLIC "-//W3C//DTD XHTML 1.0 Strict//EN"
   "http://www.w3.org/TR/xhtml1/DTD/xhtml1-strict.dtd">

<!-- Exercise 24.7: index.html -->

<html xmlns = "http://www.w3.org/1999/xhtml">
   <head>
      <title>Redirecting a Request to Another Site</title>
   </head>

   <body>
```

Fig. S24.4 Solution to Exercise 24.7: index.html. (Part 1 of 2.)

```
      <p>
         Click a link to be redirected to the appropriate page
      </p>
      <p>
         <a href = "/jhtp5/directory?page=sample1">
            Sample 1</a><br />
         <a href = "/jhtp5/directory?page=sample2">
            Sample 2</a><br />
         <a href = "/jhtp5/directory?page=sample3">
            Sample 3</a><br />
         <a href = "/jhtp5/directory?page=sample4">
            Sample 4</a>
      </p>
   </body>
</html>
```

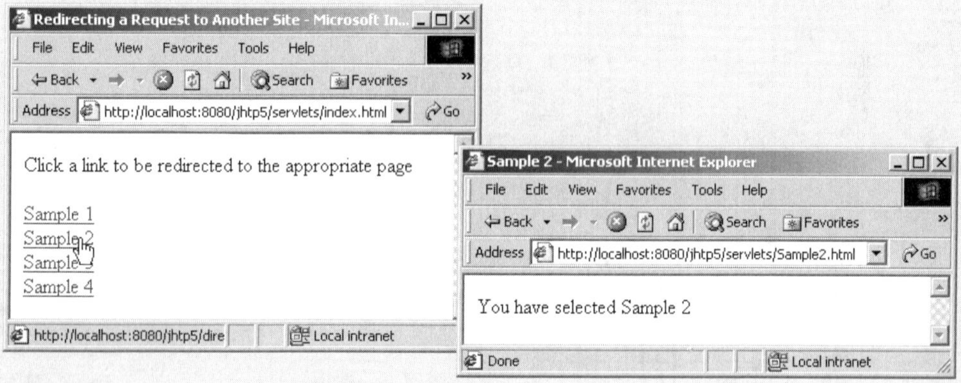

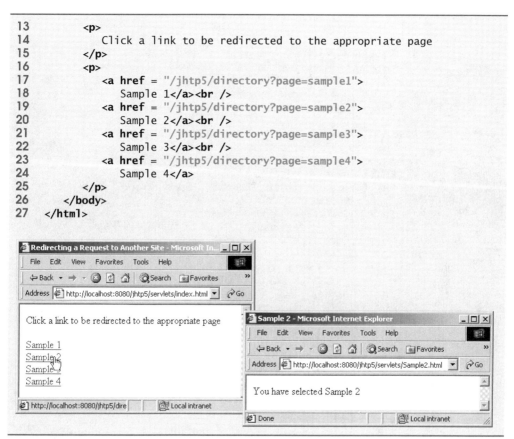

Fig. S24.4 Solution to Exercise 24.7: index.html. (Part 2 of 2.)

```
// Exercise 24.7: DirectoryServlet.java
// Program demonstrates redirection.
package com.deitel.jhtp5.servlets;

import javax.servlet.*;
import javax.servlet.http.*;
import java.io.*;

public class DirectoryServlet extends HttpServlet {

   // process "get" request from client
   protected void doGet( HttpServletRequest request,
      HttpServletResponse response ) throws ServletException, IOException
   {
      String location = request.getParameter( "page" );

```

Fig. S24.5 Solution to Exercise 24.7: DirectoryServlet.java. (Part 1 of 2.)

```
      if ( location != null )

         if ( location.equals( "sample1" ) )
            response.sendRedirect( "servlets/Sample1.html" );

         else if ( location.equals( "sample2" ) )
            response.sendRedirect( "servlets/Sample2.html" );

         else if ( location.equals( "sample3" ) )
            response.sendRedirect( "servlets/Sample3.html" );

         else if ( location.equals( "sample4" ) )
            response.sendRedirect( "servlets/Sample4.html" );

      // code that executes only if this servlet
      // does not redirect the user to another page
      response.setContentType( "text/html" );
      PrintWriter out = response.getWriter();
      out.println( "<?xml version = \"1.0\"?>" );
      out.println( "<!DOCTYPE html PUBLIC \"-//W3C//DTD " +
         "XHTML 1.0 Strict//EN\" \"http://www.w3.org" +
         "/TR/xhtml1/DTD/xhtml1-strict.dtd\">" );
      out.println( "<html xmlns = \"http://www.w3.org/1999/xhtml\">" );
      out.println( "<head>" );
      out.println( "<title>Invalid Page</title>" );
      out.println( "</head>" );
      out.println( "<p><a href = \"servlets/DirectoryServlet.html\">" );
      out.println( "Click here to choose again</a></p>" );
      out.println( "</body>" );
      out.println( "</html>" );
      out.close();

   } // end method doGet

} // end class DirectoryServlet
```

Fig. S24.5 Solution to Exercise 24.7: DirectoryServlet.java. (Part 2 of 2.)

```
<?xml version = "1.0"?>
<!DOCTYPE html PUBLIC "-//W3C//DTD XHTML 1.0 Strict//EN"
   "http://www.w3.org/TR/xhtml1/DTD/xhtml1-strict.dtd">

<!-- Exercise 24.7: Sample1.html -->

<html xmlns = "http://www.w3.org/1999/xhtml">
<head>
   <title>Sample 1</title>
</head>

<body>
```

Fig. S24.6 Solution to Exercise 24.7: Sample1.html. (Part 1 of 2.)

```
<form method = "post" action = "/jhtp5/sample1">

   <p>You have selected Sample 1</p>

</form>

</body>
</html>
```

Fig. S24.6 Solution to Exercise 24.7: Sample1.html. (Part 2 of 2.)

```
<?xml version = "1.0"?>
<!DOCTYPE html PUBLIC "-//W3C//DTD XHTML 1.0 Strict//EN"
   "http://www.w3.org/TR/xhtml1/DTD/xhtml1-strict.dtd">

<!-- Exercise 24.7: Sample2.html -->

<html xmlns = "http://www.w3.org/1999/xhtml">
<head>
   <title>Sample 2</title>
</head>

<body>
<form method = "post" action = "/jhtp5/sample2">

   <p>You have selected Sample 2</p>

</form>

</body>
</html>
```

Fig. S24.7 Solution to Exercise 24.7: Sample2.html.

```
<?xml version = "1.0"?>
<!DOCTYPE html PUBLIC "-//W3C//DTD XHTML 1.0 Strict//EN"
   "http://www.w3.org/TR/xhtml1/DTD/xhtml1-strict.dtd">

<!-- Exercise 24.7: Sample3.html -->

<html xmlns = "http://www.w3.org/1999/xhtml">
<head>
   <title>Sample 3</title>
</head>

<body>
<form method = "post" action = "/jhtp5/sample3">

```

Fig. S24.8 Solution to Exercise 24.7: Sample3.html. (Part 1 of 2.)

```
      <p>You have selected Sample 3</p>

   </form>

   </body>
   </html>
```

Fig. S24.8 Solution to Exercise 24.7: Sample3.html. (Part 2 of 2.)

```
<?xml version = "1.0"?>
<!DOCTYPE html PUBLIC "-//W3C//DTD XHTML 1.0 Strict//EN"
   "http://www.w3.org/TR/xhtml1/DTD/xhtml1-strict.dtd">

<!-- Exercise 24.7: Sample4.html -->

<html xmlns = "http://www.w3.org/1999/xhtml">
<head>
   <title>Sample 4</title>
</head>

<body>
<form method = "post" action = "/jhtp5/sample4">

   <p>You have selected Sample 4</p>

</form>

</body>
</html>
```

Fig. S24.9 Solution to Exercise 24.7: Sample4.html.

25

JavaServer Pages (JSP)

Solutions to Selected Exercises

25.3 Write a JSP page to output the string “Hello world!” ten times.

ANS:

```
<?xml version = "1.0"?>
<!DOCTYPE html PUBLIC "-//W3C//DTD XHTML 1.0 Strict//EN"
   "http://www.w3.org/TR/xhtml1/DTD/xhtml1-strict.dtd">

<!-- Exercise 25.3 solution: HelloWorld.jsp -->

<html xmlns = "http://www.w3.org/1999/xhtml">

<head>
   <title>Printing hello world</title>
</head>

<body>
<% for( int i = 0; i < 10; i++ ) { %>

   <p>Hello world!</p>

<% } %>
</body>
</html>
```

Fig. S25.1 Solution to Exercise 25.3. (Part 1 of 2.)

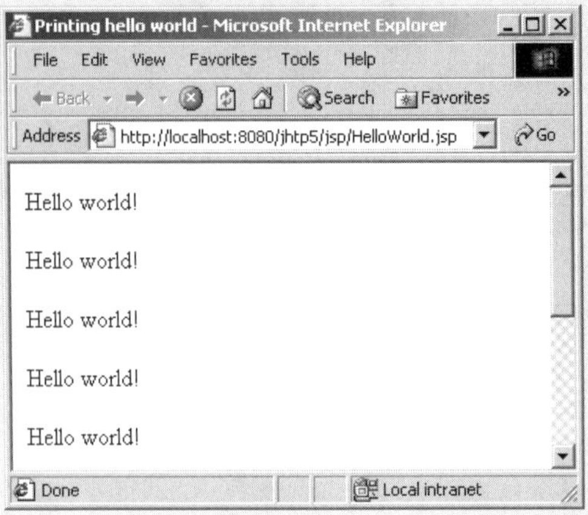

Fig. S25.1 Solution to Exercise 25.3. (Part 2 of 2.)

25.5 Rewrite Figure 25.15 to allow users to select the image. Use a JSP expression instead of the `getProperty` JSP tag.

ANS:

```
<?xml version = "1.0"?>
<!DOCTYPE html PUBLIC "-//W3C//DTD XHTML 1.0 Strict//EN"
   "http://www.w3.org/TR/xhtml1/DTD/xhtml1-strict.dtd">

<!-- Exercise 25.5 solution: adrotator2.jsp -->

<jsp:useBean id = "rotator" scope = "application"
   class = "com.deitel.jhtp5.jsp.Rotator" />

<html xmlns = "http://www.w3.org/1999/xhtml">

   <head>
      <title>AdRotator Example</title>

      <style type = "text/css">
         .big { font-family: helvetica, arial, sans-serif;
                font-weight: bold;
                font-size: 2em }
      </style>
   </head>

   <body>

      <form method = "post" action = "/jhtp5/jsp/adrotator2.jsp">

         <p>Select an book:</p>

```

Fig. S25.2 Solution to Exercise 25.5. (Part 1 of 3.)

```
            <p>
               <input type = "radio" name = "book" value = "0" />
                  Advanced Java How to Program<br />
               <input type = "radio" name = "book" value = "1" />
                  C++ How to Program<br />
               <input type = "radio" name = "book" value = "2" />
                  Internet &amp World Wide Web How to Program<br />
               <input type = "radio" name = "book" value = "3" />
                  Java Web Services for Experienced Programmers<br />
               <input type = "radio" name = "book" value = "4" />
                  Visual Basic .NET How to Program<br />
            </p>

            <p><input type = "submit" value = "Submit" /></p>

         </form>

         <hr />

         <p>
            <% if ( request.getParameter( "book" ) != null )
                  rotator.setLink( Integer.parseInt(
                     request.getParameter( "book" ) ) );
            %>

            <a href = <%= rotator.getLink() %> >

               <img src = <%= rotator.getImage() %> alt = "advertisement" />
            </a>
         </p>
      </body>
   </html>
```

Fig. S25.2 Solution to Exercise 25.5. (Part 2 of 3.)

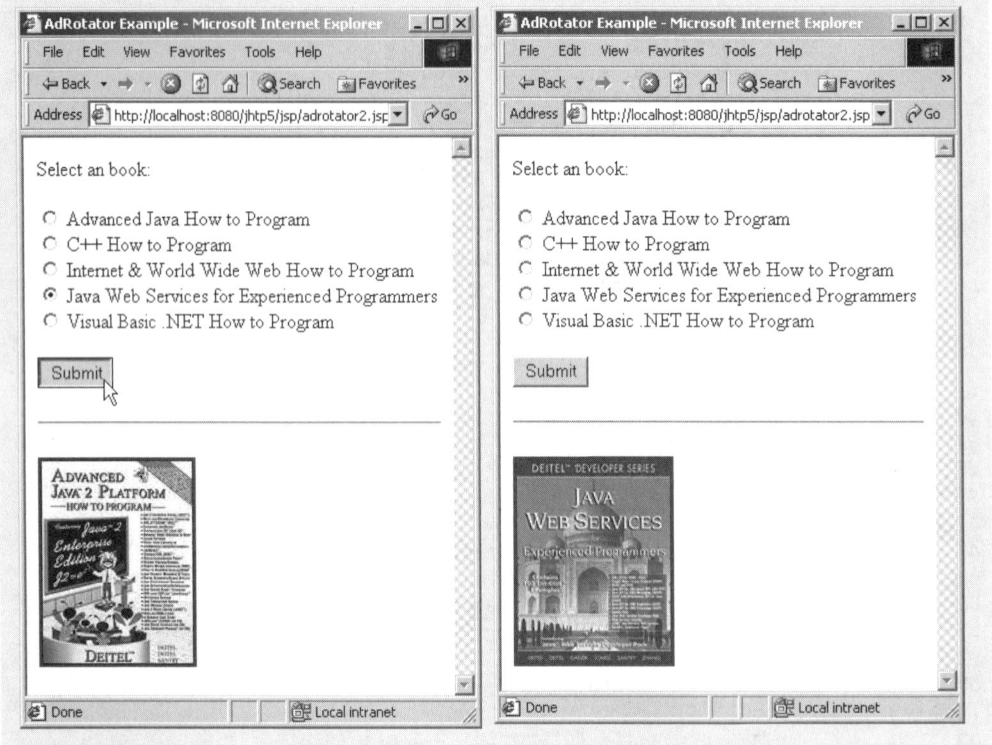

Fig. S25.2 Solution to Exercise 25.5. (Part 3 of 3.)

25.7 Reimplement the Web application of Fig. 24.20 (favorite animal survey) using JSPs.

ANS:

```
<?xml version = "1.0"?>
<!DOCTYPE html PUBLIC "-//W3C//DTD XHTML 1.0 Strict//EN"
   "http://www.w3.org/TR/xhtml1/DTD/xhtml1-strict.dtd">

<!-- Exercise 25.7 solution: animalSurvey.jsp -->

<%-- page settings --%>
<%@ page errorPage = "animalSurveyErrorPage.jsp" %>
<%@ page import = "com.deitel.jhtp5.jsp.beans.*" %>

<%-- beans used in this JSP --%>
<jsp:useBean id = "voteData" scope = "request"
   class = "com.deitel.jhtp5.jsp.beans.VoteDataBean" />

<html xmlns = "http://www.w3.org/1999/xhtml">

```

Fig. S25.3 Solution to Exercise 25.7: animalSurvey.jsp. (Part 1 of 3.)

```
   <head>
      <title>Animal Survey</title>
   </head>

   <body>
      <% // begin scriptlet

         String animalType = request.getParameter( "animal" );

         if ( animalType != null ) {

            voteData.addVote( Integer.parseInt( animalType ) );

      %> <%-- end scriptlet to insert fixed template data --%>

            <jsp:forward page = "animalSurveyResults.jsp" />

      <% // continue scriptlet

         } // end if

         else {

      %> <%-- end scriptlet to insert fixed template data --%>

            <form action = "animalSurvey.jsp" method = "get">
               <p>What is your favorite pet?</p>

               <p>
              <input type = "radio" name = "animal"
                 value = "1" /> Dog<br />
              <input type = "radio" name = "animal"
                 value = "2" /> Cat<br />
              <input type = "radio" name = "animal"
                 value = "3" /> Bird<br />
              <input type = "radio" name = "animal"
                 value = "4" /> Snake<br />
              <input type = "radio" name = "animal"
                 value = "5" checked = "checked" /> None
           </p>

           <p><input type = "submit" value = "Submit" /></p>
            </form>

      <%  // continue scriptlet

         } // end else

      %> <%-- end scriptlet --%>
   </body>
```

Fig. S25.3 Solution to Exercise 25.7: animalSurvey.jsp. (Part 2 of 3.)

```

</html> <!-- end XHTML document -->
```

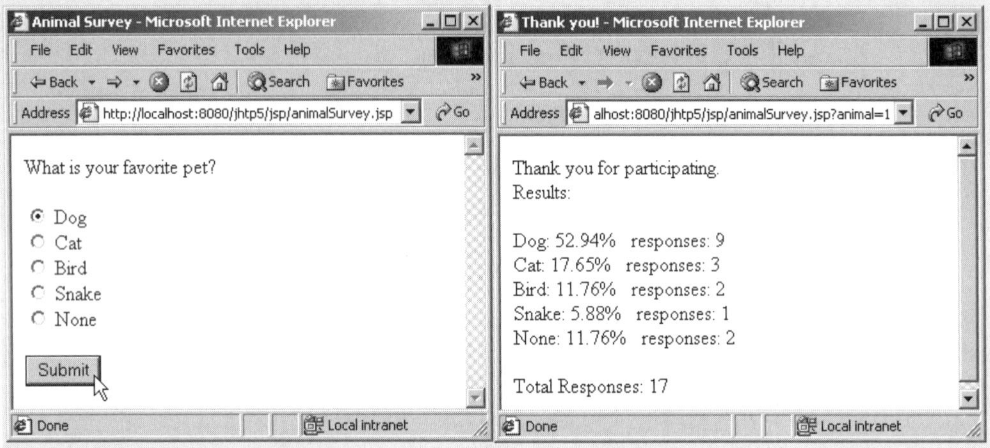

Fig. S25.3 Solution to Exercise 25.7: animalSurvey.jsp. (Part 3 of 3.)

```
<?xml version = "1.0"?>
<!DOCTYPE html PUBLIC "-//W3C//DTD XHTML 1.0 Strict//EN"
   "http://www.w3.org/TR/xhtml1/DTD/xhtml1-strict.dtd">

<!-- Exercise 25.7 solution: animalSurveyErrorPage.jsp -->

<%-- page settings --%>
<%@ page isErrorPage = "true" %>
<%@ page import = "java.util.*" %>
<%@ page import = "java.sql.*" %>

<html xmlns = "http://www.w3.org/1999/xhtml">

   <head>
      <title>Error!</title>

      <style type = "text/css">
         .bigRed {
            font-size: 2em;
            color: red;
            font-weight: bold;
         }
      </style>
   </head>

   <body>
```

Fig. S25.4 Solution to Exercise 25.7: animalSurveyErrorPage.jsp. (Part 1 of 2.)

```
      <p class = "bigRed">

      <% // scriptlet to determine exception type
         // and output beginning of error message
         if ( exception instanceof SQLException )
      %>

            An SQLException

      <%
         else if ( exception instanceof ClassNotFoundException )
      %>

            A ClassNotFoundException

      <%
         else
      %>

            An exception

      <%-- end scriptlet to insert fixed template data --%>

         <%-- continue error message output --%>
         occurred while interacting with the database.
      </p>

      <p class = "bigRed">
         The error message was:<br /><%= exception.getMessage() %>
      </p>

      <p class = "bigRed">Please try again later</p>
   </body>

</html>
```

Fig. S25.4 Solution to Exercise 25.7: animalSurveyErrorPage.jsp. (Part 2 of 2.)

```
<?xml version = "1.0"?>
<!DOCTYPE html PUBLIC "-//W3C//DTD XHTML 1.0 Strict//EN"
   "http://www.w3.org/TR/xhtml1/DTD/xhtml1-strict.dtd">

<!-- Exercise 25.7 solution: animalSurveyResults.jsp -->

<%-- page settings --%>
<%@ page errorPage = "animalSurveyErrorPage.jsp" %>
<%@ page import = "java.util.*" %>
<%@ page import = "java.text.*" %>
<%@ page import = "com.deitel.jhtp5.jsp.beans.*" %>
```

Fig. S25.5 Solution to Exercise 25.7: animalSurveyResults.jsp. (Part 1 of 2.)

```

<%-- VoteDataBean to obtain  --%>
<jsp:useBean id = "voteData" scope = "request"
   class = "com.deitel.jhtp5.jsp.beans.VoteDataBean" />

<html xmlns = "http://www.w3.org/1999/xhtml">

   <head><title>Thank you!</title></head>

   <body>
   <p>Thank you for participating.<br />Results:</p>

   <% // start scriptlet
      DecimalFormat twoDigits = new DecimalFormat( "0.00" );
      List voteList = voteData.getAnimalVotes();
      Iterator voteListIterator = voteList.iterator();
      AnimalBean animal;

      while ( voteListIterator.hasNext() ) {
         animal = ( AnimalBean ) voteListIterator.next();
         int votes = voteData.getTotalVotes();
         String percentage = twoDigits.format(
            ( double ) animal.getVotes() / votes * 100 );

   %> <%-- end scriptlet; insert fixed template data --%>

         <%= animal.getAnimal() %>:
         <%= percentage %>%   responses:
         <%= animal.getVotes() %> <br />

   <% // continue scriptlet

      }  // end while

   %> <%-- end scriptlet --%>

   <p>Total Responses: <%= voteData.getTotalVotes() %></p>

   </body>

</html>
```

Fig. S25.5 Solution to Exercise 25.7: animalSurveyResults.jsp. (Part 2 of 2.)

```
// Exercise 25.7 solution: AnimalBean.java
// JavaBean to store data for animal votes.
package com.deitel.jhtp5.jsp.beans;

public class AnimalBean {
   private String animal;
```

Fig. S25.6 Solution to Exercise 25.7: AnimalBean.java. (Part 1 of 2.)

```
   private int votes;

   // set animal name
   public void setAnimal( String name )
   {
      animal = name;
   }

   // get animal name
   public String getAnimal()
   {
      return animal;
   }

   // set number of votes
   public void setVotes( int number)
   {
      votes = number;
   }

   // get the guest's last name
   public int getVotes()
   {
      return votes;
   }

} // end class AnimalBean
```

Fig. S25.6 Solution to Exercise 25.7: AnimalBean.java. (Part 2 of 2.)

```
// Exercise 25.7 solution: VoteDataBean.java
// Class VoteDataBean makes a database connection and supports
// inserting and retrieving from the database.
package com.deitel.jhtp5.jsp.beans;

import java.io.*;
import java.sql.*;
import java.util.*;

public class VoteDataBean {
   private Connection connection;
   private Statement statement;

   // set up database connection and prepare SQL statements
   public VoteDataBean() throws Exception
   {
      // specify database location
      System.setProperty( "db2j.system.home", "C:/CloudScape_5.0" );

```

Fig. S25.7 Solution to Exercise 25.7: VoteDataBean.java. (Part 1 of 3.)

```java
      // load the Cloudscape driver
      Class.forName( "com.ibm.db2j.jdbc.DB2jDriver" );

      // connect to the database
      connection = DriverManager.getConnection(
         "jdbc:db2j:animalsurvey" );

      // create Statement to query database
      statement = connection.createStatement();
   }

   // update votes
   public void addVote( int value ) throws SQLException
   {
      // update total for current survey response
      String query = "UPDATE surveyresults SET votes = votes + 1 " +
         "WHERE id = " + value;
      statement.executeUpdate( query );
   }

   // return an ArrayList of AnimalBeans
   public ArrayList getAnimalVotes() throws SQLException
   {
      ArrayList voteList = new ArrayList();

      // get results
      String query = "SELECT surveyoption, votes, id FROM surveyresults" +
         " ORDER BY id";
      ResultSet resultsRS = statement.executeQuery( query );

      while ( resultsRS.next() ) {
         AnimalBean animal = new AnimalBean();

         animal.setAnimal( resultsRS.getString( 1 ) );
         animal.setVotes( resultsRS.getInt( 2 ) );

         voteList.add( animal );
      }

      return voteList;
   }

   // get total of all survey responses
   public int getTotalVotes() throws SQLException
   {
      // get total of all survey responses
      String query = "SELECT sum( votes ) FROM surveyresults";
      ResultSet totalRS = statement.executeQuery( query );
      totalRS.next();

```

Fig. S25.7 Solution to Exercise 25.7: VoteDataBean.java. (Part 2 of 3.)

```
         return totalRS.getInt( 1 );
      }

      // close SQL statements and database connection
      public void finalize()
      {
         // attempt to close statements and database connection
         try {
            statement.close();
            connection.close();
         }

         // handle database exceptions by returning error to client
         catch( SQLException sqlException ) {
            sqlException.printStackTrace();
         }
      } // end of finalize method

   } // end class VoteDataBean
```

Fig. S25.7 Solution to Exercise 25.7: VoteDataBean.java. (Part 3 of 3.)

End User License Agreements

Prentice Hall License Agreement and Limited Warranty

READ THE FOLLOWING TERMS AND CONDITIONS CAREFULLY BEFORE OPENING THIS SOFTWARE PACKAGE. THIS LEGAL DOCUMENT IS AN AGREEMENT BETWEEN YOU AND PRENTICE-HALL, INC. (THE "COMPANY"). BY OPENING THIS SEALED SOFTWARE PACKAGE, YOU ARE AGREEING TO BE BOUND BY THESE TERMS AND CONDITIONS. IF YOU DO NOT AGREE WITH THESE TERMS AND CONDITIONS, DO NOT OPEN THE SOFTWARE PACKAGE. PROMPTLY RETURN THE UNOPENED SOFTWARE PACKAGE AND ALL ACCOMPANYING ITEMS TO THE PLACE YOU OBTAINED THEM FOR A FULL REFUND OF ANY SUMS YOU HAVE PAID.

1. GRANT OF LICENSE: In consideration of your purchase of this book, and your agreement to abide by the terms and conditions of this Agreement, the Company grants to you a nonexclusive right to use and display the copy of the enclosed software program (hereinafter the "SOFTWARE") on a single computer (i.e., with a single CPU) at a single location so long as you comply with the terms of this Agreement. The Company reserves all rights not expressly granted to you under this Agreement.

2. OWNERSHIP OF SOFTWARE: You own only the magnetic or physical media (the enclosed media) on which the SOFTWARE is recorded or fixed, but the Company and the software developers retain all the rights, title, and ownership to the SOFTWARE recorded on the original media copy(ies) and all subsequent copies of the SOFTWARE, regardless of the form or media on which the original or other copies may exist. This license is not a sale of the original SOFTWARE or any copy to you.

3. COPY RESTRICTIONS: This SOFTWARE and the accompanying printed materials and user manual (the "Documentation") are the subject of copyright. The individual programs on the media are copyrighted by the authors of each program. Some of the programs on the media include separate licensing agreements. If you intend to use one of these programs, you must read and follow its accompanying license agreement. You may not copy the Documentation or the SOFTWARE, except that you may make a single copy of the SOFTWARE for backup or archival purposes only. You may be held legally responsible for any copying or copyright infringement which is caused or encouraged by your failure to abide by the terms of this restriction.

4. USE RESTRICTIONS: You may not network the SOFTWARE or otherwise use it on more than one computer or computer terminal at the same time. You may physically transfer the SOFTWARE from one computer to another provided that the SOFTWARE is used on only one computer at a time. You may not distribute copies of the SOFTWARE or Documentation to others. You may not reverse engineer, disassemble, decompile, modify, adapt, translate, or create derivative works based on the SOFTWARE or the Documentation without the prior written consent of the Company.

5. TRANSFER RESTRICTIONS: The enclosed SOFTWARE is licensed only to you and may not be transferred to any one else without the prior written consent of the Company. Any unauthorized transfer of the SOFTWARE shall result in the immediate termination of this Agreement.

6. TERMINATION: This license is effective until terminated. This license will terminate automatically without notice from the Company and become null and void if you fail to comply with any provisions or limitations of this license. Upon termination, you shall destroy the Documentation and all copies of the SOFTWARE. All provisions of this Agreement as to warranties, limitation of liability, remedies or damages, and our ownership rights shall survive termination.

7. MISCELLANEOUS: This Agreement shall be construed in accordance with the laws of the United States of America and the State of New York and shall benefit the Company, its affiliates, and assignees.

8. LIMITED WARRANTY AND DISCLAIMER OF WARRANTY: The Company warrants that the SOFTWARE, when properly used in accordance with the Documentation, will operate in substantial conformity with the description of the SOFTWARE set forth in the Documentation. The Company does not warrant that the SOFTWARE will meet your requirements or that the operation of the SOFTWARE will be uninterrupted or error-free. The Company warrants that the media on which the SOFTWARE is delivered shall be free from defects in materials and workmanship under normal use for a period of thirty (30) days from the date of your purchase. Your only remedy and the Company's only obligation under these limited warranties is, at the Company's option, return of the warranted item for a refund of any amounts paid by you or replacement of the item. Any replacement of SOFTWARE or media under the warranties shall not extend the original warranty period. The limited warranty set forth above shall not apply to any SOFTWARE which the Company determines in good faith has been subject to misuse, neglect, improper installation, repair, alteration, or damage by you. EXCEPT FOR THE EXPRESSED WARRANTIES SET FORTH ABOVE, THE COMPANY DISCLAIMS ALL WARRANTIES, EXPRESS OR IMPLIED, INCLUDING WITHOUT LIMITATION, THE IMPLIED WARRANTIES OF MERCHANTABILITY AND FITNESS FOR A PARTICULAR PURPOSE. EXCEPT FOR THE EXPRESS WARRANTY SET FORTH ABOVE, THE COMPANY DOES NOT WARRANT, GUARANTEE, OR MAKE ANY REPRESENTATION REGARDING THE USE OR THE RESULTS OF THE USE OF THE SOFTWARE IN TERMS OF ITS CORRECTNESS, ACCURACY, RELIABILITY, CURRENTNESS, OR OTHERWISE.

IN NO EVENT, SHALL THE COMPANY OR ITS EMPLOYEES, AGENTS, SUPPLIERS, OR CONTRACTORS BE LIABLE FOR ANY INCIDENTAL, INDIRECT, SPECIAL, OR CONSEQUENTIAL DAMAGES ARISING OUT OF OR IN CONNECTION

WITH THE LICENSE GRANTED UNDER THIS AGREEMENT, OR FOR LOSS OF USE, LOSS OF DATA, LOSS OF INCOME OR PROFIT, OR OTHER LOSSES, SUSTAINED AS A RESULT OF INJURY TO ANY PERSON, OR LOSS OF OR DAMAGE TO PROPERTY, OR CLAIMS OF THIRD PARTIES, EVEN IF THE COMPANY OR AN AUTHORIZED REPRESENTATIVE OF THE COMPANY HAS BEEN ADVISED OF THE POSSIBILITY OF SUCH DAMAGES. IN NO EVENT SHALL LIABILITY OF THE COMPANY FOR DAMAGES WITH RESPECT TO THE SOFTWARE EXCEED THE AMOUNTS ACTUALLY PAID BY YOU, IF ANY, FOR THE SOFTWARE.

SOME JURISDICTIONS DO NOT ALLOW THE LIMITATION OF IMPLIED WARRANTIES OR LIABILITY FOR INCIDENTAL, INDIRECT, SPECIAL, OR CONSEQUENTIAL DAMAGES, SO THE ABOVE LIMITATIONS MAY NOT ALWAYS APPLY. THE WARRANTIES IN THIS AGREEMENT GIVE YOU SPECIFIC LEGAL RIGHTS AND YOU MAY ALSO HAVE OTHER RIGHTS WHICH VARY IN ACCORDANCE WITH LOCAL LAW.

ACKNOWLEDGMENT

YOU ACKNOWLEDGE THAT YOU HAVE READ THIS AGREEMENT, UNDERSTAND IT, AND AGREE TO BE BOUND BY ITS TERMS AND CONDITIONS. YOU ALSO AGREE THAT THIS AGREEMENT IS THE COMPLETE AND EXCLUSIVE STATEMENT OF THE AGREEMENT BETWEEN YOU AND THE COMPANY AND SUPERSEDES ALL PROPOSALS OR PRIOR AGREEMENTS, ORAL, OR WRITTEN, AND ANY OTHER COMMUNICATIONS BETWEEN YOU AND THE COMPANY OR ANY REPRESENTATIVE OF THE COMPANY RELATING TO THE SUBJECT MATTER OF THIS AGREEMENT.

Should you have any questions concerning this Agreement or if you wish to contact the Company for any reason, please contact in writing at the address below.

Robin Short
Prentice Hall PTR
One Lake Street
Upper Saddle River, New Jersey 07458